POSITIVE BEHAVIOR SUPPORTS FOR ADULTS WITH DISABILITIES IN EMPLOYMENT, COMMUNITY, AND RESIDENTIAL SETTINGS

Second Edition

POSITIVE BEHAVIOR SUPPORTS FOR ADULTS WITH DISABILITIES IN EMPLOYMENT, COMMUNITY, AND RESIDENTIAL SETTINGS

Practical Strategies That Work

By

KEITH STOREY, Ph.D., BCBA-D

Juvo Autism and Behavioral Health Services, Oakland, CA

and

MICHAL POST, M.A.

San Francisco State University, CA

CHARLES C THOMAS • PUBLISHER, LTD.
Springfield • Illinois • U.S.A.

Published and Distributed Throughout the World by

CHARLES C THOMAS · PUBLISHER, LTD.
2600 South First Street
Springfield, Illinois 62704

© 2019 by CHARLES C THOMAS · PUBLISHER, LTD.

ISBN 978-0-398-09284-9 (paper)
ISBN 978-0-398-09285-6 (ebook)

First Edition, 2014
Second Edition, 2019

Library of Congress Catalog Card Number: 2019014841 (print)
2019016178 (ebook)

*With THOMAS BOOKS careful attention is given to all details of manufacturing
and design. It is the Publisher's desire to present books that are satisfactory as to their
physical qualities and artistic possibilities and appropriate for their particular use.
THOMAS BOOKS will be true to those laws of quality that assure a good name
and good will.*

Printed in the United States of America
MM-C-1

Library of Congress Cataloging-in-Publication Data

Names: Storey, Keith 1956– author. | Post, Michal, 1949– author.
Title: Positive behavior supports for adults with disabilities in employ-
    ment, community, and residential settings : practical strategies that
    work / by Keith Storey, PH.D., BCBA-D, Juvo Autism and
    Behavioral Health Services, Oakland, CA and Michal Post, M.A.,
    San Francisco State University, CA.
Description: Second Edition. | Springfield, IL : Charles C Thomas,
    Publisher, Ltd., [2019] | Revised edition of the authors' Positive
    behavior supports for adults with disabilities in employment, com-
    munity, and residential settings, {2015] | Includes bibliographical
    references and index.
Identifiers: LCCN 201904841 (print) | LCCN 2019016178 (ebook) |
    ISBN 9780398092856 (ebook) | ISBN 9780398092849 (paper)
Subjects: LCSH: People with disabilities—Psychology. | Positive psy-
    chology. | People with disabilities—Services for. | People with dis-
    abilities–Social conditions. | People with disabilities–Employment. |
    Social work with people with disabilities.
Classification: LCC HV1568 (ebook) | LCC HV1568 .S699 2019
    (print) | DDC 362.4/048019—dc23
LC record available at https://lccn.lloc.gov/2019014841

To Joyce Forte. Trusted mentor, role model, colleague, and friend over many years. Of all the people that I have met in the education field that there is no one that I respect or admire more than Joyce. She is probably the best K–12 teacher that I have ever seen (and I have seen a lot of outstanding teachers). Many thanks!
K.S.

To my students who have taught me and given me precious insight throughout my career, Keith Storey who never gives up in his dedication to educate and publish this knowledge for future generations, Terrence, my son, for his love and ongoing support, and in memory of my father from whom, through his unwavering kindness, I have experienced "true goodness."
M.P.

PREFACE

Scope

The scope of this book is to provide an overview of positive behavior supports for adults with disabilities in a written format that is directed to support providers who can immediately put the information to use. We have tried to write in a nontechnical format and include real-life examples for using positive behavior supports in employment, community, and residential settings. It is generic across disability labels and should be of interest to those working with adults with disabilities in any capacity. In the chapters, we have deliberately included "older" references that we see as being both important and relevant today, as well as to provide an understanding of how this field of study has built upon "classic research" for establishing the basis of positive behavior supports. In some cases, where there are not examples from the literature including adults with disabilities, we have included empirical studies and discussion article references illustrating positive behavior supports in school settings.

Plan

In this book each chapter follows the sequence of:

- Key Point Questions
- Window to the World Case Studies
- Best Practice Recommendations
- Discussion Questions
- Employment, Community, and Residential Based Activity Suggestions
- References Cited in Chapter
- Empirical Research Supporting that the Interventions Presented in Chapter are Evidence Based Practices (this is not included in Chapters 1 and 2 as these chapters are not focused on interventions)
- General References Regarding Topics in Chapter

Purpose

This book is intended to give support providers the knowledge and skills for providing positive behavior supports in employment, community, and residential settings and thereby improve the quality of life for the individuals that they support. The rubber meets the road, not only in how to support adults with disabilities, but also in how to implement positive behavior supports so that positive quality of life outcomes occur. This book responds to a critical need for highly qualified personnel who will become exemplary professionals in positive behavior supports for adults with disabilities because of their knowledge and skills in supporting adults with varying disabilities in employment, community, and residential settings.

An advantage of this book is that universities, agencies and organizations preparing support providers can easily use it in courses or trainings that address positive behavior supports, as it covers methodology that is seldom covered in detail in most texts. Those who are already support providers will find the information to be practical and easily implemented in applied settings. We see three main groups who would primarily be interested in using this book:

1. College instructors teaching courses in Applied Behavior Analysis, Transition and Employment, Rehabilitation, Career Counseling, Special Education, Social Services, Mental Health, or other related areas.

College instructors are likely to choose our book based upon:
   a. The consistent format throughout the book.
   b. The "practicality" and "readability" of the book for college students.
   c. The comprehensive analysis and coverage of developing positive behavior supports and services for adults with disabilities.
   d. The direct applicability of the information to applied settings.
2. Individuals working in the disability field.
3. Individuals studying to work in the disability field.

CONTENTS

POSITIVE BEHAVIOR SUPPORTS FOR ADULTS WITH DISABILITIES IN EMPLOYMENT, COMMUNITY, AND RESIDENTIAL SETTINGS

Chapter 1

OVERVIEW OF POSITIVE BEHAVIOR SUPPORTS

Key Point Questions

1. What is Applied Behavior Analysis?
2. What are Positive Behavior Supports?
3. How are Positive Behavior Supports different than other approaches?
4. Why are Positive Behavior Supports important?
5. What are Barriers to the Implementation of Applied Behavior Analysis and Positive Behavior Supports?
6. How do Applied Behavior Analysis and Positive Behavior Supports relate to the learning of Adults with Disabilities?
7. How are Applied Behavior Analysis and Functional Skills related?
8. What are evidence-based practices?

WINDOW TO THE WORLD CASE STUDY ONE

Mabel is 24 years old, has a diagnosis of Autism Spectrum Disorders, and works at an upscale clothing store. Mabel is very knowledgeable about women's clothing fashions and enjoys working at the store. She is looked upon as a very good and conscientious worker. Not only can she answer very detailed questions from customers but she is very meticulous about making sure that the clothes are displayed correctly and she returns items quickly to the racks.

Recently however, Mabel has started developing some behavior problems that are of increasing concern. When the store gets busy and the items to be restocked start piling up Mabel has been getting agitated. She will start muttering obscenities about the customers under her breath and if a customer interrupts her to ask a question when she is returning items to the rack, she will increasingly "snap" at the customer.

The supervisor, Ms. Hui, has called in Martha, Mabel's job coach, and told her in no uncertain terms that though Mabel has been a valued employee this behavior cannot continue and that if it occurs again, Mabel will be terminated. Martha is in a panic. She understands job analysis and job supports but she has no background in positive behavior supports. Martha contacts her supervisor at the supported employment agency, Mr. Rhodes, but he, too, has no background in positive behavior supports and also does not know what to do. It appears that Mabel's job is about to come to an unfortunate end.

WINDOW OF THE WORLD CASE STUDY TWO

Herbert is a 40-year-old adult who is labeled as having a severe intellectual disability and he also has mild Cerebral Palsy which makes his walking a bit unsteady. After living in a state institution and then in group homes for individuals with intellectual disabilities, Herbert's two siblings realized that he was unhappy and getting depressed living in a group home with five other adults with intellectual disabilities and having to share a bedroom.

A new agency, Innovative Behavior Interventions, has just opened up in the town and Herbert's siblings contacted them. Ms. Ehl, the supported living director of IBI, did a Person Centered Plan with Herbert and his siblings and it became clear, through the Person Centered Planning (PCP) process that Herbert really wanted to live in his own apartment. Herbert worked full time at a local law firm where he delivered mail and supplies, did copying, and prepped rooms for meetings. Between the income from his job and the trust fund that his parents had set up for him, he had the financial ability to rent a nice apartment. Additionally, IBI provided full-time supported living services when he was not at work.

Herbert enjoyed his new apartment and the supported living supports from IBI. However, Herbert has started getting upset in his apartment. He will sometimes yell out, and then start jumping around, and end by hitting his head very hard with objects in the apartment. This behavior is very upsetting to both Herbert and the supported living staff. Ms. Ehl wonders if IBI made a mistake in providing support to Herbert. Ms. Ehl and the supported living staff have never worked before with someone like Herbert, with such serious behavior problems. Ms. Ehl has decided to meet with the executive director of IBI and to recommend that IBI withdraw its supported living services to Herbert.

KEY POINT QUESTION #1:
WHAT IS APPLIED BEHAVIOR ANALYSIS?

The foundation of Positive Behavior Supports is Applied Behavior Analysis (ABA). Applied Behavior Analysis is derived from the work of B. F. Skinner (1953, 1971). Skinner was a psychologist who advocated that the focus of interventions should be on the behavior of individuals rather than on internal states (O'Donohue & Ferguson, 2001). Behavior may be defined as observable actions that a person does. Sitting in a seat, completing a work task correctly, making a sandwich, cursing, and greeting a supervisor at work appropriately are all observable behaviors (verbal behaviors are classified as behaviors as well). These are all behaviors that can be changed (for better or worse). Being motivated, trying hard, and being unruly are not observable behaviors and thus cannot be directly changed.

John Watson is often credited as being the first behavioral psychologist. In his 1913 manifesto he wrote that, "Psychology, as the behaviorist views it, is a purely objective experimental branch of natural science. Its theoretical goal is the prediction and control of behavior." For Positive Behavior Supports, the key words are "prediction" and "control." Good support providers[1] are effective at predicting what will work in their situations (such as using picture schedules, reinforcing positive behaviors, ignoring some behaviors, etc.) and then controlling the environment so that these behaviors occur. Sometimes support providers have concerns with the concept of control and they view control as being a bad thing. However, not positively controlling

---

1. We will use the term "support providers" throughout the book and we mean to include job coaches, residential staff, family members, social workers, case managers, and others who provide support to adults with disabilities in employment, community, and residential settings.

the situation only leads to anarchy and poor performance for the adult in their situation. For instance, by doing things such as having set routines, clear expectations about how to behave, and praising the person for completing tasks the support provider is "controlling" the behavior of the adult. Having a support provider controlling a situation in this way is good support and is not deceitful or wrong. In other words, the focus is on the cause and effect relationship between the environment and the behavior of the individual (Nye, 1992). This cause and effect is not a one way process as there is the issue of counter control where the behavior of the individual also influences the environment (e.g., the behavior of the support provider).

As they read this, many support providers may be thinking "I do this every day." Good support providers use these types of strategies all the time. In this book, we are presenting a coherent and systematic approach to understanding the purpose of Positive Behavior Supports and how support providers can implement these strategies to arrive at the desirable results for carefully targeting the behaviors that need changing, as opposed to a "hit and miss" strategy that many support providers use.

Applied Behavior Analysis

In behavior analysis, it is assumed that the behavior of individuals is lawful. This means that people do things for a reason such as being previously reinforced for a behavior (such as completing work tasks successfully) or being punished for a behavior (such as talking back to a supervisor at their work site). In other words, individuals have a history of being reinforced or punished for certain behaviors and this history influences their current behavior. For example, if Hart is consistently reinforced for preparing dinner for himself and his roommate by receiving positive feedback from the roommate on the quality of the food, and having the roommate do the dishes after dinner, then Hart is likely to continue to prepare good meals for himself and his roommate. A person who does not receive this reinforcement for preparing quality dinners is less likely to consistently prepare good dinners.

The three basic assumptions of applied behavior analysis are:

1. All behavior is learned or is a physiological response such as sneezing due to allergies.

2. Behavior can be changed by altering antecedents and/or consequences.
3. Factors in the environment (the work site, community setting, or home) can be changed to increase and maintain specific behaviors or to decrease specific behaviors.

Behavior analysts agree that people feel and think, but they do not consider these events (feeling and thinking) as causes of behavior. For instance, a person may engage in certain "undesirable" behaviors 1 (such as talking back to the job coach or refusing to complete in work tasks).[2] To analyze these behaviors as "feelings" of the person is not helpful as it is an inference as to the causes, and the support provider cannot directly change the feelings of an individual.

Applied behavior analysis focuses on the behavior of people. Behavior is not considered to be an expression of inner causes like personality, cognition, and attitude. Poor performance on work tasks, talking out loud to one's self while shopping, or refusing to brush one's teeth are analyzed as problems of behavior rather than examples of a person having a "poor attitude." Interventions for undesirable behaviors are directed at changing environmental events (support providers' behaviors or the setup in the home) to improve behavior (e.g., to increase desirable behavior). For example, using a self-management strategy to increase on-task performance or to eliminate asking questions to coworkers at inappropriate times could change the worker's undesirable behaviors for the better, and by doing so could change the "poor attitude" of the worker. But this is accomplished only by changing specific behaviors of the worker (which was accomplished by changing the environment of the worker through teaching self-management skills to the individual).

So, the focus is not only on the behaviors of the adult with a disability but also on understanding why the person engages in certain behaviors (e.g., the function of the behavior which is described in more detail in Chapter 3).

Kazdin (2008) succinctly summarizes this issue:

---

2. In this text we will use the terms "desirable" and "undesirable" in describing behavior. A variety of terms have been used in the professional literature such as difficult, acting out, maladaptive, disruptive, challenging, good/bad, appropriate/inappropriate, at-risk, target behavior, and problem behavior. Basically, these terms have been used to describe behavior that we see as being either desirable or undesirable from the viewpoint of the support providers.

Even today, even at our most scientifically precise, we can't always or even often locate the exact source of a behavior problem. . . . We know how to change behavior for the better, regardless of its exact cause, and our best bet is to just go ahead and change it. Instead of treating the child as if there's something wrong inside her that needs to be fixed, let's treat the behavior as the something wrong, and address it directly. In practice, that means locating the problem in the relationship between the child and the situation around him, in how he interacts with other people and things (which might well include flaws in the therapy or how it's delivered). (p. 169)

Factors that Influence Behavior

There are two factors that influence behavior: antecedents (what occurs before a behavior) and consequences (what occurs after a behavior).

Antecedents become effective at producing desirable behavior only when they are a signal for a predictable consequence. For instance, if Delwyn knows that he gets points for each time that he completes a cleaning task for his apartment, and that points can be traded in for backup reinforcers (backup reinforcers are things or activities that are delivered at a later time such as desired activities, objects, or food items), then he may be more likely to complete cleaning tasks.

Consequences affect behavior by strengthening the behavior (increasing its probability) or by weakening the behavior (decreasing its probability). In the example above, the cleaning task behavior was strengthened through positive reinforcement (the token economy). The behavior of not completing cleaning tasks could be weakened (decreased) through consequences with the use of punishment (a response cost system where Delwyn fines himself points for not completing cleaning tasks).

How Applied Behavior Analysis Fits into Today's Focus on Positive Behavior Supports for Adults with Disabilities

Baer, Wolf, and Risley (1968, 1987) have outlined key dimensions of applied behavior analysis and here we highlight how these fit into the application of positive behavior supports.

APPLIED: Applied Behavior Analysis is focused on practical issues that are of importance and are socially relevant. Research in applied behavior analysis occurs in "real life" settings such as supported employment or supported living situations rather than in laboratory settings (which is often known as Experimental Analysis of Human Behavior and is focused on basic experimental and transactional research with animal or human participants).

BEHAVIORAL: As indicated earlier in the chapter, applied behavior analysis focuses on the physical/observable behavior of individuals and references to inner states and causes are not deemed useful in that they do not serve as causes of behavior. Skinner made the distinction between overt behavior (which is observable) and covert behavior (that which occurs "within the skin").

ANALYTICAL: Applied behavior analysis looks for the condition or stimulus (what happens in the environment) which is responsible for the effect on the behavior (what the person does in response). In positive behavior supports this is often analyzing the function of the behavior (why the adult does something), the setting events (what is going on in the home), and the consequences (did the behavior increase or decrease).

TECHNOLOGICAL: The intervention procedure is described in enough detail for others to do the same thing in their setting. A study on positive behavior supports should describe the intervention clearly and in enough detail so that the readers can apply the intervention in the same way in their own situation.

CONCEPTUAL: Procedures are related to concepts of effective interventions rather than a collection of tricks. For example, functional assessment analyses of the behavior of an adult in terms of understanding if that adult is engaging in a behavior to obtain or to avoid. This understanding (the adult engaging in undesirable behavior in order to get attention from the support provider) then leads to procedures or interventions that are more likely to be effective (the support provider praising the adult for desirable behavior).

EFFECTIVE: The effect upon the behavior of the adult and their learning must be meaningful. For instance, decreasing aggressive behavior by Teeda from 20 to 5 times a day may be statistically significant but is not meaningful in a socially important context. There is an extensive body of research indicating that applied behavior analysis procedures are effective in providing positive behavior supports for increasing desirable behavior in employment, community, and residential settings (Filter & Horner, 2009; Wheeler & Richey, 2013).

Positive behavior support strategies are clearly scientifically based research for programs and teaching methods (Cook & Odom, 2013).

GENERALITY: Do the effects of the intervention carry over across people, settings, behavior, and times? From the example of aggression above it would be important to eliminate Teeda's aggressive behavior across people (different support providers), settings (work, community, and home), behaviors (all types of aggression such as verbal and physical), and times (morning, afternoons, and evenings).

What is the Science of Applied Behavior Analysis?

In applied behavior analysis there is an emphasis on objective description with a focus on observable events. There is also a focus on absolute unit-based measurement, e.g., behaviors that have clear and limited extensions in space and time and also have easy to determine onsets and offsets (Baer, 1986). These factors are described in more detail in Chapter 2.

Applied behavior analysis relies upon experimental analysis to determine if interventions are effective or not. This analysis often involves the use of single case research designs (also known as single subject designs) that involve one or a small number of participants and the design involves data that are taken frequently over an extended time period which allows for detailed analysis of variables that might be affecting the behavior (Kazdin, 2011). In single case designs the replication of the effect of the intervention is very important. In other words, the experimenter demonstrates repeatedly that it is the intervention that is causing the change in the behavior of the adult and not something else. For example, it is the support provider increasing her rate of praise for an adult picking out correct items from the shopping list in the grocery store rather than something that the support provider may be doing at home before the shopping trip that is increasing the rate of the correct selection of items.

Applied behavior analysis stresses the understanding of functional relations between the adult and the environment. The behavior of individuals is not random (though there is some variance in behavior as people are not always consistent in what they do, people can have good days and bad days due to a variety of reasons) and there are lawful relationships between what is happening in the environment (at work, at home, and in the community) and adult behavior. For example, factors such as food intake (if a worker did not eat breakfast) or sleep patterns (if the person did not sleep well the night before) can influence worker behavior and performance at the job site.

By understanding the relationship between the environment and the adult it becomes possible to establish effective supports. For example, if the job coach receives a text message from Cyrus (or from his supported living staff) that he has not slept well the night before, then it may be beneficial to adjust schedules, demands, work tasks, and/or reinforcers (Durand, 1998).

It is important to emphasize that behavior of a person is always changing. As someone learns skills (or the antecedents or consequences change), their behavior changes. For example, factors such as falling into a poor peer group, doing drugs, learning positive social skills, and learning a new job task at work are all things that are likely to change behavior (some for the better, some not so). The more that support providers understand these changes the better off they will be in developing instruction and other supports for individuals.

KEY POINT QUESTION #2:
WHAT ARE POSITIVE BEHAVIOR SUPPORTS?

Bradley (2009) writes that,

> As an applied science of human behavior, PBS unites the precision of a careful, analytical examination of the functions of problem behavior, a broader framework of person-centered values and processes, and an emphasis on teaching alternative skill repertoires. PBS involves a conceptual shift in our approach to addressing difficult behavior associated with disabilities away from a simple reduction of the occurrence of such behavior (e.g., punishment) to a comprehensive strengths-based teaching approach that considers the person and his or her total life span or ecology. (p. vi)

Dunlap, Sailor, Horner, and Sugai (2009) define Positive Behavior Supports as "a broad approach for organizing the physical, social, educational, biomedical, and logistical supports needed to achieve basic lifestyle goals while reducing problem behaviors that pose barriers to these goals." (p. 3). Kincaid, Dunlap, Kern, Lane, Bambara, Brown, Fox, and Knoster (2016) have comprehensively defined Positive Behavior Supports as:

PBS is an approach to behavior support that includes an ongoing process of research-based assessment, intervention, and data-based decision making focused on building social and other functional competencies, creating supportive contexts, and preventing the occurrence of problem behaviors. PBS relies on strategies that are respectful of a person's dignity and overall well-being and that are drawn primarily from behavioral, educational, and social sciences, although other evidence-based procedures may be incorporated. PBS may be applied within a multi-level framework at the level of the individual and at the level of larger systems (e.g., families, classrooms, schools, social service programs, and facilities). (p. 71)

The purpose of this book is to provide support providers the skills to implement positive behavior interventions in work, residential, and community settings. Developing and maintaining appropriate behavior can often be challenging in any setting supporting adults with disabilities. Individuals may not do their work tasks, act out, talk back to the boss, and disrupt home life or community instruction. This is all too common. And, all too often, the focus of interventions is on eliminating undesirable behaviors. Implementers of Positive Behavior Support strategies reason that the best way to decrease undesirable behaviors is by increasing desirable behaviors, and by giving individuals skills and supports so that they do not need to engage in undesirable behaviors. This approach is known as Positive Behavior Supports. For example, if Raul is being very disruptive at work in the cafeteria line then the behaviors to be increased would be being polite and staying in the line.

KEY POINT QUESTION #3: HOW ARE POSITIVE BEHAVIOR SUPPORTS DIFFERENT THAN OTHER APPROACHES?

Other approaches, while not from an applied behavior analysis perspective per se (such as Outward Bound programs or the work of William Glasser), are often very compatible with and can complement applied behavior analysis interventions. Not all other approaches have a strong (or any) empirical basis for their effectiveness. For instance, interventions for individuals with Autism Spectrum Disorders such as dolphin therapy, sensory integration therapy, Auditory Integration Therapies, or electromagnetic therapy may or may not be effective interventions but they have little, if any, empirical evidence that they are effective interventions. Applied behavior analysis does have an extensive empirical basis for its effectiveness in work, home, and community settings for adults with or without disabilities.

KEY POINT QUESTION #4:
WHY ARE POSITIVE BEHAVIOR SUPPORTS IMPORTANT?

Having a well-organized home, work, or community setting in which adults are positively engaged is, in many ways, *the* key to being a successful support provider. Support providers need skills in this area and need to be able to implement positive behavior support strategies that are empirically valid. Too many support providers rely upon a "bag of tricks" (and often it is a limited bag of tricks) and when those tricks do not work, then they are at a loss as to what to do. Positive behavior supports provide not only the frame work but also the "how to" in providing effective interventions for individuals with undesirable behaviors and there is a strong empirical base proving their effectiveness (Kazdin, 2013).

KEY POINT QUESTION #5:
WHAT ARE BARRIERS TO THE IMPLEMENTATION OF APPLIED BEHAVIOR ANALYSIS AND POSITIVE BEHAVIOR SUPPORTS?

There is often resistance from support providers to applied behavior analysis and positive behavior support approaches. There is often a misunderstanding of the concepts of applied behavior analysis, as well as staff resistance to applied behavior analysis and positive behavior support approaches. For example, Reitman (1998) analyzed five false assumptions in Kohn's book, "Punished by Rewards: The Trouble with Gold Stars, Incentive Plans, A's, Praise, and Other Bribes" (1993). These false assumptions are: (a) Behavior analysis is exclusively derived from animal research; (b) behavior analysts characterize individuals as passive agents to be manipulated; (c) behavior analysis is a behavior control technology; (d) behavior analysts are uninterested in and ignorant of the causes of behavior; and (e) behavior analysts are unconcerned about the protection and welfare of people that they serve. In addition, Kazdin (2013) analyzes the myths and red herrings of applied behavior analysis such as: (a) reward programs do not work, (b) the individual will become dependent on incentives, rewards, and praise, (c) applied behavioral interventions do not work with everyone, (d) applied behavior analysis ignores the roots of the problems, and (e) the focus on over behaviors ignores affect and cognition.

Table 1.1 outlines perceived barriers to changing behavior. This resistance may be in regards to the causes of, and procedures necessary to change the behavior of adults with disabilities (Tingstrom, 1989). For example, the applied behavior analysis approach of functional assessment to determine why individuals are engaging in behavior may be in conflict of support providers who may view the internal states (such as depression) or mental cognition (such as trouble thinking positively about a situation) as the primary causes of behavior. They believe that these internal characteristics must be modified in order to change behavior (Tingstrom & Edwards, 1989).

Tingstrom and Edwards (1989) identified other reasons for teacher resistance to behavioral approaches in school settings and these apply to support providers of adults with disabilities are well. These common misconceptions are:

1. Behavioral approaches require the use of complicated, time-consuming data collection procedures.
   Response: Not necessarily. Chapter 2 outlines data collection procedures that are often simple and not time-consuming.
2. Behavioral approaches do not work with many adults with disabilities.
   Response: There is extensive research that applied behavior analysis approaches work with all types of adults (with or without disabilities) and for adults with all types of disabilities.
3. Behavioral interventions result in a permanent need for external reinforcement.
   Response: While some adults may need ongoing external reinforcement (e.g., that which is delivered by others such as a support provider), other individuals do not, as naturally occurring reinforcers often take the place of external reinforcement (e.g., being nice to someone and being socially skilled with others may lead to friendships which are naturally reinforcing).
4. Behavioral approaches are appropriate for "behavior" problems but not for teaching skills to adults with disabilities.

Response: Controlling for undesirable behavior problems allows for skills learning. Again, there is a large body of empirical evidence that behavioral approaches are effective for teaching skills to adults with disabilities as well (Bellamy, Homer, and Inman, 1979; Storey & Miner, 2017).

KEY POINT QUESTION #6: HOW DO APPLIED BEHAVIOR ANALYSIS AND POSITIVE BEHAVIOR SUPPORTS RELATE TO THE LEARNING OF ADULTS WITH DISABILITIES?

Just as applied behavior analysis is focused on observable events, so is learning. While we often talk about adults with disabilities "thinking" or "knowing," it is only through their observable behavior that we can tell if they have learned skills (whether they be job skills, social skills, community living skills, etc.). For instance, a support provider may say Ngor really understands adding and subtracting. The support provider "knows" this because Ngor correctly balances his checkbook once a month (e.g., an observable behavior).

The overall purpose of positive behavior supports in employment, community, and home settings is to create environments that are conducive to learning and positive functioning. For example, if a supported living provider is spending most of the time dealing with Sheldon's undesirable behavior, she has little time for helping Sheldon learn functional skills that he needs to be successful in his home, such as cooking, cleaning, and recreating.

KEY POINT QUESTION #7: HOW ARE APPLIED BEHAVIOR ANALYSIS AND FUNCTIONAL SKILLS RELATED?

Independence, productivity, and integration are valued outcomes for all individuals with disabilities. The opportunity to live, learn skills, and participate in normalized settings contributes to the development of skills that enhance community functioning and attainment of these outcomes.

"What to teach?" is the initial question that needs to be addressed when making instructional decisions involving adults with disabilities. The general goal of all instruction must be to enhance a person's capacity to function successfully in the community. To that end, instruction should consist of skills that enable a person to function in employment, residential, community living, and recreational/leisure domains. Thus, any skill taught needs to be referenced to one (or more) of these domains and meet the test of being personally meaningful and valuable to specific individuals. When skills are selected in this manner, their functionality or practical utility is virtually assured.

Functional teaching activities are instructional programs that involve skills of immediate usefulness to individuals and employ teaching materials that are real rather than simulated (Wehman, Renzaglia, & Bates, 1985). In other words, the skills must be immediately useful (e.g., learning to greet a job interviewer appropriately). In considering if a skill is functional or not you need to ask if that skill is necessary to function effectively in community settings (one of the four domains). For example, learning how to use public transportation to get to a job site is functional because the individual can immediately use the skill to get to work. Learning how to put pegs in a peg-board (once you are over the age of 3) is nonfunctional because the individual is unlikely to need to use that skill in a community environment. Another way to analyze functionality is to ask, "If the person cannot perform the skill does someone else have to do it for them?" For instance, if someone cannot brush their teeth then someone else will have to brush their teeth for them. Table 1.2 provides further analysis of the context relevance in which skills should be taught.

Lewis (1997) provides examples of individuals being taught skills that are nonfunctional and age-inappropriate. These include:

- He can put 100 pegs in a board in less than 20 minutes, but, he can't put quarters in a vending machine.
- He can sort blocks by color; but, he can't sort clothes; whites from colors for washing.
- He can walk a balance beam frontwards, sideways and backwards; but, he can't walk up the steps to the gym.

KEY POINT QUESTION #8:
WHAT ARE EVIDENCE-BASED PRACTICES?

Scientifically-based research results in replicable and applicable findings from research that used appropriate methods to generate persuasive, empirical conclusions. The use of the best available research results (evidence) allows service providers, as well as decision-makers (funding sources, heads of agencies, and other administrators), to make informed decisions based upon empirical evidence. All too often programs are "fad" driven and use practices that are either untested or demonstrated to be ineffective. The National Autism Center's National Standards Report (2009/2015) stated that evidence-based practice involves the integration of research findings with (a) professional judgment and data-based clinical decision-making, (b) values and preferences of families, and (c) assessing and improving the capacity of the system to implement the intervention with a high degree of accuracy. This report is very useful as it provides guidelines for evaluating whether or not an intervention is an Evidence-Based Practice or not. It identifies 11 treatments as "Established" (i.e., they were established as effective) for individuals with Autism Spectrum Disorders (ASD).

The following interventions are Established Treatments:
- Antecedent Package
- Behavioral Package
- Comprehensive Behavioral Treatment for Young Children
- Joint Attention Intervention
- Modeling
- Naturalistic Teaching Strategies
- Peer Training Package
- Pivotal Response Treatment
- Schedules
- Self-management
- Story-based Intervention Package

BEST PRACTICE RECOMMENDATIONS

1. It is important to focus on observable adult behaviors (such as social behaviors) rather than upon thoughts or other inner states that are not observable.
2. Support providers should be focused on increasing functional skills for adults with disabilities and achieving quality of life outcomes.

DISCUSSION QUESTIONS

1. What is learning? How do you know when a person has learned something?
2. Can support providers only change their behavior or can they change the behavior of the adults that they support as well?
3. Can nonpositive behavior support approaches be effective in supporting adults in employment, community, and residential environments? What is the empirical data base for these approaches?
4. Are there certain support provider behaviors that are most effective for implementing positive behavior supports?
5. What skills do adults with disabilities need to be effective participants in employment, community, and residential settings?

ADULT LEARNING AND COMMUNITY ACTIVITY SUGGESTIONS

1. Observe a support provider and list what behaviors they are engaging in that are enhancing the learning of the adult with a disability. How are these behaviors related to prediction and control?
2. Observe a work setting and list feelings and thoughts that workers are engaging in. Describe how you know that the feelings and thoughts are occurring.
3. Interview support providers about what types of positive behavior supports they prefer and find effective. Put these suggestions into different categories for analyzing.
4. Interview adults with disabilities about what types of positive behavior supports they prefer and find effective. Put these suggestions into different categories for analyzing.

REFERENCES

Baer, D. M. (1986). In application, frequency is not the only estimate of the probability of behavioral units. In T. Thompson & M. D. Zieler (Eds.), *Analysis and integration of behavioral units* (pp. 117–136). Hillsdale, NJ: Lawrence Erlbaum Associates.

Baer, D. M., Wolf, M. M., & Risley, T. R. (1968). Some current dimensions of applied behavior analysis. *Journal of Applied Behavior Analysis, 1,* 91–97.

Baer, D. M., Wolf, M. M., & Risley, T. R. (1987). Some still-current dimensions of applied behavior analysis. *Journal of Applied Behavior Analysis, 20,* 313–327.

Bellamy, G. T., Horner, R. H., & Inman, D. P. (1979). *Vocational habilitation of severely retarded adults: A direct service technology.* Baltimore, MD: University Park Press.

Bradley, R. (2009). Foreword. In W. Sailor, G. Dunlap, G. Sugai, & R. Horner (Eds.), *Handbook of positive behavior support* (pp. v–viii). New York: Springer.

Cook, B. G., & Odom, S. (2013). Evidence-based practices and implementation science in special education. *Exceptional Children, 79,* 135–144.

Daniels, A. C. (2001). *Other people's habits: How to use positive reinforcement to bring out the best in people around you.* New York: McGraw-Hill.

Dunlap, G., Sailor, W., Horner, R. H., & Sugai, G. (2009). Overview and history of positive behavior support. In W. Sailor, G. Dunlap, G. Sugai, & R. Horner (Eds.), *Handbook of positive behavior support* (pp. 3–16). New York: Springer.

Durand, V. M. (1998). *Sleep better!: A guide to improving sleep for children with special needs.* Baltimore, MD: Paul H. Brookes Pub. Co.

Filter, K. J., & Horner, R. H. (2009). Function-based academic interventions for problem behavior. *Education and Treatment of Children, 32,* 1–19.

Kazdin, A. E. (2008). *The Kazdin method for parenting the defiant child.* Boston, MA: Houghton Mifflin.

Kazdin, A. E. (2011). *Single-case research designs: Methods for clinical and applied settings* (2nd ed.). New York: Oxford University Press.

Kazdin, A. E. (2013). *Behavior modification in applied settings* (7th ed.). Long Grove, IL: Waveland Press.

Kincaid, D., Dunlap, G., Kern, L., Lane, K. L., Bambara, L. M., Brown, F., Fox, L., & Knoster, T. P. (2016). Positive behavior support: A proposal for updating and refining the definition. *Journal of Positive Behavior Interventions, 18,* 69–73.

Kohn, A. (1003). *Punished by rewards: The trouble with gold stars, incentive plans, A's, praise, and other bribes.* New York: Houghton-Mifflin.

Lewis, P. (1997). A case for teaching functional skills. *TASH Newsletter, 23*(3), 19.

National Autism Center. (2009, 2015). *National standards report.* National Autism Center, Randolph: MA.

Nye, R. D. (1992). *The legacy of B. F. Skinner: Concepts and perspectives, controversies and misunderstandings.* Wadsworth: Belmont, CA.

O'Donohue, W., & Ferguson, K. E. (2001). *The psychology of B. F. Skinner.* Thousand Oaks, CA: Sage Publications.

Reitman, D. (1998). Punished by misunderstanding: A critical evaluation of Kohn's punished by rewards and its implications for behavioral interventions with children. *The Behavior Analyst, 21,* 143–157.

Sailor, W., Goetz, L., Anderson, J., Hunt, P., & Gee, K. (1988). Research on community intensive instruction as a model for building functional generalized skills. In R. H. Horner, G. Dunlap, & R. L. Koegel (Eds.), *Generalization and maintenance: Life-style changes in applied settings* (pp. 67–98). Baltimore, MD: Paul H. Brookes Publishing Co.

Skinner, B. F. (1953). *Science and human behavior.* New York: MacMillan.

Skinner, B. F. (1971). *Beyond freedom and dignity.* New York: Knopf.

Storey, K., & Miner, C. (2017). *Systematic instruction of functional skills for students and adults with disabilities* (2nd ed.). Springfield, IL: Charles C Thomas Publisher, Ltd.

Tingstrom, D. H. (1989). Increasing acceptability of alternative behavioral interventions through education. *Psychology in the Schools, 26,* 194–201.

Tingstrom, D. H., & Edwards, R. (1989). Eliminating common misconceptions about behavior psychology: One step toward increased academic productivity. *Psychology in the Schools, 26,* 194–202.

Watson, J. B. (1913). Psychology as the behaviorist views it. *Psychological Review, 20,* 158–177.

Wehman, P., Renzaglia, A., & Bates, P. (1985). *Functional living skills for moderately and severely handicapped individuals.* Austin, Texas: Pro-Ed.

Wheeler, J. J., & Richey, D. D. (2013). *Behavior management: Principles and practices of positive behavior supports* (3rd ed.). Upper Saddle River, NJ: Prentice Hall.

Table 1.1
Perceived Barriers to Changing Behavior

Perceived Barrier	*Response*
People have to want to change	People change all the time even when they don't want to and often when they don't realize the change. These changes occur because people are constantly influenced by what people do and say to them (e.g., the environment).
Behavior is not an adequate guide to what a person is really like	We do not know what people are thinking and feeling, the only access we have is to their behavior (e.g., what they say or do). Behavior is all we have and behavior is all we need.
People resist change	When the immediate consequences of doing anything are negative, it is difficult to get a person to change. When the immediate consequences are positive, people want to change.
Controlling the behavior of others is controlling them	The word control may bring to mind restriction, repression, domination, and rule (e.g., coercion). As a support provider it is impossible to escape controlling the behavior of others. Control is a problem only when some form of force or seduction is used to get a person to do something that is illegal, immoral, or unethical. Without some control in a person's life there would be chaos.
A deliberate attempt to change the behavior of others is manipulation	Manipulation means to influence shrewdly or deviously. Devious manipulation is wrong but shrewdly means having keen insight and being astute (which are good skills for support providers to have).
Change is up to the person	To change the behavior of others you must change what you do. By changing what you do, you change the environment for those around you, which in turn changes them.
You have no right to change the behavior of others	Effective support is about changing the behavior of others.
Only feelings cause behavior	Feelings are effects of behavior, not causes. The best way to change a feeling is to change a behavior.
The laws of behavior don't apply to everybody	Everybody is different but the laws of behavior respect the fact that everyone is different.

Adapted from Daniels (2001).

Table 1.2
Context Relevance

1. A skill to be learned has immediate utility for the individual; it either produces something useful for the person or is part of a broader skill that does so.
2. A skill has desirability for the adult; it produces something for the person that would likely be chosen by that individual if an appropriate choice were arranged.
3. A skill is acquired in a social context; its acquisition is the product of interactions with more than a single (care-giving) person.
4. A skill is acquired in the actual, physical contexts in which the skin will ultimately be requested of the individual.
5. A skill has practicality for the adult; the skill is likely to be needed and practiced with some reasonable frequency.
6. A skill is appropriate to the adult's age; it will facilitate the individual's functioning in integrated circumstances.
7. A skill is adaptable; its cluster of topographical boundaries are sufficiently diffuse to enable the individual to respond to the needs of different stimulus configurations (situations) with appropriate adaptations, including different exemplars of materials where needed.

Adapted from Sailor, Goetz, Anderson, Hunt, & Gee. (1988).

Chapter 2

MEASURING BEHAVIOR

Key Point Questions

1. Why is it important to collect data?
2. How do you operationally define behavior and why is it important to do so?
3. What are dimensions of behavior for measurement purposes?
4. What are good ways to collect data?
5. Hoe do you know if behavior has changed?
6. How do you best present data for analysis?
7. How can you use technology in data collection?

WINDOW TO THE WORLD CASE STUDY ONE

Godfrey is 29 years old and has a new job working as an accountant for a large law firm. He has been identified as having a psychiatric disability and he found this job with assistance from a Department of Rehabilitation counselor and a Disabled Student Program Services specialist at the local community college. Godfrey is an excellent accountant but he is concerned as he has not done well in his previous jobs as an accountant. In his previous jobs, Godfrey was fired as he would sometimes stand at his desk and make verbal threats to people that were not there or would sing songs with explicit lyrics. In talking with his Rehabilitation counselor and DSPS specialist, Godfrey was unable to identify when these behaviors occurred or under what circumstances. So, the three of them agreed that Godfrey would take some data on when these behaviors both occurred and did not occur so that they would have relevant information to develop an appropriate intervention to help Godfrey. They decided to set up Godfrey's smart phone to vibrate every ten minutes. At that point in time, Godfrey would record whether he was engaged in either of the inappropriate behaviors or in an appropriate behavior, where he was, and what work task he was engaged in.

Godfrey collected this information over a two week period and then met with the counselor and DSPS specialist. As they reviewed the data, they discovered Godfrey had engaged in the inappropriate behaviors four times and, in each instance, it was when he received multiple work requests within a short time period. This allowed the three of them to analyze what was Godfrey's response when he was given multiple work requests (he became stressed and confused on how to handle the situation) and what the function of the behavior was (avoidance, as the coworkers quickly left him alone and dropped the requests). The three of them then came up with several strategies for Godfrey. First, they role played the situation with him and developed some positive social skills for him to use in that situation (explain to the coworkers that he had multiple requests, that he would prioritize them, and send out an email shortly with projected completion times). Then he would decide if this strategy was successful each time that it occurred and would immediately email or call the counselor and DSPS specialist to let them know. If this strategy was successful, he would self-deliver a small reinforcer immediately (a breath mint) and then, when at home, he would order his favorite pizza for dinner.

WINDOW TO THE WORLD CASE STUDY TWO

Merle is an adult with an intellectual disability who has recently moved from a state-run institution into a supported living situation where she has a roommate and receives 24-hour support. The supported living agency staff was aware that Merle engaged in aggressive behaviors when they agreed to support her, but the staff believes that her behavior is getting worse (and more than they can handle), and now wondering if it was a mistake to try and support her. A meeting is set up in two weeks to consult with personnel from the state Developmental Disabilities agency to decide whether or not Merle should return to the state institution.

Florence Korb, who is a supported living staff member, is not so sure that the aggressive behaviors are actually increasing. She believes that Merle is the first person that they have supported who has aggressive behaviors and that the staff is not well skilled to handle her behavior and, therefore, is becoming increasingly frustrated that the aggression has not stopped. Florence decides to have her staff collect two types of data. First, they use frequency counts to record each incident of aggression and also they rate the behavior on a scale of 1-10 (with 10 being the most intensive). At the meeting with the staff from the state Developmental Disabilities agency and the supported living staff, Florence presents her findings which indicate that the aggressive behavior is remaining constant (a mean of 2.2 incidents per day) and that the rating of the intensity of the behavior is also pretty constant (a mean of 4.3 per incident). Florence suggests that they continue to support Merle in her apartment but, also, bring in a consultant who has expertise in functional assessment and positive behavior supports in order to better understand why Merle is engaging in these aggressive behaviors and to determine what can best be done to help Merle to be successful in her new living situation. All of the staff agrees that they need the expertise in these areas.

KEY POINT QUESTION #1:
WHY IS IT IMPORTANT TO COLLECT DATA?

The only trustworthy way to know if the behavior of a person has changed is if you use a reliable measurement (data collection) system. With appropriate data collection you can determine the extent to which the skill or behavior of concern is performed prior to instruction (as shown in Figure 2.1) and also reflects any changes in the behavior after the intervention (as shown in Figure 2.2). The change in behavior can be provided in graphs and also described in words (Rae had a mean of 5.2 occurrences of noncompliance per hour at work before the intervention and a mean of 0.3 occurrences per hour following the intervention).

Measurement is the process used to assign values to variables. For example, "Most of the time" becomes 80% of the time or 8 out of 10, and "Hardly ever" becomes 10% of the time or 1 out of 10 opportunities. These measurements are specific and allow for deciding if behavior has changed or not. If the behavior has changed, a decision can be made as to whether it has changed for the better or for the worse.

While it is tempting to rely upon human judgment or general impressions to evaluate the extent to which behavior is performed or whether change has occurred, human judgments may distort the relative amount of behavioral concern. For example, an adult with a disability may have episodes of aggression so intense that support providers may recall them as occurring very often even when they are relatively infrequent. In contrast, a different adult may have episodes of aggression so frequently that support providers may become accustomed to a high rate and perceive them as being less frequent than they really are.

KEY POINT QUESTION #2: HOW DO YOU OPERATIONALLY DEFINE BEHAVIOR AND WHY IS IT IMPORTANT TO DO SO?

Measurement should be:

1. *Valid:* An accurate gauging of a dimensional quality (accuracy). The measurement system should measure what it is supposed to. For example, in measuring aggressive behavior you could record the number of hits which would be an accurate measure while recording the number of noncompliant behaviors would not be an accurate measure of aggression.
2. *Reliable:* The capacity of the assessment method to yield the same measurement value when repeated measurement is made of the behavior (stability). For example, if five different support providers are collecting data on Lily's aggressive behavior but they are all defining aggression differently, then their data will not be reliable and will not provide an accurate representation of Lily's behavior. The data collection then becomes a waste of everyone's time and an example of "garbage in, garbage out."

Issues in Measurement

Defining the unit of measure

For measurement purposes, constructs may be thought of as concepts that cannot be directly measured. For example, "being good" is a construct. Direct measures of behavior that represents being good could include following supervisor directions at work, speaking appropriately to authority figures, or getting to work on time. These measures could be used to represent "being good."

One of the problems with many definitions of the behavior to be assessed is the ambiguity of the wording. Definitions of behavior are often written so that few, if any, can read them and "know" what behavior they should actually be measuring. Precisely defined behaviors are stated in terms that are observable and measurable.

OBSERVABLE: You can see the behavior occur (e.g., "thinking" is not observable, while "complying with a job coach's direction" is observable). Table 2.1 presents examples of observable and nonobservable behaviors.

MEASURABLE: You can quantify the frequency, duration, or other measures of the behavior (e.g., counting the number of times a week that a person is on time to work can easily be quantified).

> EX: Increasing Nova's "desired" behavior or decreasing Nova's "undesired" behavior are not target behaviors that are stated in observable and measurable terms; the behaviors are not directly observable since the observer does not have a precise behavior (what is "desired" or "undesired" behavior) to observe.

> EX: "Nova is at work on-time" is precise and may be easily observed and measured (she is either at work on time or is not).

A definition should meet three criteria:

(1) OBJECTIVITY: This refers to observable characteristics of behavior or environmental events. The behavior and the environment are described in terms that do not require a person collecting data to infer, or guess, what is meant. A definition should not refer to inner states of the individual such as aggressiveness or emotional disturbances. Covert feelings or states are not objective. For example, "hitting others" is overt and can be observed and measured. "Feeling angry at others" is a state that is difficult to define, observe, and accurately measure.

(2) CLEAR: The definition of the behavior should be so unambiguous that it can be read, repeated, and paraphrased by observers. For example, stating that a person "will behave" while riding the bus is not a clearly defined target behavior and may be interpreted quite differently by different observers, or may change across time for an

observer. Stating that the individual "will stay seated while riding the bus" is clear and unambiguous.

(3) COMPLETE: The definition must delineate the boundary conditions so that the responses to be included and excluded can be enumerated. The definition tells both what is included and excluded from the definition. This clarity is very important in order for observers to know what to record as occurrences of the behavior (throwing a chair at someone counts as aggression towards others) as well as what not to record (throwing a chair out the window does not count as aggression towards others). This means that the definition of the behavior includes both positive examples (also known as occurrences) of what the behavior *is* and negative examples (nonoccurrences) of what the behavior *is not.* These examples and nonexamples help to ensure that all people collecting data are consistent in measuring behaviors as there are often "gray areas" in deciding if a behavior is a positive (occurrence) example or not. For instance, when recording aggressive behavior by a person, it may be decided that only physical acts towards another person are "aggression." Physical acts towards oneself (hitting oneself in the head) or threatening another person ("I'm going to punch you") may be defined as negative (nonoccurrence) examples of the behavior for this person. The person may engage in a behavior that has not occurred before (e.g., squirting toothpaste toward another person) and the team of data collectors can then decide if that counts as aggression for future recording. Without this agreement, you may have some staff members counting verbal threats as aggression while others are not. Thus, you would be getting unreliable data that does not accurately represent the person's behavior. Table 2.2 presents examples of operational definitions of behavior taken from professional journal articles. Table 2.3 presents an operational definition of aggression along with positive and negative examples.

KEY POINT QUESTION #3: WHAT ARE DIMENSIONS OF BEHAVIOR FOR MEASUREMENT PURPOSES?

There are three approaches to measurement: Observational, Standardized Tests, and Survey (Questionnaire/Interview). This chapter and book will focus on observational methods as they are most relevant and most frequently used in positive behavior supports. Dimension of behavior represent the construct that you are trying to measure. For instance, "desirable behavior" is a construct while specific behaviors could be following directions, interacting with coworkers appropriately, completing housework, and so forth. Each one of these behaviors represents possible measures of the construct of "desirable behavior" though, of course, no one measure completely represents the construct as a whole. Then, specific measurement systems (discussed after this section) are available to use to collect data on behaviors.

Measurement Via Observational Procedures

Type (Goal for Target Behavior)

First you need to define the purpose and the process of measurement. You need to consider this *before* you begin your data collection. What is the overall goal you are trying to accomplish considering target skills and behavioral concerns? There are seven types of goals:

1. *Description.* Are you wanting to describe the current state of the behavior?
2. *Increase.* Are you wanting to see if the behavior increases?
3. *Decrease.* Are you wanting to see if the behavior decreases?
4. *Acquisition.* Are you wanting to see if the individual learns a new skill?
5. *Maintenance.* Are you wanting to see if a person continues to perform a behavior over time?
6. *Generality.* Are you wanting to see if a person can generalize what they have learned (across time, settings, people, and/or behaviors)?
7. *Fluency.* Are you wanting to know how proficient an individual is (such as being able to prepare meals that are nutritious and edible)?

The purpose of your data collection will determine what method of data collection best meets your needs. For instance, using frequency counts would probably be helpful in determining if a behavior has increased or decreased but might not be good in determining fluency.

Dimensions of Behavior

There are a variety of dimensions of behavior and these then relate to the specific observational method that may be chosen to record the behavior of individuals.

1. Frequency

Frequency is the number of occurrences for a specified period of time. This may also be expressed as the rate of behavior which is the mean number of occurrences per minute or other standard of time such as an hour or work day.

Examples of Frequency:

- Number of times a person attends a club in the community.
- Number of objects thrown by an individual.
- Number of times a work task is completed by an employee.

Advantages in Using Frequency Data:

1. Extremely sensitive to behavior changes.
2. Convert behavior counts to a standard or constant scale (responses per minute).
3. Relatively simple to score and evaluate.

Disadvantages in Using Frequency Data:

1. Ongoing behaviors such as smiling, sitting in one's seat, lying down, and talking are difficult to record simply by counting because each response may occur for a different amount of time (talking to a peer for 15 seconds and to another peer for 30 minutes would each be scored as one instance of talking).
2. Very rapid behaviors may be difficult to count (a person who is tapping their pencil on their desk).

2. Percent

Percent is the number of occurrences of the behavior divided by opportunity. Percentage can be used for skills or behaviors having differing opportunities across days or observation times. Figure 2.3 provides an example of a data collection system for percentage.

Examples of Percent:

- Percent of work tasks performed correctly.
- Percent of times a person arrives back from lunch break on time.
- Percent of times when a person greets coworkers appropriately.

Advantages in Using Percent Recording:

1. Percent converts unequal opportunities to respond across sessions or days to a common scale, thereby "equalizing" the number of opportunities to respond for purposes of data summation and evaluation.
2. They are an efficient means of summarizing large numbers of responses.
3. They are a simple way to summarizing overall performance on a graph or chart.
4. They are often more familiar to people than other measures and therefore facilitate communication of performance.

Disadvantages in Using Percent Recording:

1. They make no reference to the time over which a behavior was observed, thus limiting what can be said about response proficiency.
2. Percentages place upper and lower limits (i.e., 100% and 0%) on reporting data and do not refer to the actual number of responses or opportunities to respond.
3. Percentages can mask trends in the data by not revealing when a response occurs during a particular observation period.
4. Percentages should not be used when the total number of opportunities to respond is less than 20, in which case one change in the numerator will produce greater than a 5% change.

3. Latency

Latency is from the beginning of a discriminative stimulus (such as a supervisor direction to switch work tasks) to the initiation of the response or behavior (time from cue to onset of behavior, how long does it take the worker to start work on the other task).

Examples of Latency:

- Number of seconds it takes a person to get on the bus once the doors open.
- Number of minutes it takes a person to get out of bed in the morning once they turn off the alarm.
- Number of seconds it takes an individual to pay for an item at the store once the clerk tells them how much the total cost is.

Advantages in Using Latency Recording:

1. Appropriate measure with compliance problems.
2. Appropriate for assessing delays in responding to discriminative stimuli.

Disadvantages in Using Latency Recording:

1. Can be difficult to accurately measure.

4. Duration

Duration is the time of responding (time from the onset of the behavior to the termination of the behavior).

Examples of Duration Recording:

- Number of minutes it takes a worker to complete a work task.
- Number of minutes engaged in conversation with coworkers.
- Number of minutes of "on-task" behavior by a worker.

Duration may involve the total time of a behavior across occurrences (how many minutes a worker was on-task during a one hour work period) or maybe per occurrence (how long a worker was on-task before going "off-task"). Using duration data per occurrence can also allow for the collection of frequency of behavior as well as duration.

Advantages in Using Duration Recording:

1. Good for determining if behavior that requires a time period or length of interaction (such as interacting appropriately with co-workers) has occurred or changed.

Disadvantages in Using Duration Recording:

1. Data collector needs to be in constant observation of the person being observed.
2. Need a device for determining start and stop times.

5. Lasting Effect of Behavior

This represents a permanent physical product (or artifact) that the person produces.

Examples of Lasting Effects of Behavior:

• Samples of work completed (such as number of items returned to shelves from the checkout counter).
• Videotapes of worker performance.

Advantages:

1. Efficient.
2. Easy to go back to product to evaluate.

Disadvantages:

1. Prone to problems if product produced via alternative behavior (such as someone else doing a work task).

6. Intensity

This represents the forcefulness or severity of a behavior. It usually requires some automated-quantitative apparatus (such noise level) or a subjective rating of the behavior.

Examples of Intensity:

- The loudness of a scream.
- How hard the individual hit his hand against the wall.

Advantages:

1. Can add an important dimension of assessment when combined with other types.

Disadvantages:

1. Can be too subjective and differences in scoring can occur across time or across observers.

7. Subjective Measures

These often use Likert-type rating scales (e.g., rate from 1–10) to add subjective data to objective data (Storey & Horner, 1991; Wolf, 1978).

Examples of Subjective Measures:

- Rating from 1-10 of how loud a person yelled (with 1 being lowest and 10 being loudest).
- Rating of 1-10 of how effective the social skills program was on increasing a worker's positive social interactions with coworkers (with 1 being not effective at all and 10 being very effective).

8. Multiple Measures

Multiple measures involve using more than one of the measures above in order to obtain a more complete measurement of performance. This can be important as often the measurement needs to describe a complex situation or construct.

Examples of Multiple Measures:

- Social Integration (might include frequency and duration of interactions and a subjective rating of the quality of the interactions).

- Work Task Competence (might include percent of tasks completed and duration of how long it took the worker to complete the tasks).

KEY POINT QUESTION #4:
WHAT ARE GOOD WAYS TO COLLECT DATA?

Training Observers

An often overlooked component of data collection is that you can't necessarily expect a support provider to go and collect reliable and valid data without any training. With any data collection system, you should:

1. Discuss the purpose of the data collection as well as any logistical issues related to data collection (e.g., where to observe the individual from, what if the person asks what you are doing, etc.).
2. Discuss the operational definition and positive and negative examples of the behavior. Try to get rid of "gray areas" if possible by deciding if a specific behavior is a positive or negative example of the behavior. For instance, deciding that attempting to hit someone but missing is a negative example of aggression.
3. Practice using the data collection system through role playing and/or videotapes of the individual. Discuss individual occurrences of the behavior during the videotape and come to agreement across observers.
4. Have observers independently score from role playing/videotapes and then compare with other observers (this is known as interobserver agreement). Try to get at 80% agreement or higher.
5. Conduct data collection on the individual in the situation in which data will be collected. Compare data across observers.
6. Retrain, as necessary, as new examples of the behavior may occur. There is often "observer drift" where observers may intentionally or unintentionally change their interpretation of the operational definition of the behavior or of the examples and nonexamples.

1. Event Recording

Event recording involves continuous observation. The number of "events" or occurrences of the behavior are counted. This is the total number of times behavior occurred during predetermined observation period. It is important to have a clear start and a clear stop time of the behavior (for example, hand flapping).

Figure 2.1 presents an event recording data form. In this example, George has had 4 occurrences of "talking out" behavior during meal preparation, 8 while doing the dishes, 0 during dinner time, 3 while taking a walk after dinner, and 1 while playing a card game with his roommate.

Advantages:

1. Most common.
2. Good when event is obvious or produces a permanent product.
3. Good when event is low to moderate frequency.

Disadvantages:

1. Less effective when event has several different behaviors.
2. Problem if behavior occurs too frequently.
3. No time information.
4. The observer must be continuously observing the person during the observation period.

2. Duration Recording

This is the length of time for each occurrence of the target behavior within a predefined observation period (may be either total duration or duration per occurrence). Usually a stopwatch, computer, or an automatic recording device is needed.

Figure 2.4 presents an example of Harry's work engagement during the first hour after lunch across three days. Over the 60-minute time period, his on-task work engagement was 9 minutes, 24 minutes, and 30 minutes.

Advantages:

1. Easy to score

Disadvantages:

1. Very intense as data collector must be constantly focused on individual.
2. May be difficult to measure behaviors of very short duration.

3. Latency Recording

Latency recording can be used to measure the time it takes a person to respond to discriminative stimuli in the environment. Figure 2.5 provides an example of latency recording for compliance to job coach directions. In this example, Valerie had a mean of 88 seconds (range 30 to 200 seconds) in responding to the cue (Sd) from the supervisor for being on-task with her work.

4. Interval Recording

This is also known as time sampling. This type of recording procedure is often used when the behavior of concern or skill can (or does) occur throughout the day. The observation period is divided into intervals (such as every minute or every five minutes) and it is recorded whether the behavior occurred within the interval. It is best to choose an interval that allows the behavior to occur at least once during that interval. For example, you could observe for 10 seconds and then record for 5 seconds. The behavior is scored as having occurred or not occurred during that interval. Generally, several occurrences of the behavior within an interval are not counted separately (though it is possible to combine event recording with interval recording). You then end up with a % of intervals in which the behavior occurred.

Advantages:

1. Good for high rate of behavior.

2. Good for complex codes (such as recording 3 different types of aggressive behavior and 4 different types of noncompliance on the same data sheet).
3. Good for behaviors that are of long duration.
4. Easily converted into percentages for when observations occur across different periods of time (such as when one work task period may be 50 minutes and then on a different day 120 minutes due to the amount of work for that task).

Disadvantages:

1. May artificially truncate behavior (because you do not have information on the duration of the behavior).
2. Need to select interval small enough or could lose information.
3. Coding is intermittent so sequential information is usually lost.

5. Partial Interval Recording

This is when a behavior is recorded as having occurred if it occurs at any point during the recording interval. For instance, if the interval is one minute and the behavior occurs at 25 seconds into that interval then it is scored as having occurred.

6. Whole Interval Recording

This is when a behavior must occur during the complete interval time period in order to be counted as an occurrence of the behavior. For example, if the interval is one minute then the behavior must occur for that complete minute in order to be scored as an occurrence of the behavior.

7. Momentary Interval Recording

With momentary interval recording, the individual is observed and the behavior is scored as having occurred or not occurred only at a set point in time, such as every minute. At that minute, there is a cue for the observer (minute hand on a watch or a beep on a recording device) that cues the observer to look at the individual and record whether the behavior is occurring or not occurring at that specific point in time.

Figure 2.6 presents the example of time sampling of Graham's verbal arguments. He had a verbal argument in 8 of the 70 intervals (11% of the intervals).

KEY POINT QUESTION #5:
HOW DO YOU KNOW IF BEHAVIOR HAS CHANGED?

In order to know if behavior has changed or not some sort of summarization or analysis of the data is necessary. This may be a table, a narrative, or a graph. Without this summarization, it is only possible to make a guess if the behavior has changed or not as well as to what extent it has changed. This guessing is not a strong way to gauge change and unlikely to impress colleagues, supervisors, family members, legislators, attorneys, or other relevant people. The analysis should include a description of the behavior before the intervention and then during the intervention (Kennedy, 2005).

KEY POINT QUESTION #6:
HOW DO YOU BEST PRESENT DATA FOR ANALYSIS?

Visual representation of data in a graph is an efficient method for presenting information. It can easily be looked at and understood, and be quickly analyzed to see if change in behavior has occurred or not. Figure 2.2 provides an example of the frequency of socially appropriate remarks to peers using an A-B Single Case Research Design (Kennedy, 2005). In the figure, the Baseline Assessment (also known as the "A" phase or before the intervention having occurred) data show that socially desirable remarks occurred with a mean of 38.6 times per week (range 30-46). The intervention (also known as the "B" phase) consisted of Video Modeling and Social Skills instruction. During the intervention the employee made socially desirable remarks with a mean of 70.1 times per week (range 52-86). In addition, it is easy to look at the graph and determine that the employee's behavior is improving over time with the intervention.

A table consists of rows and columns that present numbers for analysis. Table 2.4 presents the same data as in Figure 2.2 and is one example of how data might be presented in table format. Even though

Table 2.4 contains the same data it is not as easy to analyze the behavior change as in Figure 2.2.

KEY POINT QUESTION #7:
HOW CAN YOU USE TECHNOLOGY IN DATA COLLECTION?

Technology in data collection may be "low" tech (such as a sheet of paper) or "high tech" (such as a laptop with software specifically designed for data collection). What is necessary is that the system of data collection works for the specific situation and for the people using the system. Some issues to consider in selecting the data collection system are:

1. The system is user friendly and collects reliable data.
2. It is easy and not time-consuming to summarize data from the system.
3. The more people collecting data the simpler that you want the system to be.
4. Data collection can be done covertly, if necessary so that the person does not change their behavior because they know that someone is taking data. For example, a support provider may reach into a pocket and push a button on a smart phone with the person unaware data has been collected. Covert data collection can also help to keep the person being stigmatized in work or community settings with someone obviously taking data on them.

Equipment/Procedures such as a smart phone or laptop with observation software, a notebook, wrist counters, a clipboard, a small pad of paper, moving coins from one pocket to another may be used for collecting data. These systems can be preset for the appropriate data collection methodology such as a data sheet being shrunk in size so that it fits into a day planner.

There are a variety of software programs and "apps" available for data collection. Tablets and smartphones can download apps that can be used for direct observation data collection. An app such as Behavior Tracker can be used to collect anecdotal, frequency, duration, or interval data and then present a graphic display of the data collection. Something as simple as the Notes app on a smartphone can be used to keep frequency counts and to record anecdotal data.

The increased availability of digital video use on smart devices can also be useful in assessment, analysis of data, and instruction. The use of video collection through these smart devices make using video throughout the assessment process accessible for most teachers. The video can be viewed later, for as many times as necessary, to give staff the opportunity to establish interrater reliability, analyze data, and/or archive for later use. Table 2.5 provides the web sites for different software and apps.

No matter what system is being used, certain elements should be present for data collection. These are:

1. The person's name.
2. Date.
3. Condition (baseline or intervention).
4. Skill or behavior being recorded with operational definition.
5. Observer collecting data (this is important if different people are collecting data on the same individual).
6. The representation of the system for data collection (how the format is set for actual collection of the data).
7. Summarization of the data. This may be for a specific class, or on a daily, weekly, and so on basis.

BEST PRACTICE RECOMMENDATIONS

1. Only collect data on important behaviors.
2. Collect data on desirable as well as undesirable behaviors.
3. Analyze your data and use it for decision making, otherwise, don't bother to waste your time collecting data you do not use.
4. Collect data on Individual Plan goals.
5. Use data collection systems that are described in the method section of professional journal articles. Professional journals are a good source for illustration of valid and well tested methods (see suggested journals in the Appendix).

DISCUSSION QUESTIONS

1. What is the best way to determine if the behavior of an individual has changed?

2. How often should data be collected and analyzed?
3. Who should collect data?
4. What are good ways to share data analysis with other support providers, administrators, family members, and the person with the disability?
5. What are important and meaningful behaviors to take data on?

WORK, COMMUNITY, AND RESIDENTIAL ACTIVITY SUGGESTIONS

1. Choose an undesirable behavior of an individual and write an operational definition with positive and negative examples.
2. Compare your operational definition with similar ones in the method section of professional journals articles.
3. Choose a positive support provider skill (such as praising an individual or providing feedback) and collect data on how often you engage in that behavior.
4. Have multiple people collect data on an individual at the same time. Compare the results to see how reliable they are across the observers (Kennedy, 2005).

REFERENCES CITED IN CHAPTER

Carter, D. R., & Horner, R. H. (2007). Adding functional behavioral assessment to first step to success: A case study. *Journal of Positive Behavior Interventions, 9,* 229–238.

Christophersen, E. R., Arnold, C. M., Hill, D. W., & Quilitch, H. R. (1972). The home point system: Token reinforcement procedures for application by parents of children with behavior problems. *Journal of Applied Behavior Analysis, 5,* 485–497.

Dracobly, J. D., & Smith, R. G. (2012). Progressing from identification and functional analysis of precursor behavior to treatment of self-injurious behavior. *Journal of Applied Behavior Analysis, 45,* 361–374.

Ellingson, S. A., Miltenberger, R. G., Stricker, J., Galensky, T. L., & Garlinghouse, M. (2000). Functional assessment and intervention for challenging behaviors in the classroom by general classroom teachers. *Journal of Positive Behavior Interventions, 2,* 85–97.

Kennedy, C. (2005). *Single-case designs for educational research.* Boston, MA: Allyn & Bacon.

Lehardy, R. K., Lerman, D. C., Evans, L. M., O'Connor, A., & Lesage, D. L. (2013). A simplified methodology for identifying the function of elopement. *Journal of Applied Behavior Analysis, 46,* 256–270.

Peters, L. C., & Thompson, R. H. (2013). Some indirect effects of positive practice overcorrection. *Journal of Applied Behavior Analysis, 46,* 613–625.

Storey, K., & Horner, R. H. (1991). An evaluative review of social validation research involving persons with handicaps. *Journal of Special Education, 25,* 352–401.

Tiger, J. H., Fisher, W. W., & Bouxsein, K. J. (2009). Therapist- and self-monitored DRO contingencies as a treatment for the self-injurious skin picking of a young man with asperger syndrome. *Journal of Applied Behavior Analysis, 42,* 315–319.

Wolf, M. M. (1978). Social validity: The case for subjective measurement or how applied behavior analysis is finding its heart. *Journal of Applied Behavior Analysis, 11,* 203–214.

Wong, S. E., Terranova, M. D., Bowen, L., Zarate, R., Massel, H. K., & & Liberman, R. P. (1987). Providing independent recreational activities to reduce stereotypic vocalizations in chronic schizophrenics. *Journal of Applied Behavior Analysis, 20,* 77–81.

GENERAL REFERENCES REGARDING TOPICS IN CHAPTER

Alberto, P. A., & Troutman, A. C. (2013). *Applied behavior analysis for teachers* (9th ed.). Englewood Cliffs, NJ: Prentice-Hall.

Bambara, L., M., Janney, R., & Snell, M. E. (2015). *Behavioral support* (3rd ed.). Baltimore, MD: Paul H. Brookes.

Barlow, D. H., Nock, M. K., & Hersen, M. (2009). *Single-case experimental designs: Strategies for studying behavior change* (3rd ed.). New York: Allyn & Bacon.

Brown, F., Anderson, J., & De Pry, R. L. (2014). *Individual positive behavior supports: A standards-based guide to practices in school and community settings.* Baltimore: Paul H. Brookes Publishing.

Dunlap, G., & Carr, E. G. (2007). Positive behavior support and developmental disabilities: A summary and analysis of research. In S. L. Odom, R. H. Horner, M. Snell & J. Blacher (Eds.), *Handbook of developmental disabilities* (pp. 469–482). New York: Guilford.

Durand, V. M. (2014). *Autism spectrum disorder: A clinical guide for general practitioners.* Washington, DC: American Psychological Association.

Gast, D. L., & Ledford, J. L. (2014). *Single subject research methodology in behavioral sciences* (2nd ed.). New York, NY: Routledge.

Horner, R. H., Dunlap, G., & Koegel, R. L. (1988). *Generalization and maintenance: Lifestyle changes in applied settings.* Baltimore, MD: Paul Brookes.

Kearney, A. J. (2015). *Understanding applied behavior analysis: An introduction to ABA for parents, teachers, and other professionals* (2nd ed.). Philadelphia, PA: Jessica Kingsley Publishers.

Koegel, L. K., & LaZebnik, C. (2014). *Overcoming autism: Finding the answers, strategies, and hope that can transform a child's life.* New York: Penguin Books.

Miltenberger, R. G. (2016). *Behavior modification: Principles and procedures* (6th ed.). Boston, MA: Cengage Learning.

National Autism Center. (2009, 2015). *National standards report.* National Autism Center, Randolph: MA

National Autism Center. (2009). *Evidenced-based practice and autism in the schools.* National Autism Center, Randolph: MA.

Odom, S. L., Brantlinger, E., Gersten, R., Horner, R. H., Thompson, B., & Harris, K. R. (2005). Research in special education: Scientific methods and evidence-based practices. *Exceptional Children, 71,* 137–148.

Odom, S. L., Cox, A. W., & Brock, M. E. (2013). Implementation science, professional development, and Autism Spectrum Disorders. *Exceptional Children, 79,* 233–251.

Sturmey, P., & Didden, R. (2014). *Evidence-based practice and intellectual disabilities.* Hoboken, NJ: Wiley-Blackwell.

Taubman, M., Leaf, R., & McEachin, J. (2011). *Crafting connections: Contemporary Applied behavior analysis for enriching the social lives of persons with autism spectrum disorder.* New York, NY: DRL Books, Inc.

Tincani, M., & Bondy, A. (2014). *Autism spectrum disorders in adolescents and adults: Evidence-based and promising interventions.* New York: The Guilford Press. Maryland: Paul H. Brookes Publishing.

Winston, M. (2016). *Adventures in special education and applied behavior analysis.* Cornwall-on-Hudson, NY: Sloan Publishing.

Table 2.1
Examples of Observable and Nonobservable Behaviors

Examples of Observable Behaviors	*Examples of Nonobservable Behaviors*
Jenny will complete her assignments during work time.	Jenny will be a good worker during work times.
Bruce will use his fork to eat his food during lunch time.	Bruce will be polite during lunch time.
Salomea will talk to coworkers during break times.	Salomea will be cooperative with oworkers.
Evan will ask for a break when he is angry.	Evan will think before he acts when he is angry.
Jeff will wait for his turn during when boarding the bus.	Jeff will get along with others when boarding the bus.
Matthew will put away all dishes from the dishwasher before leaving the house in the evenings.	Matthew will remember to do his chores.

Table 2.2
Examples of Definitions of Behavior

Self-Injury:	Openhanded slaps to the head or face, punches to the head or face, and head banging against stationary objects (Dracobly & Smith, 2012).
Talking to Oneself:	Any vocalization not directed at another person but excluding physiological functions such as coughing (Wong, Terranova, Bowen, Zarate, Massel, & Liberman, 1987).
Skin Picking:	Skin picking: (a) closing his thumb and any finger around any portion of his body, (b) rubbing his hands or fingers against his skin, or (c) inserting his fingers into his nose (Tiger, Fisher, & Bouxsein, 2009).
Compliance:	Engaging in requested behavior within 10 seconds of a given request. (Ellingson, Miltenberger, Stricker, Galensky, & Garlinghouse, 2000).
Elopement:	Moving the body completely across the threshold of a doorway. (Lehardy, Lerman, Evans, O'Connor, & Lesage, 2013).
Stereotypy;	Flapping his hands or arms, rocking his torso or body, repeated and nonfunctional shaking of his head, jumping and turning in circles, and banging, tapping, mouthing, waving, or repeated dropping of session materials. (Peters & Thompson, 2013).

Table 2.3
Behavioral Definition of Aggression with Positive and Negative Examples

Global Definition:
Aggression is verbal or physical behavior towards another person that results in or has the potential to result in harm to that person.

Positive (occurrence) Examples:
> Poking eye of another person.
> Slapping another person.
> Hitting another person with object.
> Pulling ear of another person.
> Banging heads of other people together.

Negative (non-ccurrence) Examples:
> Saying thank you.
> Hugging.
> Smashing objects.
> Removing glasses and breaking them.
> Laughing.

Table 2.4
Frequency of Socially Desired Remarks by an Employee to Coworkers

Week	Frequency	Phase
1	41	Baseline
2	46	Baseline
3	41	Baseline
4	35	Baseline
5	30	Baseline
6	52	Intervention
7	59	Intervention
8	57	Intervention
9	65	Intervention
10	70	Intervention
11	75	Intervention
12	75	Intervention
13	81	Intervention
14	81	Intervention
15	86	Intervention

Table 2.5
Observation Apps and Software

ABC data and ABC Logbook (http://cbtaonline.com)
Yacker-Tracker noise detector (http://www.yackertracker.com)
Behavior Snap (http://www.behaviorsnap.com/)
Behavior Tracking Pro http://www.behaviortrackerpro.com/
Decibel 10 (www.skypaw.com)
Central Reach (www.centralreach.com)

Figure 2.1
Event Data Sheet

Person: George
Behavior: Talking Out
Operational Definition: Any statement made by the person that interrupted or interfered with instruction or disrupted coworker' attention to task (on-task engagement). (adapted from Carter & Horner, 2007).

Time Period	Occurrences	Activity	Data Collector
5:00 – 5:45	/ / / /	Meal preparation	Keith
5:45 – 6:15	0 occurrences	Dinner time	Keith
6:15 - 6:45	/ / / / / / / /	Doing the dishes	Keith
6:45 - 7:45	/ / /	Walk after dinner	Michal
7:45 - 8:00	no data collection	Bathroom time	n/a
8:00 - 9:00	/	Playing card game	Michal

Figure 2.2
Frequency of Socially Appropriate Remarks to Peers

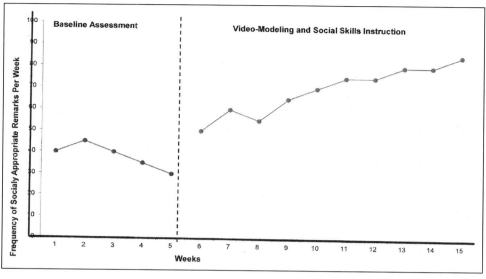

Figure 2.3
Percent Data Sheet

Individual: Haing

Behavior: Correct completion of work tasks.

Operational Definition: Work tasks are completed to specification of supervisor and meet quality control check.

Date	# opportunities	# behavior	Percentage	Activity	Data Collector
9/9	20	10	50%	Filing	Keith
9/10	20	12	60%	Filing	Keith
9/11	20	15	75%	Filing	Keith
9/12	20	18	90%	Filing	Keith

Figure 2.4
Duration Data Sheet

Individual: Harry
Behavior: Work Engagement
Operational Definition: Orienting toward the work activities, engaging physically or verbally with materials, objects, tasks, or coworkers as appropriate; or engaging in appropriate activities approved by the supervisor (adapted from Carter & Horner, 2007).

Date	Start Time	Stop Time	Total Time	Activity	Data Collector
9/6	8:14	8:19	5 min	Circle Time	Michal
9/6	8:22	8:23	1 min	Circle Time	Michal
9/6	8:31	8:35	4 min	Circle Time	Michal
9/7	8:10	8:21	11 min	Circle Time	Michal
9/7	8:23	8:36	13 min	Circle Time	Michal
9/8	8:11	8:32	21 min	Circle Time	Keith
9/8	8:35	8:44	9 min	Circle Time	Keith

Figure 2.5
Latency Data Sheet

Individual: Valerie
Behavior: Compliance
Operational Definition: Engaging in requested behavior within 10 seconds of a given request. (Ellingson, Miltenberger, Stricker, Galensky, & Garlinghouse, 2000).

Date	Cue (Sd)	Time to Response	Activity	Data Collecte
2/29	Go to kitchen	45 sec	Start making lunch	Keith
2/29	Get bread out	33 sec	Making lunch	Keith
2/29	Get cheese and ham out of fridge	68 sec	Making lunch	Keith
2/29	Put lunch food and materials away	30 sec	Clean up	Keith
3/1	Put cell phone away	200 sec	Time to start work tasks	Michal
3/1	Get materials out	150 sec	Work time	Michal

Figure 2.6
Interval Data Sheet

Individual: Graham
Behavior: Bickering
Operational Definition: Verbal arguments louder than the normal speaking voice between any individuals (adapted from Christophersen, Arnold, Hill, & Quilitch, 1972)

Time	1	2	3	4	5	6	7	8	9	10
9:00	0	+	0	0	0	0	0	0	0	0
9:10	+	0	+	0	0	0	0	0	0	0
9:20	0	+	+	+	0	0	0	0	0	0
9:30	+	0	0	0	0	0	0	0	0	0
9:40	0	0	0	0	0	0	0	+	0	0
9:50	0	0	0	0	0	0	0	0	0	0
10:00	0	0	0	0	0	0	0	0	0	0

Record a + if the behavior occurred. Record a 0 if the behavior did not occur.
Type 1: Whole Interval: + = behavior occurred during the whole interval time period.
Type 2: Partial Interval: + = behavior occurred at some point during the interval time period.
Type 3: Momentary Interval: + = behavior occurred at beginning of the interval time period.

Chapter 3

FUNCTIONAL ASSESSMENT AND ANALYSIS

Key Point Questions

1. What are the functions of behavior?
2. What role do antecedents and consequences play in the understanding of behavior?
3. What is ABC analysis?
4. How should interviews be used in determining the function of the behavior?
5. How should direct observations be used in determining the function of the behavior?
6. How should systematic manipulations be used in determining the function of the behavior?
7. How do you determine replacement behaviors that serve the same function as the undesirable behaviors?

WINDOW TO THE WORLD CASE STUDY ONE

Margarita is a thirty something adult with a severe intellectual disability. She was living with her parents until recently when they moved into an elder care situation and it was no longer possible for Margarita to continue to live with them. Margarita has moved into a supported living situation where she is living in a house (bought by Margarita's parents for her) with a roommate, Alma, who is without a disability. Alma lives in the house rent free and provides support to Margarita in the evenings (Margarita receives support from a supported living agency in the mornings and on the weekends). Margarita works five days a week at the city housing bureau where she receives support from a supported employment agency job coach. She is doing well in her new living situation except sometimes she engages in unusual behaviors such as yelling and waiving her arms, throwing herself into furniture, and has started dropping plates onto the kitchen floor to break them. Alma and the supported living staff are concerned as these behaviors have been increasing.

Fortunately, the supported living agency has contracted with Dr. Haymes who has a strong background in applied behavior analysis and functional assessment. After performing a comprehensive functional assessment, Dr. Haymes hypothesized that Margarita was acting out in order to get attention from Alma and the supported living staff. Part of the functional assessment involved interviewing Margarita's parents. The parents shared that in the evenings and weekends, when Margarita was living with them, they would often do activities together at home or in the community and often with a variety of friends.

After these interviews and observations (including an observation in the home), Dr. Haymes decides that the function of Margarita's undesirable behavior is to get attention. She developed this hypothesis statement: "When Margarita is at home and does not receive positive social interactions at least four times an hour from Alma or supported living staff, Margarita engages in undesirable behavior in order to get attention."

Based upon this information and hypothesis statement, Dr. Haymes decided upon a two-pronged approach. First, she thought that it was important to teach positive attention-getting skills to Margarita. Since Margarita is nonverbal, Dr. Haymes developed an app for Margarita's smart phone and tablet where Margarita had only to press an icon and a voice would say, "Hi, I would like some attention and would like to do an activity with you." This provided Margarita with a positive way to initiate getting attention. Second, Dr. Haymes set up a system so that Alma's phone would vibrate every 30 minutes in the evenings and mornings during the work week, and throughout the day during the weekends, for the supported living staff. This vibration served as a prompt to alert staff to initiate, at that point in time, an interaction with Margarita, or to make a positive comment if they were already engaged in an activity. Because of these two interventions, Margarita's undesirable behaviors decreased to zero and, not surprisingly, her positive social interaction with Alma and the supported living staff also increased, making the home environment more pleasant for everyone.

WINDOW OF THE WORLD CASE STUDY TWO

Gayther is a 28-year-old adult with Autism Spectrum Disorders. Gayther works in a hospital where he preps and sterilizes equipment for surgery. Gayther is ideal for this important job because of his attention to detail and obsession for cleanliness. At his first six-month review, Gayther's supervisor, Ms. Lazaro, was so pleased with Gayther's performance she put him on permanent status and gave him a raise.

However, recently, two problems have developed that are of concern to the supervisor. First, the entire staff in the sterilization area take a break together in the adjacent break room at the same time every day. Gayther becomes visibly upset during these times and will sometimes suddenly bolt out of the room. Second, when there is a staff meeting (such as going over the surgery schedule for the week) where Gayther has to be present, he will often start making loud repetitive statements over and over that have no relevance to the meeting ("Have you ever been to Istanbul?") and Ms. Lazaro often has to ask him to leave the meeting, providing the information individually to Gayther later.

Ms. Lazaro talks with Gayther's job coach, Ms. Forte, (Ms. Forte usually stops in once a week to check in with Gayther and Ms. Lazaro to see if any work performance problems have developed). Ms. Lazaro discusses these concerns with Ms. Forte, who makes sure to observe Gayther as soon as possible. When observing Gayther, Ms. Forte uses the Functional Assessment Observation Form (O'Neill et al., 2015) and, also, interviews Gayther and some coworkers using the interview form provided by O'Neill et al. (2015). The collected data on this form provide Ms. Forte with a clear analysis of what is happening. Gayther is engaging in the undesirable behaviors in order to escape from the two situations. First, in the break room, the table and kitchen area often have spills or food left on them. Second, during the meetings, Gayther is usually sitting very close to coworkers with varying degrees of hygiene and many times they brush up against him. With his obsession with cleanliness, Gayther finds it difficult to maintain in these two situations so he often engages in the undesirable behaviors in order to remove himself from the uncomfortable situations (escape behaviors).

With this information, Ms. Forte develops several strategies for Gayther. First, she teaches Gayther relaxation and visualization strategies to use during meetings. She meets with Gayther outside of work and teaches him how to count and breathe deeply and engage in muscle tensing and relaxation. They role play this technique with some friends who sit close to Gayther and brush up against him. Also, during this role play, she teaches him to visualize himself going to his work area immediately after the meeting and using hand wipes to clean his hands and areas of his clothes where others may have brushed up against during the meeting. This intervention combines antecedent and consequence strategies. For the break room situation, Ms. Forte, Gayther, and Ms. Lazaro come up with a variety of strategies. First, signs are put up reminding people to clean up spills; Ms. Lazaro then develops a sign-up sheet for workers to clean the break room on a daily basis. Third, Ms. Forte role plays the relaxation and visualization strategies with Gayther, who then practices them in the break room area. Additionally, Gayther decides to add a self-reinforcement strategy where the dirtier the break room is, the greater the reinforcement is that he gives himself. If he handles the situation appropriately, he gives himself extra computer time at home or buys a special desert to have for dinner. These strategies prove successful for Gayther and he is now much better at handling these and similar situations. Moreover, he now has confidence these strategies are effective and he has helped to develop them.

KEY POINT QUESTION #1:
WHAT ARE THE FUNCTIONS OF BEHAVIOR?

Research has increasingly shown that many behaviors, traditionally viewed as undesirable, are used to convey social intent, or in other words serve a function for the adult with a disability (Cipani, 2018; Filter & Horner, 2009; Waller, 2009). For example, a supported employee may "mouth off" to a supervisor in order to escape or avoid work tasks or other work demands. Undesirable behaviors are frequently misinterpreted by support providers as nonfunctional and in need of immediate suppression. However, once these individuals are taught alternative behaviors that are more adaptive (that build skills for the person and serve the same function) than the undesirable, the undesirable behaviors often rapidly disappear (Chandler & Dahlquist, 2015).

Determining the function of any undesirable behavior is critically important to understanding and developing an intervention (whether formal or informal). Functional assessment is *the key* to effective behavioral support. Functional assessment should lead to a focus on preventing undesirable behaviors from occurring rather than waiting for the behavior to occur and then punishing it. Because the focus of assessment is on determining the function of the behavior, intervention is more likely to be successful because the focus is on replacing disruptive behavior with appropriate behaviors that serve the same function (O'Neill, Albin, Storey, Horner, & Sprague, 2015).

A functional assessment is a process whereby informed hypothesis statements are developed about relationships between events in the environment and the occurrence of a person's undesirable behaviors (Larson & Maag, 1998). Table 3.1 provides examples of hypothesis statements. These relationships have been characterized as involving either: (a) the operations of a reinforcement contingency, including both positive and negative reinforcement; or (b) controlling antecedent stimulus in the environment (Foster-Johnson & Dunlap, 1993).

Current perspectives on undesirable behaviors call for identifying the specific function or functions served by undesirable behavior. The two major functions behaviors may serve are: (a) to obtain something desirable, (b) to escape or avoid something undesirable.

A functional analysis is an assessment method for identifying the relationship between behaviors and the setting, antecedent, and consequent events that maintain the behaviors. The difference between functional assessment and functional analysis is that a functional assessment includes interviews and/or direct observations while a functional analysis involves systematic manipulations of environmental events.

A complete functional analysis involves three strategies: (a) interview, (b) direct observation, and (c) systematic manipulations.

It is often possible to understand the function of a behavior with interviews and simple observations and then there is no need for a complete functional analysis. For instance, seeing a person who yells "no" to a staff person's request and then turns his back on the staff person, the function of the behavior is clearly understood to escape the task request. There would be no need to conduct a formal functional analysis.

The purpose of the functional assessment is to understand the function served by the undesirable behavior and to plan interventions based on that function.

A functional analysis is complete when five main outcomes are accomplished:

1. A clear description of the undesirable behavior(s), including classes (classes of behavior are groups of behavior that are of the same topography and serve the same function such as hitting, kicking, biting may be classed as "aggressive behaviors") or sequences of behaviors that frequently occur together.
2. Identification of the events, times, and situations that predict when the undesirable behavior(s) *will* and *will not* occur across the full range of typical daily routines (knowing when undesirable behavior does not occur, such as when a worker is engaged on a specific work task, can provide information that is as important as knowing when undesirable behavior does occur).
3. Identification of the consequences that maintain the undesirable behaviors (that is, what function(s) the behavior appears to serve for the student).
4. Development of one or more summary statements or hypotheses that describe specific behaviors, the specific type of situations in which they occur, and the outcomes or reinforcers maintaining them in that situation.
5. Collection of direct observation data that support the summary statements that have been developed.

In addition, the functional assessment:

1. Provides information on practical functional and social skills that will help enable the person to succeed in the criterion environment.
2. Contains an ecological emphasis that looks at the person functioning in his or her work, residential, and/or community environments.
3. Examines the process of learning and performance.
4. Suggests intervention techniques that may be successful.
5. Specifies ongoing assessment procedures (see Chapter 2) that can evaluate intervention progress.

6. Avoids stressing deficits of the person in isolation from what is happening in the work, residential, or community environment.
7. Avoids reporting scores or labels.
8. Assessment is not episodic, it is formative as it interacts with ongoing instruction and evaluation.

The objective of the above procedures is to develop effective and positive (skill building) interventions. Because the process is based on some "value-laden" assumptions, it is important that these be made clear (see Table 3.2 for a summary of these values). Foster-Johnson and Dunlap (1993) and O'Neill et al. (2015) have reported that functional assessment procedures are based on the following basic assumptions.

First, adults with disabilities do not engage in undesirable behaviors on a random basis. There is logic to their behavior and functional assessment is an attempt to understand that logic. Undesirable behaviors are not abnormalities, but are reasonable adaptations necessitated by the abilities of the individual and the limitations of their environment to support them. For example, an individual who is verbally aggressively towards their coworkers (with the function being to get their attention) may not have the necessary social skills to initiate interactions in a more appropriate fashion (Gresham, 1997).

A second assumption of functional assessment is that the objective is not to define and eliminate undesirable behavior, but to understand the structure and function of that behavior in order to teach and develop effective alternative behaviors that are desirable. According to O'Neill et al. (2015), functional assessment will identify: a) unnecessary situations that prompt the undesirable behavior; b) new skills one can teach that will make undesirable behaviors unnecessary; and c) effective staff responses to the both desirable and undesirable behaviors. This focus is more likely to be effective than interventions which simply attempt to reduce undesirable behavior. This focus also promotes greater awareness of, and therefore better, manipulation of ecological components of the person's environment.

A third assumption is that undesirable behavior is related to the "context" in which it occurs. Undesirable behaviors occur in response to some stimulus or situation that can be identified. Therefore, changes in the circumstances can be important in changing the behavior. Context refers to all the events and sensations that might affect a person including: environmental events, instructions, staff behavior, peer interactions, activities, physiological, and emotional conditions (e.g., anxiety, fatigue, pain, hunger). By assuming that behavior is related to context, the focus of responsibility remains on those who work with the person. Service providers must examine the environment in which the individual functions and not, as is too often the case, use circular definitions to explain away undesirable behavior (such as behavior difficulties cannot be attributed to broad personality characteristics or states, or be blamed on other factors such as a poor home life or biological factors).

It is important to understand that individual behaviors may serve multiple functions for a person. For example, talking back to a supervisor may allow the employee to gain social attention in one situation (the function being to get) and in another situation to escape a difficult work task (the function being to avoid). This understanding helps to facilitate the process of developing and implementing an appropriate and effective intervention. Thus, an intervention such as sending the employee home for talking back to the supervisor when trying to get attention would be appropriate (it would be punishing the behavior) but would not be successful when the employee is talking back in order to escape the difficult work task (the employee would be negatively reinforced and the behavior would be likely to occur more frequently when the employee is presented with a difficult task).

KEY POINT QUESTION #2:
WHAT ROLE DO ANTECEDENTS AND CONSEQUENCES PLAY IN THE UNDERSTANDING OF THE FUNCTION OF BEHAVIOR?

As noted in Chapter 1, antecedents are what occur before a behavior and consequences are what occur after a behavior. The purpose of functional assessment is to understand how the antecedents and consequences are influencing the occurrence of the undesirable behavior.

Antecedents evaluate specific environments (busy work time versus slow work time), health (allergies), and home (did the person have breakfast before going to work), that predict the occurrence as well as the nonoccurrence of the undesirable behaviors (and also the prediction of desirable behavior).

Consequences increase, maintain, or decrease behavior. Understanding the consequences that occur after the undesirable behavior can be very important in functional assessment and in developing effective interventions. For example, if an adult is shopping in a store in a crowded situation and becomes agitated and the support provider has the person leave, then the person has been reinforced (e.g., negative reinforcement for the escape behavior) and in the future is more likely to engage in this undesirable behavior when in a crowded situation in a store.

KEY POINT QUESTION #3: WHAT IS ABC ANALYSIS?

In the ABC analysis, the A stands for antecedent, the B for behavior, and the C for consequence. The collection of data in this easy to use process can be helpful in analyzing the function of the behavior when there is one undesirable behavior and it occurs consistently. Figure 3.1 provides an ABC data sheet where escape is the undesirable behavior. The potential problem with an ABC analysis is that there may be a large amount of data collected, making it difficult to summarize and evaluate. For instance, in Figure 3.1, while there are nine instances of behavior, it is hard to look at the information on the data sheet and tell what the function of the behavior is or to determine a pattern to the behavior. And this is data for only one day. Similar data over a ten-day period would be even more difficult to evaluate.

KEY POINT QUESTION #4: HOW SHOULD INTERVIEWS BE USED IN DETERMINING THE FUNCTION OF THE BEHAVIOR?

The first step in performing a functional assessment is to conduct an in-depth interview with support providers, as well as with parents and other people knowledgeable about the person such as employers, coworkers, friends, and so on. Interviewing the adult may also be appropriate in many instances. There are a number of structured interview formats available (Dunlap, Kern-Dunlap, Clarke, & Robbins, 1991; Kern, Dunlap, Clarke, & Childs, 1995; O'Neill et al., 2015) which assist in identifying alternative replacement behaviors, setting events commonly associated with incidences of undesirable behavior, and observed social and environmental consequences of behaviors. The primary purpose of interview data is to begin to develop hypotheses about behavioral functions of undesirable behavior being exhibited by the individual. Taking the time to carefully interview will also assist support providers and others in examining their own actions as they relate to undesirable behaviors. It is with the interview that the intervention and training process actually begins. Table 3.3 lists important questions for a functional assessment interview. At this point in the functional assessment process, it is also important for the assessor to think about potential medical issues that may be contributing to the undesirable behavior. If there are medical conditions present (e.g. sleep disorders, allergies, dietary, etc.), support providers will need to work closely with medical practitioners in addressing the problems. The interview should also attempt to identify other ecological and historical variables that commonly contribute to the undesirable behavior of the adult, such as the support provider's behavioral history with the person, academic and learning difficulties, inconsistent past use of behavioral interventions, and potential family or living environment variables such as history of domestic violence, abuse, or neglect.

KEY POINT QUESTION #5:
HOW SHOULD DIRECT OBSERVATIONS BE USED IN DETERMINING THE FUNCTION OF THE BEHAVIOR?

Following the interview, systematic observation should be conducted using systems designed to contribute to hypothesis formation and validation. These systems may include a variety of direct observation methods including Antecedent Behavior Consequence data collection sheets (Cipani, 1993), scatter plots (Touchette, MacDonald, & Langer, 1985), and functional assessment observations systems (O'Neill et al., 2015).

The Functional Assessment Observation form (FAO) (O'Neill et al., 2015) is useful for collecting direct observation data. Figure 3.2 provides an example of the FAO form from O'Neill et al. (2015) for an adult named Peter. In this example, data has been collected over four days (9/12 through 9/15). The first section of the form lists the time frames for data collection (in this example it is of one-hour time periods). The second section lists undesirable behaviors (biting wrists, hitting face, and grabbing/pushing). The third section lists predictors (e.g., antecedents) for the behavior. The fourth section has the perceived functions of the behavior (get/obtain or escape/avoid). The fifth section lists the consequences. Then there is a section for comments. At the bottom of the form there is a section for scoring the frequency of the behavior per day. The first time an undesirable behavior occurs the appropriate boxes are marked with a number 1. For the occurrence, a number 1 is marked in each of the behavior, predictor, perceived functions, and consequence sections of the form. In this example, the first occurrence was biting wrist and grabbing/pushing which happened during the 8-9 time period. The predictor was shaving. The perceived function was to escape the activity. The consequence was that Peter was blocked and redirected. Then the number 1 in the events section was crossed off. Then each occurrence of the undesirable behavior is marked with a 2, then a 3, and so on. In this example, there were 7 occurrences of undesirable behavior during the first day. During the second day the first occurrence in this example is scored as an 8. This allows an overlay of data on the observation form so that patterns of behavior can more easily be analyzed.

In Figure 3.2, there are clear patterns for the undesirable behavior. First, the biting wrist and grabbing/pushing behaviors occurred together during shaving which suggests that they are members of the same response class and serve the same function (escape from the activity). The consequence was that staff would block the behavior and redirect Peter. The biting wrist and hitting face behaviors occur together when Peter is alone or not receiving attention and the perceived function is to get attention. The consequence was that staff would bock and redirect Peter. Another clear pattern is that there were no incidents of undesirable behavior during the 9-10 and 12-1 time periods. This information is just as important as knowing when undesirable behavior is occurring because it allows analysis of what is happening during these times so that Peter does not have to engage in undesirable behaviors. This understanding can help lead to interventions in other classes that are positive and proactive.

KEY POINT QUESTION #6:
HOW SHOULD SYSTEMATIC MANIPULATIONS BE USED IN DETERMINING THE FUNCTION OF THE BEHAVIOR?

One way to develop and/or verify hypothesized functions of behavior is to engage in functional analysis, also referred to as systematic manipulations (O'Neill et al., 2015). Functional analysis has been differentiated from functional assessment as a process in which the identified variables are directly manipulated in order to verify or clarify hypothesized relationships. The direct manipulations are conducted in the context of reversal or alternating treatment designs and have been referred to as experimental analysis or hypothesis testing (Dunlap et al., 1993). For instance, it could be hypothesized that when a support provider stands within one foot of Immanuel and gives him a directive that he becomes aggressive. In order to test this hypothesis, the support provider could alternate standing within one foot of Immanuel and then further away while giving him directives. By doing this, the support provider can evaluate if he does become aggressive when she is within one foot but does not when she is further away. Table 3.4 provides guidelines for conducting a systematic manipulation in a functional analysis.

KEY POINT QUESTION #7: HOW DO YOU DETERMINE REPLACEMENT BEHAVIORS THAT SERVE THE SAME FUNCTION AS THE UNDESIRABLE BEHAVIORS?

The primary goal of functional assessment is to identify the function of undesirable behavior. Once the function of the behavior is understood then it is possible to effectively develop strategies which replace undesirable behaviors with more adaptive alternative behaviors (also known as skill building or replacement behaviors). When the intervention is based on the function of the undesirable behavior, the general strategy is to both weaken the maintaining consequence and strengthen a positive skill building behavior that services the same function (Mace, Yankanich, & West, 1989). For example, if Freda is engaging in the behavior of throwing things in her home in order to get attention from her supported living provider, the replacement behavior could be teaching Freda appropriate methods of getting support provider attention, such as how to appropriately ask for help. The support provider could also give Freda attention at times when she is engaged in tasks at home, such as cooking which would make it less necessary for Freda to engage in undesirable behaviors to get attention and would also reinforce Freda's task completion behavior.

All too often the intervention chosen is based upon the topography of the behavior (what the observable behavior is, such as hitting or throwing things) rather than the function of the behavior. For example, a support provider may immediately terminate a community activity any time that an adult curses (the topography of the behavior). While this may be an effective intervention for some individuals, for a person who is engaging in the behavior in order to escape from a difficult performance situation, such as using a new ATM machine, the intervention of terminating the activity is ineffective due to the support provider inadvertently reinforcing the escape behavior. In this situation, the adult will then be more likely to curse in the future when presented with a difficult task.

The focus on teaching replacement behavior is proactive. In other words, the intervention takes place when the undesirable behavior is not occurring and is focused on making desirable behaviors more probable. This is in contrast to nonfunctional interventions which are mainly focused on decreasing undesirable behavior (Carr, Robinson, & Palumbo, 1990). The problem with a focus on nonfunctional interventions is that, while an undesirable behavior may be decreased, if the person does not have a desirable behavior to replace it with then the individual may engage in a different undesirable behavior that services the same function. For instance, if Mausolus hits his head in order to get staff attention and this undesirable behavior is eliminated through the use of punishment, then Mausolus still has no desirable way of getting staff attention, therefore, he may then pound his head in order to get staff attention. Table 3.5 provides examples of replacement behaviors that serve the same function as the undesirable behaviors.

In developing replacement behaviors, it is important that the replacement behavior is functionally equivalent to the undesirable behavior (it services the same function). The replacement behavior should:

1. Be as efficient for the person as the undesirable behavior (Horner, Sprague, O'Brien, & Tuesday-Heathfield, 1990).
2. Be something that the person chooses or wants to do.
3. Be skill building for the person.

BEST PRACTICE RECOMMENDATIONS

1. The function of the undesirable behavior should be understood before developing an intervention.

2. Interventions should teach positive (or replacement) behaviors that serve the same function as the undesirable behavior so that the person then has positive skills that they can use, and do not have to rely upon undesirable behaviors.

EMPLOYMENT, COMMUNITY, AND RESIDENTIAL ACTIVITY

1. Observe different undesirable behaviors in an employment, community, or residential setting and classify each behavior according to what you think its function is (to get or to avoid).
2. Ask support providers in that environment as to what they perceive the function of the undesirable behavior to be. See if their perceived function matches with yours.

DISCUSSION QUESTIONS

1. Are there other functions of behavior other than to get or to avoid?
2. Do interventions have to be based upon the function of the behavior to be successful?
3. How do you set up support guidelines for support providers when different adults may be engaging in the same undesirable behavior but for different functions?
4. What is wrong with reducing undesirable behaviors?

REFERENCES

Carr, E. G., Robinson, S., & Palumbo, L. W. (1990). The wrong issue: Aversive versus nonaversive treatment. The right issue: Functional versus nonfunctional treatment. In A. C. Repp & N. N. Singh (Eds). *Perspectives on the use of nonaversive and aversive interventions for persons with developmental disabilities* (p. 361–379). Sycamore, IL: Sycamore Publishing Company.

Chandler, L. K., & Dahlquist, C. M. (2015). *Functional assessment: Strategies to prevent and remediate challenging behavior in school settings* (4th ed.). Upper Saddle River, NJ: Merrill/Pearson.

Cipani, E. (1993). *The Cipani behavioral assessment and diagnostic system.* Bellevue, WA: Edmark Publishers.

Cipani, E., (2018). *Functional behavioral assessment, diagnosis, and treatment: A complete system for education and mental health settings* (3rd ed.). New York: Springer Pub.

Dunlap, G., Kern-Dunlap, L., Clarke, S., & Robbins, F. R. (1991). Functional assessment, curricular revision, and severe behavior problems. *Journal of Applied Behavior Analysis, 24,* 387–397.

Dunlap, G., Kern, L., dePerczel, M., Clarke, S., Wilson, D., Childs, K. E., White R., & Falk, G. D. (1993). Functional analysis of classroom variables for students with emotional and behavioral disorders. *Behavioral Disorders, 18,* 275–291.

Filter, K. J., & Horner, R. H. (2009). Function-based academic interventions for problem behavior. *Education and Treatment of Children, 32,* 1–19.

Foster-Johnson, L., & Dunlap, G. (1993). Using functional assessment to develop effective, individualized interventions for challenging behaviors. *Teaching Exceptional Children, 25,* 44–50.

Gresham, F. M. (1997). Social competence and students with behavioral disorders: Where we've been, where we are, and where we should go. *Education and Treatment of Children, 20,* 233–249.

Horner, R. H., Sprague, J. R., O'Brien, M., & Tuesday-Heathfield, L. (1990). The role of response efficiency in the reduction of problem behaviors through functional equivalence training: A case study. *Journal of the Association for Persons with Severe Handicaps, 15,* 91–97.

Kern, L., Dunlap, G., Clarke, S., & Childs, K. E. (1995). Student-assisted functional assessment interview. *Diagnostique, 19,* 29–39.

Larson, P. K., & Maag, J. W. (1998). Applying functional assessment in general education classrooms: Issues and recommendations. *Remedial and Special Education, 19,* 338–349.

Mace, F. C., Yankovich, M. A., & West, B. (1989). Toward a methodology of experimental analysis and treatment of aberrant classroom behaviors. *Special Services in the Schools, 4,* 71–88.

O'Neill, R. E., Albin, R. W., Storey, K., Horner, R. H., & Sprague, J. R. (2015). *Functional assessment and program development for problem behavior: A practical handbook* (3rd ed.). Stamford, CT: Cengage Publishing Company.

Touchette, P. E., MacDonald, R. F., & Langer, S. N. (1985). A scatter plot for identifying stimulus control of problem behavior. *Journal of Applied Behavior Analysis, 18,* 343–351.

Waller, R. J. (2009). *The teacher's concise guide to functional behavioral assessment.* Thousand Oaks, CA: Corwin Press.

Wong, S. E., Terranova, M. D., Bowen, L., Zarate, R., Massel, H. K., & Liberman, R. P. (1987). Providing independent recreational activities to reduce stereotypic vocalizations in chronic schizophrenics. *Journal of Applied Behavior Analysis, 20,* 77–81.

EMPIRICAL RESEARCH SUPPORTING THAT THE INTERVENTIONS PRESENTED IN CHAPTER ARE EVIDENCE BASED PRACTICES

Borgmeier, C., & Horner, R.H. (2006). An evaluation of the predictive validity of confidence ratings in identifying accurate functional behavioral assessment hypothesis statements. *Journal of Positive Behavior Interventions, 8,* 100–105.

Carr, E. G., & Durand, V. M. (1985). Reducing behavior problems through functional communication training. *Journal of Applied Behavior Analysis, 18,* 111–26.

Carter, D. R., & Horner, R. H. (2007). Adding functional behavioral assessment to First Step to Success: A case study. *Journal of Positive Behavior Interventions, 9,* 229–38.

Carter, D. R., & Horner, R. H. (2009). Adding function-based behavioral support to First Step to Success: Integrating individualized and manualized practices. *Journal of Positive Behavior Interventions, 11,* 22–34.

Chezan, L., Drasgow, E., & Martin, C. (2014). Discrete-trial functional analysis and functional communication training with three adults with intellectual disabilities and problem behavior. *Journal of Behavioral Education, 23,* 221–246.

Day, H. M., Horner, R. H., & O'Neill, R. E. (1994). Multiple functions of problem behaviors: Assessment and intervention. *Journal of Applied Behavior Analysis, 27,* 279–289.

Day, R. M., Rea, J. A., Schussler, N. G., Larsen, S. E., & Johnson, W. L. (1988). A functionally based approach to the treatment of self-injurious behavior. *Behavior Modification, 12,* 565–589.

Delgado-Casas, C., Navarro, J. I., Garcia-Gonzalez-Gordon, R., & Marchena, E. (2014). Functional analysis of challenging behavior in people with severe intellectual disabilities. *Psychological Reports, 115,* 655–669.

Dunlap, G., Kern, L., dePerczel, M., Clarke, S., Wilson, D., Childs, K. E., White, R., & Falk, G. D. (1993). Functional analysis of classroom variables for students with emotional and behavioral challenges. *Behavioral Disorders, 18,* 275–291.

Durand, V. M., & Carr, E. G. (1987). Social influences on "self-stimulatory" behavior: Analysis and treatment application. *Journal of Applied Behavior Analysis, 20,* 119–132.

Gregori, E., Rispoli, M., Gerow, S., & Lory, C. (2018). Treatment of self-injurious behavior in adults with intellectual and developmental disabilities: A systematic review. *Journal of Developmental and Physical Disabilities, 30,* 111–139.

Ingram, K., Lewis-Palmer, T., & Sugai, G. (2005). Function-based intervention planning: Comparing the effectiveness of FBA indicated and contra-indicated interventions plans. *Journal of Positive Behavior Interventions, 7,* 224–236.

Lambert, J. M., Bloom, S. E., Kunnavatana, S. S., Collins, S. D., & Clay, C. J. (2013). Training residential staff to conduct trial-based functional analyses. *Journal of Applied Behavior Analysis, 46,* 296–300.

Lang, R., O'Reilly, M., Machalicek, W., Lancioni, G., Rispoli, M., & Chan, J. M. (2008). A preliminary comparison of functional analysis results when conducted in contrived versus natural settings. *Journal of Applied Behavior Analysis, 41,* 441–445.

Lang, R., Sigafoos, J., Lancioni, G., Didden, R., & Rispoli, M. (2010). Influence of assessment setting on the results of functional analyses of problem behavior. *Journal of Applied Behavior Analysis, 43,* 565–567.

Newcomer, L. L., & Lewis, T. J. (2004). Functional behavioral assessment: An investigation of assessment reliability and effectiveness of function-based interventions. *Journal of Emotional and Behavioral Disorders, 12,* 168–181.

Santiago, J., Hanley, G., Moore, K., & Jin, C. (2016). The generality of interview-informed functional analyses: systematic replications in school and home. *Journal of Autism and Developmental Disorders, 46,* 797–811.

Sprague, J. R., & Horner, R. H. (1992). Covariation within functional response classes: Implications for treatment of severe problem behavior. *Journal of Applied Behavior Analysis, 25,* 735–745.

GENERAL REFERENCES REGARDING TOPICS IN CHAPTER

Carr, E. G., Levin, L., McConnachie, G., Carlson, J. L., Kemp, D. C., & Smith, C. (1993).Communication-based treatment of severe behavior problems. In R. Van Houten & S. Axelrod (Eds.), *Behavior analysis and treatment* (pp. 231–267). New York: Plenum.

Carr, E. G., Levin, L., McConnachie, G., Carlson, J. I., Kemp, D. C. & Smith, C. E. (1994). *Communication-based intervention for problem behavior: A user's guide for producing positive change.* Baltimore: Paul H. Brookes.

Carr, E. G., Reeve, C. E., & Magito-McLaughlin, D. (1996). Contextual influences on problem behavior in people with developmental disabilities. In L. K. Koegel, R. L. Koegel, & G. Dunlap (Eds.), *Positive behavioral support: Including people with difficult behavior in the community* (pp. 403–423). Baltimore: Paul H. Brookes.

Chandler, L. K., & Dahlquist, C. M. (2015). *Functional assessment: Strategies to prevent and remediate challenging behavior in school settings* (4th ed.). Upper Saddle River, NJ: Merrill/Pearson.

Cross, M. (2011). *Children with social, emotional and behavioral difficulties and communication problems: There is always a reason* (2nd ed.). Philadelphia, PA: Jessica Kingsley Publishers.

Filter, K. J., & Alvarez, M. E. (2011). *Functional behavioral assessment: A three-tiered prevention model.* New York, NY: Oxford University Press.

Freeman, R. L., Horner, R. H., & Reichle, J. (2002). Expanding functional assessment procedures to include physiological measurement in relation to environmental stimuli in case involving self-injurious behavior and self-restraint. In S. Schroeder, M. L. Oster-Granite, & T. Thompson (Eds.), *Self-injurious behavior: Gene-brain-behavior relationships.* Washington, DC: APA Books.

Horner, R. H. (1994). Functional assessment: Contributions and future directions. *Journal of Applied Behavior Analysis, 27,* 401–404.

Horner, R. H., & Carr, E. G. (1997). Behavioral support for students with severe disabilities: Functional assessment and comprehensive intervention. *Journal of Special Education, 31,* 84–104.

Kern, L., Dunlap, G., Clarke, S., & Childs, K. E. (1994). Student-assisted functional assessment interview. *Diagnostique, 19,* 29–39.

Lucyshyn, J. M., Olson, D. L., & Horner, R. H. (1999). Building an ecology of support for a young woman with severe problem behaviors living in the community. In J. R. Scotti & L. H. Meyer (Eds.), *Behavioral intervention: Principles, models, and practices* (pp. 269–290). Baltimore, MD: Paul H. Brookes Publishing Co.

Repp, A. C., & Horner, R. H. (1999). *Functional analysis of problem behavior: From effective assessment to effective support.* Belmont, CA: Wadsworth Publishing.

Sprague, J. R., & Horner, R. H. (1999). Low frequency, high intensity problem behavior: Toward an applied technology of functional analysis and intervention. In A. C. Repp & R. H. Horner (Eds.), *Functional analysis of problem behavior: From effective assessment to effective support* (pp. 98–116). Belmont, CA: Wadsworth Publishing.

Sugai, G., Horner, R. H., & Sprague, J. R. (1999). Functional assessment-based behavior support planning: Research-to-practice-to-research. *Behavioral Disorders, 24*(3), 253–257.

Sugai, G., Lewis-Palmer, T., & Hagan-Burke, S. (1999–2000). Overview of the functional behavioral assessment process. *Exceptionality, 8,* 149–160.

Tincani, M., Lorah, E. R., & Dowdy, A. (2018). *Functional behavioral assessment.* Austin, TX. Pro-Ed.

Table 3.1
Examples of Hypothesis Statements

1. Basil puts his head in his hands and closes his eyes in order to avoid tasks that are difficult for him.
2. Olga is likely to leave the kitchen and go to her room when her roommate reminds her that it is her turn to take out the garbage.
3. When Winston is alone or not receiving attention from a support provider, he will loudly sing to himself.
4. When there are transitions at work (from setting to setting or task to task), Tuol will refuse to move to the new setting or to leave the task that he is working on.
5. When support providers stand too close (within two feet) of Bernal, he will push them away with his hands.

Table 3.2
Values of Functional Assessment

1. Behavioral support must be conducted with the dignity of the individual as a primary regard.
   A. Functional assessment is appropriate because it acknowledges that a person's undesirable behavior is reasonable from that person's perspective.
   B. Adults do not engage in undesirable behavior because they have a disability label such as Down Syndrome, or emotional disturbance, or are regarded as obnoxious, bad, and so on.
   C. There is logic to the behavior of an individual and functional assessment is an attempt to understand that logic.
2. The objective of functional assessment is not to define and eliminate an undesirable behavior but to understand the structure and function of that behavior in order to *teach* the person how to develop positive skills, therefore not needing to engage in the undesirable behavior.
3. Functional assessment is a process for looking at relationships between behavior and the environment.
   A. It is as much an analysis of the environment (schedules, support provider behavior, physical settings) as it is of the behavior of the adult.
   B. The functional assessment should not become a process that "blames" the person for behaving in undesirable ways.

Table 3.3
Questions for a Functional Assessment Interview

1. List, describe, and prioritize behavior(s) of concern.
2. What do you think causes the behavior (e.g., what are the antecedents)?
3. What do you think is the function of the behavior?
4. How often do these behaviors occur?
5. Is there any circumstance under which the behavior does not occur?
6. Is there any circumstance under which the behavior always occurs?
7. Does the behavior occur more often during certain times of the day?
8. Does the behavior occur in response to the number of people present?
9. Does the behavior occur only with certain people?
10. Does the behavior occur only during certain tasks?
11. Could the behavior be related to any skills deficit?
12. What observable events signal that the behavior is about to occur?
13. What one thing could you do that would be likely make the undesirable behavior occur?
14. What are the consequences of the behavior?

Adapted from Dunlap, Kern-Dunlap, Clarke, & Robbins, (1991); O'Neill et al. (2015).

Table 3.4
Guidelines for Conducting Functional Analysis Manipulations

A: Identify specific variables to be assessed during manipulations.
B: Determine the level of risk that may be involved.
C: Ensure that relevant variables can be controlled and manipulated.
D: Obtain appropriate reviews and approvals.
E: Have enough staff available to maintain safety during sessions.
F: Determine specific criteria for terminating sessions if needed.
G: Consider the use of protective equipment for individuals and/or support providers.
H: Consider using precursor behaviors as signals for terminating sessions.
I: Employ appropriate data collection and design procedures.

Table 3.5
Examples of Matching Interventions with
Replacement Behaviors that Serve the Same Function

Function of Behavior	*Potential Interventions*
Dawn becomes aggressive towards others when she doesn't understand support provider directions (escape behavior).	Teach how to ask for help when directions are not clear.
Kristin likes to receive attention from coworkers (get behavior) but greets them inappropriately which evokes a negative response from her coworkers.	Teach appropriate greeting skills.
Johann excessively asks questions of his supervisor at work (get behavior, attention from supervisor).	Teach a self-management strategy for limited question asking and then self-recruited feedback for attention and reinforcement from the supervisor.
Roald gets very anxious in crowded settings and will cause commotion so that he is removed from the setting (escape behavior).	Teach relaxation techniques in combination with a self-management strategy.

Figure 3.1
ABC Data Sheet

Person: Hubert
Behavior: Talking to Oneself
Operational Definition: Any vocalization not directed at another person but excluding physiological functions such as coughing (Wong, Terranova, Bowen, Zarate, Massel, & Liberman, 1987).

Date	*Antecedent*	*Behavior*	*Consequence*
2/1	Working by self in office	Talking to self	Ignored by other workers
2/1	No attention from job coach for 15 minutes	Talking to self very loud	Verbal prompt from job coach to return to work task
2/1	Given work by coworker	Talking to self even when coworker is giving work	Verbal prompt from job coach to stop talking out loud

continued

Figure 3.1—*Continued*

Date	Antecedent	Behavior	Consequence
2/1	Walking down hallway to lunch	Singing out loud	Ignored by those in hallway
2/2	Given work by coworker	Talking to self even when coworker is giving work	Verbal prompt from job coach to stop talking out loud
2/2	no attention	Singing to self	Verbal reprimand from coworker to be quiet
2/2	Working by self in office	Talking to self	Ignored by other workers
2/2	Working by self in office	Talking to self	Ignored by other workers
2/2	Given work by coworker	Talking to self even when coworker is giving work	Verbal prompt from job coach to stop talking out loud

Figure 3.2
Example of a Completed Functional Assessment Observation Form

Functional Assessment Observation Form

Name: *Peter*

Starting Date: *9/12* Ending Date: *9/15*

Time	Behaviors: Bite wrist	Behaviors:	Behaviors: Hit face	Behaviors:	Behaviors: Grab/Push	Predictors: Demand/Request	Predictors: Difficult Task	Predictors: Transitions	Predictors: Interruption	Predictors: Alone (no attention)	Predictors: [illegible]/Self-care	Predictors:	Predictors:	Predictors:	Perceived Functions – Get/Obtain: Attention	Get/Obtain: Desired Item/Activity	Get/Obtain: Self-Stimulation	Get/Obtain:	Escape/Avoid: Demand/Request	Escape/Avoid: Activity ( )	Escape/Avoid: Person	Escape/Avoid:	Other/Don't Know	Actual Conseq.: Block/Redirect	Actual Conseq.:	Comments (If nothing happened in period, write initials)
8-9	*1 2 8 9 13*				*1 2 8 9 13 16*						*1 2 8 9 13 16*									*1 2 8 9 13 16*				*1 2 8 9 13 16*		
9-10																										VK
10-11	*3 10 17*		*3 10 17*							*3 10 17*					*3 10 17*									*3 10 17*		
11-12	*4 14*		*4 18*							*4 14 18*					*4 14 18*									*4 14 18*		
12-1																										VK
1-2	*5 11 15*		*5 6 11 15*							*5 6 11 15*					*5 6 11 15*									*5 6 11 15*		
2-3	*7 12 19*		*7 12 19*							*7 18 19*					*7 12 19*									*7 12 19*		
Totals	16		12		6																					

Events:	~~1~~ ~~2~~ ~~3~~ ~~4~~ ~~5~~ ~~6~~ ~~7~~	~~8~~ ~~9~~ ~~10~~ ~~11~~ ~~12~~	~~13~~ ~~14~~ ~~15~~	~~16~~ ~~17~~ ~~18~~ ~~19~~ 20 21 22 23 24 25
Date:	*9/12*	*9/13*	*9/14*	*9/15*

Chapter 4

REINFORCEMENT

Key Point Questions

1. What is positive reinforcement?
2. What is negative reinforcement?
3. What are criticisms of using reinforcement?
4. What are applications of reinforcement?
5. What are guidelines for using reinforcement?
6. What are different types of reinforcement?
7. How do you use reinforcement to increase behaviors?
8. How do you use reinforcement to decrease behaviors?

WINDOW TO THE WORLD CASE STUDY ONE

Mayer is a supported employee who is working at a plant nursery warehouse. Mayer is labeled as having Autism Spectrum Disorders, though his coworkers (all without disabilities) would classify him as "weird" or "a bit strange." Mayer's job is to prune plants at the large warehouse and he does a great job doing this. It is at break times that Mayer runs into difficulties. Mayer is more than a little obsessed with movies about farming and that is what he wants to talk about. Mayer will interrupt the conversations of others to talk about these farming movies (actually more of a long monologue). Since there is only one break room where everyone, at the same time, takes their morning, lunch, and afternoon breaks, it can be difficult for his coworkers to avoid him.

Some of the coworkers have started complaining to their supervisor. Mayer has a job coach, Rachel, who checks in with the supervisor every couple of weeks to make sure that everything is going well with Mayer. The supervisor mentions the coworker concerns to Rachel. She goes out to the work site to talk with Mayer and to observe one break time. It is clear to Rachel that Mayer needs some social skills instruction as well as a reinforcement system. She decides to use the SkillStreaming approach (Goldstein & McGinnis, 1997) to teach Mayer some skills to help him understand social situations and to develop alternative behaviors other than talking about movies on farming. She and Mayer agree that he should decrease his talking about farm movies but Mayer doesn't want to eliminate it as, after all, this is what he is most interested in. Rachel decides to use a Differential Reinforcement of Low Rates of Behavior (DRL) reinforcement strategy for Mayer. Mayer keeps some pennies in his left front pocket of his pants. Every time that he talks about farm movies he moves a penny to his right front pocket. If at the end of the day Mayer has three or fewer pennies in his right pocket, then he gets to reinforce himself by watching a movie that night about farming. If he has four or more pennies, then he does not get to watch a movie about farming that night. Since Mayer wants to watch a movie about farming each night, he is careful to stop talking about farming movies once he has three pennies. In addition, through the social skills training, Mayer has learned to limit his talking about farm movies to no more than three sentences for each occurrence. The combination of social skills instruction and the DRL reinforcement schedule results in an immediate decrease in his talking about farm movies and also results in an increase in Mayer talking about topics that are of interest to his coworkers. Mayer enjoys these positive interactions and decides to limit his talking about farming to once per day at work.

WINDOW TO THE WORLD CASE STUDY TWO

Ida has recently moved from a state institution to an apartment where she receives supported living services. As part of these services, Ida is learning how to shop for groceries. Previous to moving into her apartment Ida had never been shopping for groceries and, in fact, had almost never been in the community outside of the institution. When in the grocery store with the supported living service coach, Ida often starts flapping her hands and jumping up and down. This, of course, interrupts shopping skills instruction and causes quite a scene causing negative reactions from customers and staff with customers clearing out of the area. The behavior seems to be escalating and a few times Ida has grabbed fruit or other items and thrown them on the floor.

The supported living staff is becoming very concerned and starting to think that Ida shouldn't go shopping any more. The supported living director, Mr. Roosevelt, contacts the behavioral specialist in the agency, Ms. Haun. On Ida's next two shopping trips with her support coach, Ms. Haun tags along. She observes the situation using the Functional Assessment Observation Form discussed in Chapter 3. Based upon these observations, it becomes clear to Ms. Haun that Ida becomes overstimulated by all of the lights, noise, and movements of other shoppers and staff. The hand-flapping behaviors are the first in the escalation of the behaviors. The function of her behaviors is to avoid the lights, noise, and movements (Ida has also learned that when she engages in these behaviors staff quickly terminates her shopping (a negative reinforcement paradigm).

Based upon this analysis, Ms. Haun decides upon a combination of strategies to help Ida. First, is to teach Ida relaxation techniques when she starts to get overstimulated at the grocery store. These include deep breathing, tensing and relaxing muscles, and counting slowly to five. Ms. Haun practices these techniques with Ida in her apartment and once she has mastered the skills there they practice in the grocery store when she is not shopping there. Second, Ms. Haun develops a reinforcement strategy where the support staff praises Ida for having her hands on the shopping cart while they gently place their hands on her arm, shoulder, or back when they are praising her. This is a Differential Reinforcement of Incompatible Behavior (DRI) reinforcement strategy (Ida cannot have her hands on the shopping cart and flapping her hands at the same time, and reinforcing the hands-on cart behavior could stop Ida's escalation behaviors). Third, staff make sure that they have Ida's smart phone with her when she goes shopping and if she appears to be getting agitated, they remind her that she can listen to calming music with her ear plugs, if she would like. With the implementation of these three combined strategies, Ida's undesirable behaviors in the grocery store quickly come to an end and the staff is able to assist Ida in learning how to shop for groceries.

KEY POINT QUESTION #1:
WHAT IS POSITIVE REINFORCEMENT?

Positive reinforcement is an event or stimulus presented after a response has been performed that increases the frequency of the behavior it follows (Kazdin, 2013). In other words, positive reinforcement is a process. You can only see that reinforcement has happened when an individual's behavior increases following the delivery of the reinforcer. If the behavior doesn't increase, what you presented isn't a reinforcer. For instance, if Delwyn is learning to select fresh fruit in the grocery store and the support provider praises him ("Delwyn, it was great that you put back the melon that wasn't ripe and chose a different one that is ripe"), and if the support provider's praise is reinforcing for Delwyn, then he will be more likely to appropriately pick a ripe melon in the future (an increase in his behavior).

Another way to analyze reinforcement is that you are arranging conditions under which a person gets things rather than is being given things. Though reward and reinforcement are sometimes used interchangeably, an important distinction to recognize is that people are rewarded, but behavior is reinforced. In other words, you can say something nice to a person, and they may appreciate it, but that does not necessarily mean that their specific behavior will increase.

It is important to note that not all items or events are reinforcers for everyone. One person may like praise from a support provider, another not. One employee may like choosing the order in which to do tasks, another may prefer that the supervisor set the schedule. Once again, unless the behavior increases following the presentation of the stimulus or event, then the stimulus or event is not a reinforcer.

It is very important to understand that it is as easy to inadvertently reinforce undesirable behaviors as desirable behaviors. This is tied to the function of the behavior. For instance, if Rajesh is talking to a coworker rather than doing a work task, and the function is to obtain attention from the job coach, and the job coach says, "Rajesh, you need to work and not talk to others," then the job coach may be unwittingly reinforcing the talking behavior.

The determination to use positive reinforcement to change behavior of individuals with a disability is both a philosophical and pragmatic decision. This determination stems from not only knowing reinforcement is effective, but also making a philosophical decision that using reinforcement is a more desirable and humane way to change adult behavior than the absence of any reinforcement or through the use of punishment.

KEY POINT QUESTION #2:
WHAT IS NEGATIVE REINFORCEMENT?

Negative reinforcement is the contingent removal of an aversive stimulus immediately following a response that increases the future rate and/or probability of the response (Alberto & Troutman, 2017). The key words in this definition are *increases* and *removal.* Both positive and negative reinforcement increase behavior. Negative reinforcement refers to the increase in the frequency of a response by removing an aversive event immediately after the response has been performed.

With positive reinforcement, when a person performs a behavior, the support provider gives the person something they like (such as praise, a food item, or an object) that increases the behavior. With negative reinforcement, when a person performs a behavior, the support provider removes something that the person dislikes (the aversive stimulus) which results in an increase in the behavior. For example, a supported employee will have to check in directly with her supervisor if she arrives more than 5 minutes late for work. The supported employee does not like the stern correction from the supervisor so she decides to leave her house earlier in order to get to work on time in order to avoid the chastisement. The stern verbal correction from the supervisor is the aversive stimulus which is then removed following the desired behavior (arriving on time to work). Table 4.1 provides more examples of negative reinforcement.

The use of the term "negative" can be confusing and people mistakenly believe that it means decreasing or punishing behavior (punishment is discussed in Chapter 5). However, both positive and negative reinforcement result in increases in behavior. An event is a negative reinforcer only if its removal after a response increases performance of that response. Negative reinforcement is not a judgment of something being either good or bad. It is important to remember that negative reinforcement can produce desirable behavior. Negative reinforcement works because the person performs the behavior to escape the aversive stimulus.

Contrary to popular belief, many off-task and disruptive behaviors are probably not maintained by support provider attention. Instead, individuals often use these behaviors to escape or avoid a task or situation (negative reinforcement). There are three questions to ask in order to determine if negative reinforcement contingencies are controlling undesirable behaviors:

1. Does the behavior result in the termination or postponement of specific support provider requests, instructional demands, or instructional tasks, activities, or materials? For example, the support provider is helping Marius to make a new meal and Marius gets frustrated and when the support provider shows her how to grate cheese Marius throws the grater to the floor and the support provider responds, "Marius, it looks like you are upset. Why don't you go into the living room and take a break and I'll grate the cheese?" The specific support provider request (to grate the cheese) has been terminated.

2. Is the person not competent with regard to the specific instructions, tasks, support provider requests, or materials identified in A above? For instance, if Marius does not understand what it means to "grate cheese" so she does not respond and continues to sit at the table in the kitchen without grating the cheese.

3. Does the undesirable behavior occur more frequently under those specific learning situations, tasks, materials, or support provider requests identified in A and B above (in contrast to other learning situations or tasks where the person is more capable)? For example, Betsy enjoys going to the health club to exercise. She likes lifting weights and riding the exercise bikes. These are set routines and the stimuli that she has to respond to are the same each time (such as setting the level and time on the exercise bike). In contrast, when Betsy tried the water aerobics classes, she did not like them and became aggressive towards her support provider, leaving the session early each time. This appears to have been due to the music, the instructors, and the instructor constantly changing her modeling, making it difficult for Betsy to respond appropriately and thus she became aggressive in order to terminate the aerobics class.

KEY POINT QUESTION #3:
WHAT ARE CRITICISMS OF USING REINFORCEMENT?

The use of reinforcement has not been without its criticism. Common concerns are: *Reinforcement is just bribery. They should just do it because it is good for them. Why should one person get something special when other people don't?*

First, are reinforcement and bribery the same thing? No! They do have similarity in that you are trying to encourage a person to behave in a certain manner by offering a reward. The difference is that with bribery the person is being influenced to perform a dishonest or illegal act. Using reinforcement to help an individual to learn functional skills they need to be successful in work, community, or home environments, is certainly not dishonest or illegal; indeed, it is the main role of support providers.

It is a common belief that adults with disabilities should do something because it is good for them. However, we all work under some system of reinforcement. Not everyone is "intrinsically" motivated for everything that they do. How many people would continue to work on the job if they weren't paid? However, reinforcement can be used to develop intrinsic and desirable behaviors in adults which is a good thing (Cameron & Pierce, 1994; Eisenberger & Cameron, 1996).

Third, why should one individual get something special when others don't? This brings us to the issue of developing supports and instruction specifically for the needs of an individual. One person may need some additional reinforcement to do something while another adult doesn't. This doesn't mean that you can't fade the reinforcement later, but if the person needs reinforcement to acquire a skill, it is better for the person to learn the skill using positive reinforcement rather than not learning it.

KEY POINT QUESTION #4:
WHAT ARE APPLICATIONS OF REINFORCEMENT?

The systematic use of reinforcement involves different reinforcement schedules. Just because a person does a behavior (whether desirable or undesirable) it doesn't mean that they are going to be (or should be) reinforced every time.

CONTINUOUS REINFORCEMENT. With this schedule, every instance of the behavior is reinforced. For instance, if a person is on a continuous reinforcement, every time that they engage in a specific behavior, such as getting to work on time, they would receive a reinforcer for each occurrence. Continuous reinforcement schedules are not necessarily bad. In fact, they may be very appropriate at times such as for initial skill acquisition. When a person is first learning how to do something they may be unsure of themselves or may not understand the reinforcement contingencies associated with what they are doing. Remember that continuous reinforcement generates a high rate of behavior. When a person is first learning how to do something, you usually want them to do it repeatedly so you can determine if they know how to perform the behavior; therefore, delivering continuous reinforcement may be necessary for the behavior you want to increase.

Once an individual has learned how to do something, they probably don't need to be reinforced all the time for it. You can then go to intermittent reinforcement schedules for skill proficiency and maintenance. A good way to fade support provider provided reinforcement is by pairing those reinforcers with naturally occurring reinforcers. For example, a young adult with a severe intellectual disability who has just moved into an apartment may not initially understand the connection between a behavior (putting their dishes in the dishwasher after a meal) and the reinforcer (a star on their household task chart which can be turned in for a tangible reinforcer in the evening). In this case, the support provider could pair praise for putting dishes in the dishwasher with giving the star, then immediately exchanging the star for the tangible reinforcer.

FIXED RATIO. A fixed ratio reinforcement schedule refers to reinforcement being delivered based on some frequency of responses. For example, a supported employee might be reinforced every third time that they complete a job task such as bussing a table (FR3). There are several advantages to using a fixed ratio schedule such as (a) you often get a fast response from the individual, (b) the schedule is highly predictable to the person, and (c) because it is based on frequency, there is no limit to receiving reinforcers. Sometimes though, an individual pauses after reinforcement is delivered as they know that a certain number of responses have to occur before they get reinforced again.

VARIABLE RATIO. In a variable ratio reinforcement schedule, the frequency of responses necessary to get a reinforcer, changes.

From our example above, the employee may get reinforced after one time of bussing a table, then after five times, then three times, then four times, and so on. A variable ratio schedule can be very powerful because the person doesn't know when they will be reinforced and thus are likely to continue to work hard in order to obtain the reinforcer. Some considerations in using a variable ratio schedule include: (a) you must always indicate the range of responses necessary to get a reinforcer (from the bussing example you probably don't want the worker to have to buss 50 tables before getting reinforced. It would be better to keep the range small, such as, from one to five times), (b) you need to make sure that there is a change in predictability (with a variable ratio schedule you don't want the person to know when they are going to get reinforced), (c) with variable ratio schedules you don't get pauses as with fixed ratio, and (d) behavior under control of a variable ratio schedule is extinguished more slowly than under a fixed ratio schedule.

FIXED INTERVAL. A fixed interval schedule refers to delivering a reinforcer after the same time period, such as, such as every 2 minutes or every 30 seconds. An advantage to fixed interval schedules is that they are easy to use. You can easily set a timer to go off every 10 minutes and deliver reinforcement then.

VARIABLE INTERVAL. A variable interval schedule is also time based. However, instead of reinforcement being delivered after the same interval period each time, the interval varies. For instance, with the bussing example, reinforcement for on-task bussing behavior could be delivered after 2 minutes, then after 10 minutes, then 6 minutes, then 11 minutes, and so on. Resistance to extinction is greater with intermittent reinforcement than with a fixed interval schedule.

NONCONTINGENT REINFORCEMENT. Tucker, Sigafoos, and Bushell (1998) define noncontingent reinforcement as the delivery of reinforcement on a fixed-interval (time) schedule irrespective of whether the desirable (or undesirable) behavior occurred during that interval. For example, a job coach could give a positive statement to a worker every 5 minutes no matter what worker behavior occurred during that time period. Sometimes the term "noncontingent reinforcement" is used to describe where reinforcement is used haphazardly or incorrectly. Unlike other schedules of reinforcement (DRO, DRI, or DRL which are covered later in this chapter) with noncontingent reinforcement, the behavior of the individual does not influence the delivery of reinforcement.

Tucker et al. (1998) provide these guidelines for the use of non-contingent reinforcement:

1. The reinforcement provided meets the function of the undesir-able behavior (such as staff attention).
2. The reinforcement is provided on a continuous and noncontin-gent basis.
3. The reinforcement schedule is faded to a level that is socially acceptable and ecologically valid.
4. Noncontingent reinforcement is combined with the teaching of positive alternative behaviors that serve the same function.

In a different take on noncontingent reinforcement, Pryor (1999) uses the term "jackpots" to refer to reinforcement that is of a much bigger magnitude of the normal reinforcer and is delivered noncon-tingently. For example, a supervisor at a job site could stop all work and throw a surprise party for the afternoon with food, special activi-ties, music, and so forth. Pryor notes that the use of "jackpots" can cre-ate high morale in the environment (work or home) and also can be effective in improving the behavior of individuals who may be recal-citrant, fearful, or resistant.

KEY POINT QUESTION #5:
WHAT ARE GUIDELINES FOR USING REINFORCEMENT?

This section provides general guidelines that make the use of rein-forcement more effective. Some common errors that are made in the use of reinforcement are outlined in Table 4.2.

1. *Only reinforce correct responses.* Recognize that reinforcement strengthens the behavior that it follows; don't want to inadver-tently reinforce undesirable behaviors instead of desirable ones.
2. *If you provide instruction or assistance, also provide reinforcement.* Reinforcement increases the behavior so make sure that you deliver the reinforcement after the individual performs the re-sponse correctly. Since you are delivering instruction on some-thing that is difficult for a person, you want to be sure and in-crease reinforcement for that behavior. Make sure that the rein-

forcement comes after the instruction and after the correct performance. Some general rules concerning the use of reinforcement for correct performance are presented in Table 4.3.

3. *Use a positive tone.* Vary your tone from warm and pleasant to strong and enthusiastic. The degree of reinforcement should match the importance of the response.

4. *Be brief.* You want to be brief because you do not want to interrupt the person and take them off task, or to take time out of instruction.

5. *Vary what you say.* You don't always have to say "good job." It is easy to get in a rut of saying the same word or phrase over and over and over and over, so be sure to vary your praise.

6. *Make sure that you are reinforcing.* You want to be pleasant and positive so that the person you are working with will want to interact with you and receive instruction from you. This will make your praise reinforcing and other reinforcers less necessary. So be nice!

7. *Do not reinforce simply attending to the task.* It is correct performance (i.e., outcome) that you want to reinforce. If you only reinforce attending to task (i.e., process), the correct performance may not increase. If you reinforce correct performance, the attending to task behavior will improve. Of course, it is easier to reinforce on-task behavior and this is okay, though on-task behavior does not necessarily lead to performance outcomes such as completing the task.

8. *Fade external reinforcement as soon as possible.* As a general rule, you want to eliminate external reinforcement. This isn't always possible or desirable, but it is a good goal.

KEY POINT QUESTION #6:
WHAT ARE DIFFERENT TYPES OF REINFORCEMENT?

Reinforcers may be activities (taking the dog for a walk), social (phone call to a friend), or a tangible item (food).

Participation and instruction in employment, community, and residential settings is often activity based. Activity based means that a chain or sequence of behaviors are performed which produce an outcome that is functional for the individual (for example, the sequence of getting ready for an aerobics class includes going to the locker room, getting dressed in workout clothes, going to the site for the class, participating in the aerobics class, going back to locker room, showering, putting clothes on, and leaving the building). Thus, it is possible to reinforce at different points in the sequence and/or at the end of the chain of behaviors. The activities themselves can also often serve as reinforcers for an individual.

There are a variety of ways to select reinforcers for individuals. One simple way to find out what a person likes is to ask them! Individuals are more likely to "buy in" with the intervention when they have a choice of reinforcers. However, for some adults, you may need a more structured interview to help the person understand the different reinforcers that are available (Raschke, 1981; Schanding, Tingstrom, & Sterling Turner, 2009). If the person is not able to easily tell you what they like, someone else who knows them well might be able to. Family members and friends can be good resources. Besides interviews, direct observations may be very useful in assessing reinforcement preference. These observations may involve recording foods the person prefers at mealtimes, the type of activities they prefer to engage in, or with whom they prefer to interact.

KEY POINT QUESTION #7: HOW DO YOU USE REINFORCEMENT TO INCREASE BEHAVIORS?

Externally Delivered Reinforcement

TIMING. The timing of reinforcement delivery is very important. Generally, reinforcement must be immediate if it is to be successful. The longer the delay between the behavior and the delivery of reinforcement the more likely the person will not understand the connection. With a long delay, it is also very possible that something else may happen in the meantime, consequently, the support provider will inadvertently reinforce an undesirable behavior instead of the intended desirable behavior.

CONTINGENCY. This is probably the most important consideration for delivering reinforcement. Is the reinforcement contingent on what the person does? Contingency means that when the individual does a certain behavior (such as putting away the clothes that have been washed), they get a specific reinforcer (i.e., playing the X-box with their roommate). If they do not put away the washed clothes then the roommate does not play the X-box with them.

One way to help make the connection between the reinforcement and the behavior is to label the reinforcement contingencies. In other words, tell the person why they are being reinforced. For example, if the person puts the laundry away the roommate could say "great, we've done our chores for the evening; let's have some fun and play some games on the X-box!"

The reinforcer should only be given when the specific behavior occurs. In the example above, if the person doesn't put the laundry away then they need corrective feedback (the roommate could say "we agreed upon chores for the week and one of yours was to put away the laundry which you didn't do so I don't want to play the X-box with you until you do put away the laundry") rather than reinforcement.

PREDICTABILITY. Can the person you are supporting predict when they are going to get reinforced? Usually you want the reinforcement to be predictable rather than unpredictable. This relates to the point above concerning contingency. If the person cannot predict when they are going to get reinforced, they may not consider it contingent upon their behavior and they may miss the connection.

DENSITY OF REINFORCEMENT. When an individual is learning a new skill (how to pay at the grocery store using their smart phone) or engaging in a new behavior (greeting coworkers appropriately), it is best to favor dense (lots of) reinforcement (a lot of praise and the use of activity or other reinforcers) versus thin reinforcement (only praising and using other reinforcers occasionally). Though the support provider may eventually want to fade the reinforcement (not eliminate it), it is important to initially make sure that the individual is getting enough reinforcement so that their desirable behavior increases.

SATIATION. A reinforcer may lose its power over time. For instance, a person may like salted peanuts a lot but after a few handfuls not want any more. This is known as satiation. At this point, something to drink would probably be more reinforcing than another handful of peanuts. It is important that different reinforcers be used and that they are mixed so that the person doesn't satiate on one reinforcer. Some ways to prevent satiation are: (a) having different reinforcers available for different tasks, (b) alternate reinforcers during instructional sessions, (c) gradually decrease the size or amount of the reinforcer, (d) be sure that the reinforcer being used is not something the person has easy access to at other times, and (e) change the pool of reinforcers to choose from; you don't want the individual to always pick the same reinforcer and possibly become satiated.

PREMACK PRINCIPLE. The Premack Principle is based upon using higher-probability behaviors to reinforce lower-probability behaviors. For instance, completion of a task such as cleaning the bathroom (lower-probability behavior) can be increased by following it with a snack in the kitchen (higher-probability behavior). This is also known as the "Grandmother Rule" as in "You have to eat your vegetables before you get any dessert."

GENERAL COMMENT. Remember that you *want* the person to be reinforced for desirable behaviors. A common mistake is when the support provider thinks that the person should have to work harder or do something extra to get reinforced. In this case, the support provider tries to make it as difficult as possible for the adult to get the reinforcer by continuously raising the ante. What usually happens in this case, is that the person becomes frustrated or angry because they are not receiving the expected reinforcement. This results in the person not doing what the support provider expects them and creates a "Catch-22" situation. Therefore, be sure that support providers are delivering reinforcement often enough.

Self-Delivered Reinforcement

Probably the most efficient way to deliver reinforcement is to have the person do it himself or herself! Then a support provider doesn't have to be stop instruction or support to deliver the reinforcer and the individual is more in control of his or her own behavior. Chapter 7 provides information on self-management strategies that are effective for self-delivery of reinforcement.

KEY POINT QUESTION #8: HOW DO YOU USE REINFORCEMENT TO DECREASE BEHAVIORS?

Besides increasing desirable behaviors, reinforcement can be used to decrease undesirable behaviors. For instance, if a supported employee talks frequently to their job coach during work times instead of working (with the function being to get attention from the job coach), the job coach could praise the employee when they are on-task, thus reinforcing the desirable on-task behavior which could make the undesirable off-task behavior less likely to occur. There are three methods for using reinforcement to decrease behaviors.

1. Differential Reinforcement of Incompatible Behavior (DRI)

One way to decrease undesirable behaviors is to reinforce a behavior which is desirable *and* incompatible with the undesirable behavior. For example, if LeRoy, a supported employee with ASD, only wants to stand in the break room (which makes it difficult for coworkers to interact with him), LeRoy's job coach could set up a reinforcement system for LeRoy where he is reinforced for sitting in the break room (the behaviors of standing and sitting are incompatible as LeRoy cannot be doing both at the same time).

Considerations in using DRI procedures include:

a. Make sure that the behavior reinforced is incompatible with the undesirable behavior.
b. The behavior selected for reinforcement is functional for the individual. For example, the person is reinforced by getting to go out and work in the garden after vacuuming the living room.
c. The person knows how to perform the behavior.
d. In addition, the reinforcer chosen is stronger or more powerful than the reinforcement that the person gets for performing the undesirable behavior, for instance, getting positive attention from coworkers for talking about a mutually interesting topic than receiving negative attention from coworkers for talking about a topic that is not mutually interesting.

2. Differential Reinforcement of Other Behavior (DRO)

With DRO, the person gets reinforced when the undesirable behavior does not occur. For instance, if Lajos, a supported employee, is not talking about an undesirable topic with coworkers and his smart phone vibrates then he could make a mark on an app on his phone to indicate that he was not talking about an undesirable topic (Lajos could be talking about desirable topics or not talking at all). This self-management system could then be used where Lajos would self-deliver reinforcement at a later time period based upon the number of times that he is not talking about an undesirable topic. His phone could be set to vibrate and either a Fixed Interval (FI) or Variable Interval (VI) schedule. When using DRO it is very important that the reinforcement interval selected corresponds to the behavior of the adult so that they get frequent reinforcement. For eliminating talking about undesirable topics with coworkers, a support provider might employ a DRO 5 (minute) schedule of reinforcement. If the employee does not talk about undesirable topics (absence of the behavior) out during the 5 minutes then the employee would get reinforced and a new 5-minute cycle is started (this is a FI schedule). When using DRO it is very important that the support provider select a reinforcement interval that corresponds to the person's undesirable behavior so that they get frequent reinforcement. For instance, if the employee talks about an undesirable topic every 2 minutes, using an interval of 5 minutes for reinforcement would not be effective because he would always talk about an undesirable topic before the 5-minute interval is up and never get reinforced. So, in this example, the support provider would want to choose an interval less than 2 minutes so the employee gets reinforced for not talking about undesirable topics. Once the employee is consistently being reinforced, then it would be possible to gradually increase the interval length (from 2.5 minutes to 3 minutes, to 3.5 minutes, to 4 minutes, and so on).

A problem with DRO procedures is that, though the person may not engage in the undesirable behavior such as talking about an undesirable topic, they may engage in a different behavior which is also undesirable (such as making strange noises). Inadvertently, the support provider may end up reinforcing a different undesirable behavior. So DRO procedures don't really teach the individual a specific skill to replace the undesirable behavior.

3. Differential Reinforcement of Low Rates of Behavior (DRI)

Another way to decrease behavior, but not eliminate it, is to reinforce low rates of the undesirable behavior. DRL is for when you want to decrease a behavior but not to eliminate it completely, for example, it could be problematic if a supported employee is constantly asking questions of coworkers during break times. Asking questions per se is not a bad thing. Asking 15 questions during a 15-minute break would be too much though. A job coach could set a limit of 3 questions per break period for that employee and then reinforce the employee each break period that they asked 3 or fewer questions.

BEST PRACTICE RECOMMENDATIONS

1. Reinforcement can be used to teach new behaviors or to strengthen behaviors that the person already has.
2. Reinforcement is the key to any intervention procedure and should always be included.
3. Negative reinforcement plays an important role, yet often unrecognized, in many situations.
4. Don't assume that your "reinforcer" is in fact reinforcing behavior (if the behavior does not increase then it is not a reinforcer.
5. Reinforcement is the most effective way to change any behavior.

DISCUSSION QUESTIONS

1. Do support providers have a positive effect on individuals because their motives and intentions are positive? Is having a positive attitude and using positive reinforcement the same thing?
2. Should adults with disabilities be expected to engage in desirable behavior without the use of reinforcers?
3. Are there other strategies besides the use of reinforcement that are as effective or even more effective for changing behavior?

EMPLOYMENT, COMMUNITY, AND RESIDENTIAL ACTIVITY SUGGESTIONS

1. Visit a workplace, community setting, and/or home environment and use frequency counts for scoring the number and type of reinforcers (positive and negative) that are occurring in that situation.
2. As a support provider, record the number of times that you deliver praise or other reinforcers to an individual.

REFERENCES CITED IN CHAPTER

Alberto, P. A., & Troutman, A. C. (2017). *Applied behavior analysis for teachers* (10th ed.). Englewood Cliffs, NJ: Prentice-Hall.

Bellamy, G. T., Horner, R. H., & Inman, D. P. (1979). *Vocational habilitation of severely retarded adults: A direct service technology.* Baltimore, MD: University Park Press.

Cameron, J., & Pierce, W. D. (1994). Reinforcement, reward, and intrinsic motivation: A meta-analysis. *Review of Educational Research, 64,* 363–423.

Eisenberger, R., & Cameron, J. (1996). Detrimental effects of reward: Reality or myth? *American Psychologist, 51,* 1153–1166.

Goldstein, A. P., & McGinnis, E. (1997). *Skillstreaming the adolescent: new strategies and perspectives for teaching prosocial skills.* Champaign, IL: Research Press.

Kazdin, A. E. (2013). *Behavior modification in applied settings* (7th ed.). Long Grove, IL: Waveland Press

Pryor, K. (1999). *Don't shoot the dog: The new art of teaching and training.* New York: Bantam.

Raschke, D. (1981). Designing reinforcement surveys: Let the student choose the reward. *Teaching Exceptional Children, 14,* 92–96.

Schanding, G. T., Tingstrom, D., & SterlingTurner, H. (2009). Evaluation of stimulus preference assessment methods with general education students. *Psychology in the Schools, 46,* 89–99.

Tucker, M., Sigafoos, J., & Bushell, H. (1998). Use of noncontingent reinforcement in the treatment of challenging behavior: A review and clinical guide. *Behavior Modification, 22,* 529–547.

EMPIRICAL RESEARCH SUPPORTING THAT THE INTERVENTIONS PRESENTED IN CHAPTER ARE EVIDENCE BASED PRACTICES

Almeida, D. A., Allen, R., Maguire, R. W., & Maguire, K. (2018). Identifying community-based reinforcers of adults with autism and related disabilities. *Journal of Behavioral Education, 27,* 375–394.

Borrero, J. C., Bartels-Meints, J. A., Sy, J. R., & Francisco, M. T. (2011). Fixed-time schedule effects in combination with response-dependent schedules. *Journal of Applied Behavior Analysis, 44,* 163–167.

Chowdhury, M.. & Benson, B. A. (2011). Use of differential reinforcement to reduce behavior problems in adults with intellectual disabilities: A methodological review. *Research in Developmental Disabilities, 32,* 383–394.

Krentz, H., Miltenberger, R., & Valbuena, D. (2016). Using token reinforcement to increase walking for adults with intellectual disabilities. *Journal of Applied Behavior Analysis, 49,* 745–750.

Lalli, J. S., Casey, S. D., & Kates, K. (1997). Noncontingent reinforcement as treatment for severe behavior problems: Some procedural variations. *Journal of Applied Behavior Analysis, 30,* 127–137.

Lambert, J., Bloom, S., Samaha, A., Dayton, E., & Kunnavatana, S. (2016). Effects of noncontingent reinforcement on the persistence and resurgence of mild aggression. *Psychological Record, 66,* 283–289.

Savage, M. N., Taber-Doughty, T., Brodhead, M. T., & Bouck, E. C. (2018). Increasing physical activity for adults with autism spectrum disorder: Comparing in-person and technology delivered praise. *Research in Developmental Disabilities, 73,* 115–125.

GENERAL REFERENCES REGARDING TOPICS IN CHAPTER

Clutterbuck, P. (2010). *Positive reinforcement: Activities and strategies for creating confident learners.* Bethel, CT: Crown House.

Gongola, L. C., & Daddario, R. (2010). A practitioner's guide to implementing a differential reinforcement of other behaviors procedure. *Teaching Exceptional Children, 42,* 14–20.

Groden, J., Kantor, A., Woodard, C. R., & Lipsitt, L. P. (2011). *How everyone on the Autism Spectrum, young, and old can become resilient, be more optimistic, enjoy humor, be kind, and increase self-efficacy: A positive psychology approach.* Philadelphia, PA: Jessica Kingsley Publishers.

Hoover, J. J., Vance Hall, R., & Hall, M. L. (2018). *How to select reinforcers.* Austin, TX: Pro-Ed,

Maag, J. W. (2001). Rewarded by punishment: Reflections on the disuse of positive reinforcement in schools. *Exceptional Children, 67,* 173–186.

Richman, D. M., Barnard-Brak, L., Grubb, L., Bosch, A., & Abby, L. (2015). Meta-analysis of noncontingent reinforcement effects on problem behavior. *Journal of Applied BehaviorAnalysis, 48,* 131–152.

Wehmeyer, M. L. (2013). *The Oxford handbook of positive psychology and disability.* New York: Oxford University Press.

Table 4.1
Examples of Negative Reinforcement

1. Taking medicine to relieve a headache may be negatively reinforced by the termination of pain.
2. Leaving the house to escape from an argument with one's significant other.
3. Turning off an alarm to escape from a loud noise.
4. Closing a window to shut off a draft.
5. Responding to a baby to escape from the crying.
6. Turn on the heat to escape from the cold.
7. Putting on seat belt in car to end buzzer noise.
8. Leaving the room when someone is rude or critical because this behavior has ended other aversive conversations.

Table 4.2
Common Errors in Delivering Reinforcement

1. The perception error: "Everybody likes. . . ." To use reinforcement effectively, you must know what reinforces a person's behavior. The perception error occurs when you perceive that something will reinforce a person's behavior when in fact it won't.
2. No one reinforcer works for all people. Different individuals may have different reinforcers.
3. Not making reinforcement contingent upon behavior.
4. Delaying reinforcement.
5. A "reward" may not be a reinforcer. Reinforcement is in the eye of the beholder.
6. Expecting too much behavior change before delivering reinforcement. It is much better to reinforce small changes than big changes (shaping).
7. Combining reinforcement and corrective feedback at the same time. "You did good, but. . . ." The individual will remember only what came after the "but."

Table 4.3
General Rules Concerning the use of Reinforcement for Correct Performance

1. Select a reinforcing event on the basis of initial evaluation of the individual and apparent function of events used in previous similar situations.
2. Pair all reinforcers for step completion with the naturally occurring consequences for correct performance.
   A. Delivery the reinforcer immediately upon completion of the task.
   B. Deliver reinforcement only when the person is attending to the task.
   C. Reinforcement should be delivered at the same time as assistance on the next step so that the person continues through the task without interruption (i.e., make it short and sweet).
3. Do not establish any cues other than the task and setting that signal an increased probability of reinforcement.

Note: Adapted from Bellamy, Horner, and Inman (1979).

Chapter 5

PUNISHMENT

Key Point Questions

1. What is Type One punishment?
2. What is Type Two punishment?
3. What are criticisms of using punishment?
4. How is Punishment Most Effectively Implemented?
5. What are guidelines for using punishment?
6. What are different types of punishment?

WINDOW TO THE WORLD CASE STUDY ONE

Walter is a job coach who is supporting Hakan, an employee with a mild intellectual disability, who has been doing office work at a county hospital for a month. Hakan does a good job of managing patient records and delivering patient files to different offices throughout the hospital. Walter notices that Hakan has a tendency to talk out loud to himself which draws stares and an occasional negative comment from coworkers. Walter sees that this behavior could have a negative influence upon Walter's initial evaluation and whether he might be retained as a permanent employee or let go. Walter also fears Hakan's talking to himself behavior will deter potential friendships with coworkers from developing.

Walter and Hakan team together about this behavior and decide upon a token economy that combines reinforcement and punishment to stop his talking out loud to himself. They decide to set Hakan's smart phone to vibrate on a Variable Interval schedule (so that he cannot predict when the phone will vibrate) with a mean of every five minutes (VI 5). If Hakan is not talking out loud to himself when the phone vibrates, then he pulls out a small notebook from his pocket and marks a plus. He can then reinforce himself after work with specific reinforcers that he has selected (10 points for a coffee, 50 points for a movie or DVD, 100 points for a trip to the mall, etc.).

Walter and Hakan have also agreed upon using a response cost procedure with the token economy where Hakan fines himself minus five plusses for each time that he is talking out loud to himself when his phone vibrates. Hakan wanted the fine to be costly, in comparison to the reinforcement, to strongly reduce his talking to himself. These combined procedures have an immediate positive impact as now there is direct reinforcement for the absence of the talking to himself behaviors as well as punishment for the occurrence of undesirable talking to himself behaviors.

WINDOW TO THE WORLD CASE STUDY TWO

Johann is an adult diagnosed with Autism Spectrum Disorders. Johann lives in an apartment with one roommate in a supported living situation. Johann is very set in his routine which is a double-edged sword. As long as his daily routine remains the same, everything is fine and he does well. When things change unexpectedly, then Johann is known to suddenly explode and become aggressive towards those around him. This is especially true in community settings. For instance, when he is doing his laundry in the laundromat there are specific machines that he wants to use. When he is going to the gym to workout he wants to put his clothes away in a specific locker. At the grocery store he does not like it when items are moved to a different location.

When Johann becomes aggressive the staff hold his arms to his side (fortunately he is rather short and of small stature) and turn their heads away from him until he is calm for 30 seconds. They then remove him from the situation and return to his apartment. This has the effect of punishing his aggressive behavior which is good. Unfortunately, it does not teach him positive skills for coping with similar situations and, since these situations are bound to occur in the future, Johann does not have necessary skills for handling the difficult situation.

KEY POINT QUESTION #1:
WHAT IS TYPE ONE PUNISHMENT?

Type One punishment is the presentation of a stimulus or event after a behavior that decreases the frequency of the behavior (Kazdin, 2013). Punishment can be said to have occurred only if the person's rate of emitting the behavior has been reduced. Punishment, like reinforcement, is defined solely by its effect upon behavior (that it decreases the behavior). If the behavior doesn't decrease, it isn't a punisher. For example, Eva is an adult with a learning disability who shares an apartment with Emma. Eva has been leaving clothes scattered around the living room and Emma is bothered by the messiness. Finally, she ways to Eva, "I don't like it when you leave your clothes in the living room. I prefer that our apartment is neat and clean in the common areas." After this comment from Emma, Eva makes sure not to leave her clothes in the living room. Thus, Emma's comments were a punisher for Eva's behavior as it decreased the occurrence of her leaving her clothes in the living room.

As with using reinforcement, it is important to note that not all items or events are punishing for all individuals. One person may find a reprimand from a work supervisor punishing while another person may not. One individual may find a support provider putting her hand on their shoulder to be punishing while another individual might not find being touched this way punishing at all. Once again, unless the behavior decreases following the presentation of the stimulus or event, then the stimulus or event is not a punisher.

Also, like reinforcement, it is as easy to inadvertently punish desirable as it is undesirable behaviors. This is tied to the function of the behavior. For example, Leonard loves his job at the warehouse. He works fast, does quality work, and is always well-focused on his work. His job coach stops by once every two weeks for an hour or two to check in with Leonard and his supervisor and to observe Leonard at work. When Leonard completes a task, he likes to make a comment to a coworker or the supervisor like, "Man, I finished that task fast, see how hard I'm working" in order to get attention. When the job coach observes Leonard doing this, he tells him not to make those comments as the coworkers and supervisor could see it as bragging. However, the job coach could be punishing Leonard's working hard as he would then no longer be receiving attention for his task completion.

Punishment, per se, is not necessarily either a "good" or a "bad" thing. When combined with reinforcement and other positive interventions, the use of punishment can be an effective strategy in implementing positive behavior supports. The more effective the positive interventions are, then the more effective and enhanced the mild and brief punishment procedures will be. As Horner (2002) has pointed out:

> It is important to acknowledge that punishment is a natural and ongoing part of life, and we need to better understand the role of punishment if we are to be successful in our efforts to engineer environments in which children and adults with deviant behavior are successful. Teachers, parents, employers, and friends in all parts of our society regularly deliver contingent punishers that result in reduction of specific responses. (p. 465)

KEY POINT QUESTION #2:
WHAT IS TYPE TWO PUNISHMENT?

Type Two punishment is the removal of a stimulus or event after a behavior that decreases the frequency of the behavior (Kazdin, 2013). With Type Two punishment, when a person performs a behavior, the support provider removes something that the person likes. For example, if Aspasia is constantly stopping by to ask nonwork-related questions of coworkers and is disrupting their work, the job coach decides that the function of her question asking is to get coworker attention, and tells the coworkers to ignore Aspasia's questions and say "I'm busy now." If Aspasia's question asking then decreases (as the ignoring is punishing to her), then Aspasia's behavior was decreased by the removal of the stimulus (coworker attention) after the behavior.

KEY POINT QUESTION #3:
WHAT ARE CRITICISMS OF USING PUNISHMENT?

Perhaps the most important criticism is that punishment may not be the most effective way of changing behavior for the better. Just eliminating an undesirable behavior does not necessarily mean that there will be an increase in desirable behavior. At best, punishment just stops a behavior from occurring. Just stopping an undesirable behavior doesn't solve the problem or meet the function of the behavior. As noted in Chapter 3, the function of the behavior must be addressed. Stopping one undesirable behavior, without providing the individual with a desirable behavior that serves the same function, will probably only replace the previous undesirable behavior with another undesirable behavior. By punishing undesirable behaviors without reinforcing or teaching a constructive alternative behavior, it will be easier for the individual to engage in another undesirable behavior that serves the same function as the person may not have learned positive replacement skills. Horner et al. (1990) have provided eight basic criteria in which punishment procedures should be accountable (see Table 5.1).

Punishment leads to narrow stimulus control, where the person will only refrain from engaging in the undesirable behavior when someone who has or who could punish them is present. In this case, a person might do the undesirable behavior of talking with coworkers at break times about inappropriate topics if the job coach is not present. In other words, generalization is poor when punishment alone is used. The person is unlikely to eliminate the undesirable behavior across settings, people, times, and/or behaviors.

Individuals who are punished often engage in escape or avoidance behaviors. Support providers often expect the person to stop the undesirable behavior when, in fact, it leads to escape behavior. For instance, most people do not want to be around someone who is punishing them, no matter what the situation is. For example, an adult with an intellectual disability may skip class at an adult school in order to avoid being around a teacher who makes negative comments about the person's ability to learn, or the person may engage in undesirable behaviors in order to be sent out of the presence of the teacher (a negative reinforcement paradigm is described in Chapter 4). In other words, the teacher has become an aversive stimulus for the adult with a disability.

With the use of punishment, the person is more likely to follow the punishment with an aggressive or inappropriate response than with positive reinforcement. This means that the support provider must then deal with an additional undesirable behavior. The aggressive behavior may then serve as a negative reinforcer for the person being punished, in that they are likely to be removed (escape) from the situation.

Maintenance is often poor with the use of punishment procedures. Often undesirable behaviors return when the punishment procedures are withdrawn, as the person may not engage in a desirable behavior serving the same function, especially if they have not been taught and reinforced for engaging in an alternative behavior serving the same function.

With punishment there is often an emotional or physiological arousal and side effects. For example, if Carmen hits herself and the support provider holds Carmen's hands to her side, telling her "no hitting," while turning her head away from Carmen for one minute, Carmen's heart rate is likely to increase, as well as her receiving an endorphin release, which can then inhibit Carmen's ability to learn or function appropriately for a time period afterwards. These effects can be counterproductive to learning and functioning and establishing positive relations between the support provider and that individual.

There may be side effects to the punishment, such as emotional reactions (nervousness, crying, anger, etc.). The discriminative stimuli (cues) for punishment (for example, support provider presence) may produce similar reactions in the absence of punishment. For instance, Mr. Legree is a stern, sour, unsmiling job coach who makes sarcastic comments to supported employees when they make even a minor mistake on a job task (often even when they do a job task right, such as "I'm surprised that you completed that one correctly"). Mr. Legree's supported employees are nervous that they will make a mistake when he is watching them work, consequently they sweat, become tense, and their thinking freezes. Even if supported employees are working well, they have these emotional and physical reactions going on during whenever Mr. Legree is present.

Punishment may interfere with new learning. The adult may be unresponsive to the social environment and less willing to engage in positive behaviors (why should I try when all I get is punishment). Furthermore, the use of punishment can serve as a modeling response resulting in the person being punished being more likely to use punishment themselves. Also, the support provider who uses punishment is negatively reinforced for using punishment. For instance, when Rori is cleaning her bedroom and makes rude comments to her support provider, who is trying to help her clean her bedroom, and the support provider responds to the rude comments by walking out of the room, then the support provider is being negatively reinforced by removing herself from Rori's presence (Rori, the negative stimulus is removed). Thus, there is the perpetuation of punishment and the support provider is likely to repeatedly use punishment. In addition, from Rori's perspective, it may also be a negative reinforcement paradigm (the support provider is removed from the situation and the help is terminated) so that in the future she is more likely to engage in the rude talking behavior.

Many types of aversive punishment procedures used with adults with disabilities have often been used with political prisoners and condemned by Human Rights groups. Examples of some of these aversive procedures are electric shock, plunged into ice water, verbal abuse, enforced standing, ammonia held under the nose, and hair pulling (Farmer & Stinson, 2009/2010; Repp & Singh, 1990). The use of these aversive punishment procedures is always inappropriate to use with any individual with a disability.

KEY POINT QUESTION #4:
HOW IS PUNISHMENT MOST EFFECTIVELY IMPLEMENTED?

There are a variety of variables that influence whether or not a punishment procedure will be effective:

1. *Whether or not the punishment is implemented immediately after the undesirable behavior.* The longer the delay between the undesirable behavior and the punishment the less effective the punishment will be. For example, if Delores engages in the undesirable behavior of hitting her Supported Living provider, who is helping her get ready for work in the morning, but then is told after work by the support provider that she does not want to go with her to the movie (as previously planned) because of the hitting behavior in the morning, the delay between the hitting and the not going to the movie will weaken the effect of the punishment.

2. *The intensity of the punishment.* The stronger or more aversive the punishment, the more effective it will be in decreasing the behavior. For instance, if every time Norm hits his head with his fist while playing his favorite video game on his iPad, the support provider takes away the iPad for the rest of the day, then his head hitting may stop.

3. *The schedule of the punishment.* Punishment may be delivered on schedules just like with reinforcement (fixed or variable ratio and fixed or variable intervals). For example, if George's support staff decide to turn away from him and ignore him for one minute every time that he spits at them (punishing his behavior through extinction) but sometimes they are not consistent in doing so and pay attention to him ("George, no spitting at others"), then he is on a variable ratio punishment schedule which may not be effective in decreasing his spitting behavior (as he is also sometimes getting reinforced with attention for his spitting behavior).

4. *Whether or not a desirable (e.g., an alternative or skill building behavior) that serves the same function has been taught and reinforced.* This is of critical importance. In the example of Norm's head hitting, if the function of his head hitting was to get attention from support providers when he was alone for more than five minutes (and the head hitting is eliminated through the removal of his iPad), then Norm may engage in other undesirable behaviors in order to get attention. However, by teaching Norm an appropriate method of getting attention (such as hitting an icon on his smart device that says "Hey, I want attention right now!), then Norm would have a positive skill for getting attention (and serves the same function as the head hitting).

KEY POINT QUESTION #5:
WHAT ARE GUIDELINES FOR USING PUNISHMENT?

1. Punishment should be only be used in the short term. By definition, punishment should reduce the occurrence of the undesirable behavior. If this reduction is not occurring, then the stimulus or event is not actually a punisher and its use should be immediately discontinued.
2. Punishment should only be used so that adaptive behavior can be taught to the individual.
3. The punishment should be compatible with community norms.
4. The person cannot avoid or escape from the punishment (by hiding, cheating, aggression, etc.).
5. If punishment is threatened and the undesirable behavior occurs, then the punishment must be carried out.

6. Support providers should never make a threat of punishment that they cannot follow through on or back up.
7. Punishment should be carried out in a calm manner.
8. Positive desirable behaviors should be reinforced in conjunction with the use of punishment.

The following four questions should always be asked before using behavior reduction procedures such as punishment:

1. Is the behavior change important for the person? In other words, is it socially important that this undesirable behavior be eliminated?
2. Have regulations regarding behavior reduction procedures been reviewed by those who will implement and/or oversee them?
3. Is the undesirable behavior being replaced with a functional alternative behavior in addition to the punishment?
4. Has it been assessed whether a medical problem is causing the undesirable behavior? (Lee & Axelrod, 2005)

KEY POINT QUESTION #6:
WHAT ARE DIFFERENT TYPES OF PUNISHMENT?

Extinction

Extinction is the withholding of reinforcement from a previously reinforced response. Extinction discontinues the reinforcement that follows the behavior.

Extinction has most often been used where attention from a support provider is reinforcing the undesirable behavior. For example, Kevin, an adult with a severe intellectual disability, makes strange noises and the support providers pay attention to Kevin in order to stop him from making the noises (with the function of the behavior being to get support provider attention). Kevin is thus getting reinforced for making the strange noises. If the support providers stop paying attention to Kevin when he makes the strange noises, then his noise-making behavior is on extinction (it is no longer being reinforced by the attention) and is likely to decrease or stop all together. Extinction is best used in conjunction with reinforcing other more appropriate behaviors that serve the same function.

There are six considerations before making the decision to use extinction (Benoit & Mayer, 1974):

1. Can the undesirable behavior be tolerated temporarily based on its topography (e.g., aggression) and at its current rate of occurrence?
2. Can an increase in the undesirable behavior be tolerated?
3. Is the undesirable behavior likely to be imitated by other individuals?
4. Are the reinforcers controlling the undesirable behavior known?
5. Can reinforcement be withheld? For instance, in the example above of Kevin making strange noises in order to get attention, it is known that the attention is the reinforcer controlling the behavior and it would be easy for the support staff to ignore the behavior.
6. Have alternative desirable behaviors that serve the same function been identified for reinforcement?

Characteristics of the Extinction Process

1. A behavior undergoing extinction usually decreases slowly in rate. Thus, extinction should not be used unless the support providers can afford to tolerate a gradual reduction in the undesirable behavior.
2. When reinforcement no longer follows a behavior, the undesirable behavior first occurs at a greater rate before it diminishes. This is known as extinction burst. For example, if Kevin has been getting attention from support providers when he spits at them and then they start ignoring the behavior, then Kevin's spitting behavior may initially increase before it starts decreasing.
3. The longer a person has been reinforced for a behavior, the longer it will probably take for the extinction process will work.
4. The more effort that it takes the person to engage in the undesirable behavior, the more likely that it is that the person will stop the undesirable behavior when extinction is used. For example, if Kevin has to get up, walk over to the support provider, ask them to turn around, put his hands on their shoulders and try and turn them towards him, all of this effort may be more than it is worth from his perspective.

5. Spontaneous recovery may occur. This is a process in which a behavior that has apparently disappeared through extinction suddenly reappears. For instance, a person may "check" to see how a support provider will respond when they engage in a behavior after it has been put on extinction. Kevin may occasionally spit at a support provider to see what their reaction will be and if they will pay attention to him after he spits at them. This does not mean that the use of extinction has been unsuccessful and the undesirable behavior can continue to be ignored.

Problems in Using Extinction

1. Procedure must be carried out with great consistency since even occasional reinforcement may cause the behavior to recur at a high rate. All support providers must consistently engage in the extinction program, even one incident of inadvertently reinforcing the undesirable behavior can cause the behavior to start occurring again.
2. It can be difficult to determine exactly which event is reinforcing the undesired behavior in some manner.
3. Some behaviors, in themselves, may be reinforcing (such as an individual who engages in self-stimulatory behavior for internal stimulation), and the function is not tied to getting attention, in which case ignoring the undesirable behavior will not work.
4. Some behaviors are too dangerous to ignore.
5. When some peers see an individual performing undesirable behaviors without any adverse consequences, the peers may imitate the undesirable behaviors.
6. There is limited generalization with extinction. The undesirable behavior may occur just as frequently in settings where extinction is not in effect. For example, if George's spitting at work is ignored, it may cease to occur in that setting, However, if support providers pay attention to him when he spits at home, then the undesirable behavior is likely to continue in that setting.

Time-Out

Time-out is a punishment procedure in which the ability of the individual to receive positive reinforcement is withdrawn for a pre-specified period of time following the occurrence of the undesirable behavior. Time-out does not necessarily mean that the person is removed from the situation or environment.

Nonexclusionary Time-Out

With nonexclusionary time-out, the person remains in the situation and environment but is not eligible for reinforcement during the time-out time period. This could also be as simple as the support provider not providing social reinforcement by turning away from the person. The big advantage to nonexclusionary time-out is that the person is not removed from the learning environment and can still receive instruction. For instance, when he is being taught cooking skills by his supported living provider, Yan may very mildly try to hit the support provider in order to get attention. With nonexclusionary time-out, the support provider would block the hitting and then ignore Yan for the next two minutes (loss of access to attention which is the reinforcer in this situation).

Exclusionary Time-Out

With exclusionary time-out, the person is removed from the situation for a specified amount of time. Exclusionary time-out should be used sparingly and only for chronically and seriously undesirable behaviors. The time-out environment should be boring and nonreinforcing for the individual. The person should be removed to an area where they will not be seen (and preferably not heard) by anyone except the person administering the time-out. It is very important that the person be monitored during the time-out so that other undesirable behaviors do not occur (such as the person leaving the work site).

In the above cooking example, with exclusionary time-out, the support provider would block the hitting, say "no hitting people," and have Yan sit in the living room for two minutes and then return to cooking in the kitchen.

Effective Time-Out Procedures Include the Following Common Characteristics

1. There is a high density of reinforcement in the setting. Time-out will work *only* if the learning environment is more interesting and reinforcing than the time-out situation or environment.

2. No reinforcement is available during time-out period. The support provider must be able to control that no reinforcement is delivered to the individual during the time-out.
3. Duration of the time-out period has been specified ahead of time and is brief.
4. The person is not released from time-out (e.g., become eligible for reinforcement) if the undesirable behavior is still occurring when time-out period ends. This does not mean that the entire time-out period is restarted if the person is still engaging in the undesirable behavior at the end of the time-out period, but that the time period is extended.
5. Time-out is applied immediately following the undesirable behavior.
6. Verbal interactions with the person are brief, to the point, and calm regarding the establishment of the time-out situation ("Yan, there is no hitting. You need to sit in the living room for two minutes"). The person is ignored when in time-out.
7. Detailed records are kept.
8. Time-out does not involve taking away any reinforcers from the person.
9. When the person returns from time-out (e.g., is once again eligible for reinforcement), that individual is treated exactly how they were before the undesirable behavior occurred. Reinforcement should be no easier or harder to obtain than it was before the undesirable behavior occurred (i.e., don't hold a grudge).
10. The person is taught an alternative desirable behavior than can be engaged in for receiving reinforcement so that the individual does not have to engage in the undesirable behavior.

Criticism of Time-Out Procedures

Time-out has been criticized because:

1. It fails to teach functional and desirable behaviors.
2. It decreases the person's opportunity to learn more appropriate behavior and functional skills by removing the individual from the learning environment.
3. It removes the person from the support provider's attention when the person needs that attention the most.

4. Time-out may have paradoxical effects, functioning as a negative reinforcer of undesirable behavior or as an escape mechanism when difficult or unpleasant tasks exist in the "time-in" environment.

Difference Between Extinction and Time–Out

The difference between extinction and time-out is that with extinction, reinforcement is withheld for a specific behavior that had been previously reinforced. With time-out, the person is not eligible for reinforcement for any behavior for a specific amount of time.

Response Cost

Response cost is when points, tokens, privileges, or other reinforcers already given to an individual are removed (either by the individual or by a support provider) contingent upon instances of a specific behavior or behaviors. Response cost is best used with undesirable behaviors that: (a) have been difficult to decrease or eliminate through the reinforcement of competing behaviors, and (b) are not excessively dangerous to others or materials in the environment.

For example, Amy is an adult who is identified as having a mental health disorder. Sometimes at work, Amy will ask a coworker a question about an inappropriate topic (their drug use, sex lives, etc.). These questions have often gotten Amy into serious trouble. She has tried several methods in the past to stop asking inappropriate questions but with no luck. Amy meets with Ms. Valenzuela who is a counselor provided through Amy's Employee Assistance Program. Amy and Ms. Valenzuela agree that a response cost program might be the most effective consequence strategy for Amy. Amy comes up with five organizations that are doing political work that Amy is very much opposed to. Every time that Amy asks an inappropriate question to a coworker she must write a $100 check to one of those organizations and mail it within one hour of asking the inappropriate question. Amy has Obsessive Compulsive Disorder as well, which serves to cause her to follow through on writing and sending the checks. After only three times of asking inappropriate questions and sending the checks, Amy has stopped asking inappropriate questions to coworkers as the response cost (punishment) was powerful enough to extinguish the behavior.

Response cost can be used where time-out or extinction is not a possibility. Another advantage is that it can be administered more quickly than time-out. Response cost is often used with token economies (see Chapter 7 for information on token economies). When used accurately, response cost rarely produces the extreme emotional behavior often seen as a side effect of other punishment procedures.

Guidelines for Using Response Cost

1. Specify ahead of time the undesirable behaviors that will be fined. This is useful in reducing the ambiguity that may exist when support providers provide consequences for the undesirable behavior of individuals they are supporting.
2. A single fine should not significantly deplete (bankrupt) the total number of tokens or points.
3. If a person is being fined many times, the size of the fine is probably inadequate.
4. Initial introduction of the fining procedure needs to be carefully explained and rehearsed with the individual. This will help to avoid an undue amount of instructional time spent arguing over fines and trying to collect them.
5. The response cost should occur quickly and calmly.
6. At the time of the fine, the person should be told they are losing points, how many points, and how they can be earned back.

The Disadvantages for Using Response Cost

1. Fining may be conducted in a capricious manner if contingencies are not well planned and set.
2. Support providers may fine too heavily or too much at one time.
3. The individual may become upset or defiant if having to surrender tokens or other items.

BEST PRACTICE RECOMMENDATIONS

1. Punishment procedures should always be combined with positive reinforcement and the teaching of positive alternative behaviors that serve the same function.

2. If the undesirable behavior does not quickly diminish, then the punishment intervention is not effective and should be discontinued.

DISCUSSION QUESTIONS

1. What is the difference between punishment and aversive interventions?
2. Is it ever okay to harm an individual when using punishment procedures?
3. What is an appropriate ration of reinforcement to punishment?
4. Can all undesirable behaviors be decreased without the use of punishment?

EMPLOYMENT, COMMUNITY, AND RESIDENTIAL ACTIVITY SUGGESTIONS

1. Observe an adult with a disability and record the undesirable behaviors that are occurring. List the ones that would best benefit from the use of punishment and ones that would not.
2. Interview adults (with and without disabilities) about the use of punishment in their own schooling or adult life to see whether they thought specific instances helped or hindered their academic and social behavior. What influences did punishment have on their adult lives?
3. Observe a support provider and take frequency data on that support provider's use of reinforcement and punishment. Analyze which appears to be most effective in that situation and why.

REFERENCES CITED IN CHAPTER

Benoit, R. B. and Mayer, G. R. (1974). Extinction: Guidelines for its selection and use. *The Personnel and Guidance Journal, 52,* 290–296.

Farmer, A., & Stinson, K. (2009/2010). Failing the grade: How the use of corporal punishment in U.S. public schools demonstrates the need for U.S. ratification of the Children's Rights Convention and the Convention on the Rights of Persons with Disabilities. *New York Law School Law Review, 54,* 1035–1069.

Horner, R. H. (2002). On the status of using punishment: A commentary. *Journal of Applied Behavior Analysis, 35,* 465–467.

Horner, R. H., Dunlap, G., Koegel, R. L., Carr, E. G., Sailor, W., Anderson, J., Albin, R. W., & O'Neill, R. E. (1990). Toward a technology of "nonaversive" behavioral support. *Journal of the Association for Persons with Severe Handicaps, 15,* 125–132.

Kazdin, A. E. (2013). *Behavior modification in applied settings* (7th ed.). Belmont, CA: Wadsworth/Thomson Learning.

Lee, D. L., & Axelrod, S. (2005). *Behavior modification: Basic principles* (3rd ed.). Austin, TX: Pro-Ed.

Repp. A. C., & Singh, N. N. (1990). *Perspectives on the use of nonaversive and aversive interventions for persons with developmental disabilities.* Sycamore, IL: Sycamore Publishing Company.

EMPIRICAL RESEARCH SUPPORTING THAT THE INTERVENTIONS PRESENTED IN CHAPTER ARE EVIDENCE BASED PRACTICES

Falcomata, T. S., Roane, H. S., Hovanetz, A. N., Kettering, T. L., & Keeney, K. M. (2004). An evaluation of response cost in the treatment of inappropriate vocalizations maintained by automatic reinforcement. *Journal of Applied Behavior Analysis, 37,* 83–87.

Grace, N. C., Kahng, S. W., & Fisher, W. W. (1994). Balancing social acceptability with treatment effectiveness of an intrusive procedure: A case report. *Journal of Applied Behavior Analysis, 27,* 171–172.

Hagopian, L. P., Fisher, W. W., Sullivan, M. T., Acquisto, J., & LeBlanc, L. A. (1998). Effectiveness of functional communication training with and without extinction and punishment: A summary of 21 inpatient cases. *Journal of Applied Behavior Analysis, 31,* 211–223.

Manente, C. J., & LaRue, R. H. (2017). Treatment of self-injurious behavior using differential punishment of high rates of behavior (DPH). *Behavioral Interventions, 32,* 262–271.

Mruzek, D. W., Cohen, C., & Smith, T. (2007). Contingency contracting with students with autism spectrum disorders in a public-school setting. *Journal of Developmental and Physical Disabilities, 19,* 103–114.

Rooker, G. W., Jessel, J., Kurtz, P. F., & Hagopian, L. P. (2013). Functional communication training with and without alternative reinforcement and punishment: An analysis of 58 applications. *Journal of Applied Behavior 46,* 708–722.

GENERAL REFERENCES REGARDING TOPICS IN CHAPTER

Adams, D. L., & Erevelles, N. (2017). Unexpected spaces of confinement: Aversive technologies, intellectual disability, and "bare life." *Punishment and Society, 19,* 348–365.

Ager, A., & O'May, F. (2001). Issues in the definition and implementation of "best practice" for staff delivery of interventions for challenging behavior. *Journal of Intellectual and Developmental Disability, 26,* 243–256

Azrin, N. H., & Holz, W. C. (1966). Punishment. In W. K. Honig (Ed.), *Operant behavior: Areas of research and application.* New York: Appleton-Century-Crofts.

Delfs, C. H., & Campbell, J. M. (2010). A quantitative synthesis of developmental disability research: The impact of functional assessment methodology on treatment effectiveness. *Behavior Analyst Today, 11,* 4–19.

Gershoff, E. T. (2002). Corporal punishment by parents and associated child behaviors and experiences: A meta-analytic and theoretical review. *Psychological Bulletin, 128,* 539–579.

Griffin, J. C., Palsey, T. J., Stark, M. T., & Emerson, J. H. (1988). B. F. Skinner's position on aversive treatment. *American Journal on Mental Retardation, 93,* 104–105.

Heyvaert, M., Saenen, L., Campbell, J. M., Maes, B., & Onghena, P. (2014). Efficacy of behavioral interventions for reducing problem behavior in persons with autism: An updated quantitative synthesis of single-subject research. *Research in Developmental Disabilities, 35,* 2463–2476.

Johnston, J. M. (2006). "Replacing" problem behavior: An analysis of tactical alternatives. *The Behavior Analyst, 29,* 1–11.

Lerman, D. C., & Vorndran, C. M. (2002). On the status of knowledge for using punishment: Implications for treating behavior disorders. *Journal of Applied Behavior Analysis, 35,* 431–464.

Matson, J. L., & Kazdin, A. E. (1981). Punishment in behavior modification: Pragmatic, ethical, and legal issues. *Clinical Psychology Review, 1,* 197–210.

Matson, J. L., & Taras, M. E. (1989). A 20-year review of punishment and alternative methods to treat problem behaviors in developmentally delayed persons. *Research in Developmental Disabilities, 10,* 85–104.

Vollmer, T. R. (1994). The concept of automatic reinforcement: Implications for behavioral research in developmental disabilities. *Research in Developmental Disabilities, 15,* 187–207.

Vollmer, T. R. (2002). Punishment happens: Some comments on Lerman and Vorndran's review. *Journal of Applied Behavior Analysis, 35,* 469–473.

Table 5.1
Punishment Procedures should be Accountable for Eight Basic Criteria

1. The punishment should result in durable reduction of undesirable behavior.
2. The reduction of undesirable behavior should generalize across the full range of people, places, times, and materials that the person will encounter as part of their normal daily routine.
3. The punishment should not involve the use of procedures that result in physical pain or tissue damage.
4. The procedures should be appropriate for use in regular school settings.
5. The procedures should always include systematic reinforcement and instruction of adaptive alternative behaviors.
6. The procedures used to reduce undesirable behavior should be adequately safeguarded against abuse by unskilled staff implementing procedures.
7. The technology should always include continuous monitoring, external observation, and review by a knowledgeable review panel.
8. The procedures to reduce undesirable behavior should be the least intrusive needed to be effective, and in no case exceed normal community standards of appropriateness.

Adapted from Horner, Dunlap, Koegel, Carr, Sailor, Anderson, Albin, & O'Neill, (1990).

Chapter 6

PREVENTATIVE PROCEDURES
AND INTERVENTIONS

Key Point Questions

1. What are ecological modifications?
2. What is goal setting?
3. What are token economies?
4. What is relaxation training?
5. What are modifications to instruction and supports?
6. What is anger control training?
7. What are pretask requests?

WINDOW TO THE WORLD CASE STUDY ONE

Denise is a young adult who has various disability labels (emotional disturbance, bipolar, learning disability). At her job site she does her work tasks well and she also does well in community and home living tasks (where she lived in an apartment with two roommates and receives independent living services). However, she is known to have "rage" at the drop of a hat if she believes that supervisors, coworkers, independent living staff, or community members or teachers are disrespecting her. These rages include verbal aggression and threats which sometimes escalate into physical aggression. Denise's supervisor, coworkers, and independent living staff are very concerned about this behavior and for Denise's future, especially since police had to be called to the apartment the last two times Denise has gone into a "rage." At Denise's recent Individual Program Plan team meeting, the whole team, including Denise, thought that this "rage" issue was of critical importance and needed to be dealt with immediately. The head of the Independent Living Services program, Ms. Kutasy, volunteered to come up with a plan for helping Denise.

Ms. Kutasy decides that several interventions need to be immediately implemented to develop skills for Denise. Denise realizes that her rage behavior is a serious problem and she is worried that she will end up in the prison system. Since Denise is willing to work with Ms. Kutasy, Denise agrees to meet individually with Ms. Kutasy three times a week for 30 minutes. During this time, Ms. Kutasy teaches Denise relaxation skills (visualization, deep breathing, and muscle tense/relax). Second, Denise joined an anger management group meeting twice per week in the evenings. Third, Ms. Kutasy and Denise set up a self-reinforcement system where Denise self-monitored her behavior to help her not respond to triggers or provocations from others. Reviewing the self-monitoring recorded data, both Denise and Ms. Kutasy were surprised to see the number of times per day that Denise believed that she was provoked by peers. Each time that Denise did not respond to these triggers she made a mark on a card, then for every 10 times that she did not respond she reinforced herself by downloading a song onto her smart phone. She also texted Ms. Kutasy at the end of each day to provide information on her behavior (the number of times being provoked and her number of times she did not go into a "rage"). In this way, Ms. Kutasy could support and praise the changes in Denise's behavior. Fourth, Ms. Kutasy met with the work supervisor and the independent living staff to provide training and awareness on behaviors that Denise perceived as disrespectful. This allowed the supervisor and independent living staff to change their behavior and not unintentionally illicit undesirable behavior from Denise.

Because of these interventions, Denise's rage behavior decreased significantly. Denise now had positive behaviors replacing her rage behavior and peer support in her anger management group. Further, with the changed behavior of her supervisor at work and independent living staff, she was having fewer situations that were likely to set off her rage behavior.

WINDOW OF THE WORLD CASE STUDY TWO

Teresa is a new supported living staff member for Katrina and Lisa, two adults with Autism Spectrum Disorders who live in an apartment. Teresa notices that both Katrina and Lisa like routines in their home and that there is a schedule of who will do what chores. However, chores don't get done and there is a lot of arguing about who is to do what chore and when.

After dinner one night, the three of them discuss the situation and Katrina and Lisa agree that the current situation is not working. They ask Teresa to come up with a plan to alleviate the situation. Teresa decides upon several ecological modifications for the situation. First, she clarifies the schedule so that all the chores to be done in the home are listed on a daily basis, including who will do what task on what day (the food preparation, the cooking, the dishes, cleaning the bathroom, cleaning the living room, etc.). Teresa also adds a check column to the list so that the person can check off when the chore is completed, and also for the other person to then mark a check on the sheet acknowledging that the chore has been completed.

Secondly, Teresa combines goal setting and token economies into the plan. Katrina and Lisa agree upon a token economy where each check earns a point towards individually selected reinforcers (for example, for Lisa, it is 10 points for a DVD rental, 20 points for a treat from the ice cream store down the block, and 30 points for buying her lunch at work rather than bringing her lunch from home). They also agree upon a goal of 90% completion of tasks for the week agreeing to a mutually reinforcing event, such as, dinner at a restaurant, a concert, going to a play, and so on.

KEY POINT QUESTION #1:
WHAT ARE ECOLOGICAL MODIFICATIONS?

Ecological modifications includes the systematic use of environmental variables in order to promote positive behavior change (Cowick & Storey, 2000). Support providers have control over a number of factors that may affect the behavior of individuals, such as, physical settings and setting structure, and staff-individual interactions, instructional and support methods and goals, task difficulty, and scheduling of activities. Through ecological manipulations, it is possible to prevent undesirable behaviors from occurring and also to promote positive replacement behaviors in a way that result in greater generalization and maintenance. Table 6.1 presents examples of ecological manipulations. These ecological manipulations may involve focus on:

Broader Aspects of a Person's Life

It is important to look broadly at a person's life to evaluate factors to change for increasing desirable behavior and quality of life outcomes for that individual. This evaluation may include factors such as:

1. Changing schedules or routines.
2. Resolving physical, mental health, and/or medical issues.
3. Increasing positive social contacts and relationships.
4. Performing meaningful work.

Setting Factors

Setting factors may increase the probability of desirable or undesirable behaviors and may influence the individual's ability to cope with the environmental variables. For instance, having a supported employee eat lunch with certain coworkers may influence the behavior of that person (if they like or dislike the coworkers). For instance, if Kyoko is struggling socially at work, then it might be desirable to have Kyoko paired with a coworker who has good social skills and who can serve as a desirable role model (rather than pairing her with other coworkers who are also having social difficulties).

Factors to evaluate are:

1. Places where desirable and/or undesirable behaviors are occurring.
2. Persons with whom desirable and/or undesirable behaviors are occurring.
3. Activities where desirable and/or undesirable behaviors are occurring.

Task-Related Factors

Many undesirable behaviors occur in task-related situations, so often a support provider's first interpretation is that the person is being noncompliant. An alternative explanation is that there is something about the task that is problematic for the individual. For example, by being aggressive the adult gets out of something that they consider nonfunctional (or easy, or boring, or too difficult).

Interventions that may alleviate task related factors are:

1. Breaking the task down into smaller steps.
2. Giving the individual extra assistance on certain steps that may be more difficult.
3. Change in scheduling.
4. Change everything (or as much as possible).

Response Interruption

Response interruption prevents an undesirable behavior from continuing (the behavior has to first occur before it can be stopped) by interrupting the behavior. These interruptions can include:

1. Prosthetic device (such as the use of a helmet for an individual with severe self-injurious behavior).
2. Manual blocking (the support provider standing between an aggressive individual and the intended victim).
3. Verbal cues ("Emma, you need to stop clenching your fists and take a deep breath").

Physical Exercise

Exercise has many benefits for individuals such as lowering stress levels, enhancing moods, boosting blood flow to the brain and helping it to receive oxygen and nutrients, better sleeping at night, and increasing cognitive performance (Archer & Kostrzewa, 2012; Hillman, Erickson, & Kramer, 2008). Since many adults with disabilities do not get adequate amounts of exercise, the use of quick and simple exercises as well as more extensive exercise programs such as joining a sports team or a workout group can be very beneficial for a variety of issues, including undesirable behaviors.

KEY POINT QUESTION #2: WHAT IS GOAL SETTING?

Goal setting (also known as a contract) involves the person setting specific behavioral goals they will meet along with the specific reinforcement they will receive for meeting that goal (Manly, Hawkins, Evans, Woldt, & Robertson, 2002). It is important to have a goal that is realistic, achievable, and requires effort. This can enhance motivation and reduce the occurrence of undesirable behaviors. It is recommended that the goal/contract include:

1. A task or activity the individual plans to learn or the behavior that they will engage in.
2. Specified activities and/or specific behaviors the person will engage in (defined and positively worded).
3. The degree of proficiency the individual will attain.
4. How the person will demonstrate that the learning has occurred.
5. What are the time dimensions for the goal.
6. How the goal will be measured and evaluated. Performance feedback must be used to provide ongoing information about the behavior of the individual (are they making progress towards the goal?).
7. The role and responsibilities for each person (the individual, support provider, and others such as family members or employer).
8. A written contract that is signed by all parties involved.
9. Short term goals should be initially used for quick reinforcement.
10. The goal intervention ties into self-management strategies.

KEY POINT QUESTION #3: WHAT ARE TOKEN ECONOMIES?

A reinforcement system based on tokens is referred to as a token economy. Tokens function in the same way that money does, where tokens are used to purchase back-up reinforcers. Tokens are conditioned reinforcers (they can be exchanged for a variety of objects or activities, e.g., back-up reinforcers). Tickets, stars, points or checkmarks are commonly used.

Advantages to using a token economy are:

1. Tokens/points can be distributed quickly and unobtrusively.
2. Reinforcement with tokens can develop high rates of desirable behavior.
3. Tokens can bridge the delay between the desirable behavior and the delivery of the back-up reinforcement.
4. Since tokens are backed up by a variety of reinforcers, they are less subject to satiation than other reinforcers.
5. Tokens can be delivered without interrupting instruction.
6. Tokens do not require consumption of treats or performance of behaviors that may interrupt instruction.

Table 6.2 provides general guidelines for the implementation of token economies.

KEY POINT QUESTION #4:
WHAT IS RELAXATION TRAINING?

Work, community, and home settings can be stressful and anxiety generating places for individuals for a variety of reasons, such as, crowded situations, noise levels, task demands, and social interactions. This stress can negatively impact task and social performance. Thus, strategies for reducing or eliminating stress can be beneficial for adults with disabilities.

Relaxation training involves a variety of strategies, for example, visualization, worry control, coping skills, nutrition, and exercise (Davis, Eshelman, & McKay, 2008; Shapiro & Sprague, 2009). The goal is for the individual to develop skills and strategies that reinforce behavior that is incompatible with anxiety, and is a coping skill for stress. Relaxation skills can be taught to an individual or a group. As with any intervention, not all individuals will respond successfully to relaxation training. Some of the most common relaxation methods are:

1. Tensing and relaxing muscle groups (also known as deep muscle relaxation or progressive muscle relaxation) which involves tensing and then relaxing hands or shoulders.
2. Deep breathing (also known as diaphragmatic breathing) involving the expansion of the abdomen rather than the chest when breathing.

3. Squeeze objects. These can be balls, modeling clay, or "koosh" objects.

These strategies can be used individually or together. For instance, Jacob could be taught, before entering the lunch room at work where he will have to interact with others, to tense and relax three muscle groups and to take deep breaths for 30 seconds. This could help him to reduce his stress level and to become more focused before starting to interact with coworkers in the lunch room .

KEY POINT QUESTION #5: WHAT ARE MODIFICATIONS TO INSTRUCTION AND SUPPORTS?

Making changes or modifications to instruction and supports can be a key component of positive behavior support. Many individuals engage in undesirable behaviors due to difficulty in their academic, social, or task performance and, for this reason, changes or modifications can decrease undesirable behavior.

The terms accommodations and modifications are often used interchangeably, but they represent two different changes. Accommodations provide different ways for individuals to take in (access) information or to display their knowledge or skill back to the support provider, employer, and so on. Accommodations don't alter or lower the standards, the content, performance criteria, or expectations for a task. The use of Braille, audiotaped meetings, recorded text, a note taker, and modified directions are all examples of accommodations.

Modifications are changes in the delivery, content, or completion level of tasks. They result in changing or lowering expectations and create a different standard for some individuals. Modifications do change the performance requirement for an individual. Fewer task requirements, lowering of the lifting requirements for a job, shortened work days are examples of modifications.

Wright (2005) has provided information on nine types of adaptations for curriculum modification for students with disabilities and they apply to adults with disabilities as well:

1. *Size:*
   Adapt the number of items or tasks that the person is expected to learn or complete. This might be the length or portion of a task expected to be completed.
   Example: Reduce the number of steps of a cooking task a person must learn at any one time.

2. *Time:*
   Adapt the time allotted and allowed for learning or task completion.
   Example: Individualize a timeline for completing a task, adjust the pace of learning (increase or decrease).

3. *Level of Support:*
   Increase the amount of personal assistance or instruction with a specific task.
   Example: Have coworkers provide support for learning a new task.

4. *Input:*
   Adapt the way instruction is delivered to the individual.
   Example: Use different visual aids, video modeling, use more concrete examples.

5. *Difficulty:*
   Adapt the skill level or the rules on how the individual may complete the work.
   Example: Allow the use of a calculator to figure math problems, simplify task directions, change rules on task completion.

6. *Output:*
   Adapt how the person can respond to instruction in terms of demonstrating understanding and knowledge.
   Example: Instead of answering questions from a supervisor in writing, allow a verbal response. Use a communication book for some individuals.

7. *Participation:*
   Adapt the extent to which a person is actively involved in the task.
   Example: Allow partial participation in which the person completes some parts but not all of an activity (such as eliminating parts of a cleaning task which require bending which is difficult for the person).

8. *Alternative/Modified Goals:*
   Adapt the goals or outcome expectations while using the same materials.
   Example: For a work task, expect the worker to complete parts, but not all, of the complete task. For example, cleaning the exercise equipment in the weight room at the health club, but not the mirrors (due to a visual impairment which makes it hard for the worker to determine cleanliness of the mirrors). The mirrors could then be cleaned by a coworker.

9. *Adapted Curriculum:*
   Provide different instruction and materials to meet a person's individual goals.
   Example: In a foreign language class at a community college, a student may develop a play or script that uses both authentic language and cultural knowledge of a designated time period, rather than taking a comprehensive language exam which involves reading paragraphs and answering questions.

KEY POINT QUESTION #6:
WHAT IS ANGER CONTROL TRAINING?

Some adults with disabilities have anger which can lead to poor work or social performance, aggression, and other undesirable behaviors. One strategy with strong empirical evidence of effectiveness is Aggression Replacement Training (ART) which is an intervention designed for individuals that are aggressive (Goldstein, Glick, & Gibbs, 1986). ART teaches alternative skills to anger and aggression.

The three components of ART are:

1. SkillStreaming which teaches a curriculum of ProSocial, inter-personal skills (i.e. what to do instead of aggression). Skillsteam-ing is covered in more detail in Chapter 9.
2. Anger Control Training (ACT) which teaches an individual what to do, as well as what not to do, if provoked. The goal of anger control training is to teach the individual self-control of anger. In ACT, each individual brings to each session a description of a recent anger-arousing experience which they record in a bind-er. Table 6.3 provides an example of Anger Control Training steps. For 10 sessions (usually group sessions), the individuals receive instruction in responding to their frustrations with a chain of behaviors that include:
    a. Identifying triggers (i.e., those external events and internal self-statements that provoke an anger response, such as being too close to a particular individual or having one's space sud-denly invaded).
    b. Identifying cues (i.e., those individual physical events, such as tightened muscles, flushed faces, and clenched fists, which let the individual know that the emotion he or she is experienc-ing is anger).
    c. Using reminders (i.e., self-statements, such as "stay calm," "chill out," and "cool down," or nonhostile explanations of others' behavior).
    d. Using reducers (i.e., a series of techniques that, like the use of reminders, is designed expressly to lower the person's level of anger, such as deep breathing, counting backward, imagining a peaceful scene, or imagining the long-term consequences of one's behavior).
    e. Using self-evaluation (i.e., reflecting on how well the frustra-tion was responded to by identifying triggers, identifying cues, using reminders, and using reducers and then praising or rewarding oneself for effective performance (Goldstein & Glick, 1994).
3. Moral Reasoning Training, which promotes values that respect the rights of others, and helps individuals to want to use the interpersonal and anger management skills taught. The goal of moral reasoning training is to have individuals think about mor-

al issues from different perspectives and examine their judgments, as well as those of others.

Moral reasoning training generally involves group meetings where relevant examples of moral dilemmas are presented. Each individual in the group is asked to describe the proper behavior the person in the dilemma should do, and why (Goldstein et al., 1986).

KEY POINT QUESTION #7: WHAT ARE PRETASK REQUESTS?

Pretask requests (also known as behavioral momentum) is a procedure designed for situations in which an adaptive pattern of responding competes with undesirable behaviors. Pretask requests are an antecedent strategy in that the procedure is used to keep the undesirable behavior from occurring. Pretask requests can be effective in transitions, acquisition of skills, and in breaking a chain of undesirable behaviors (Singer, Singer, & Horner, 1987).

For example, for an adult who has difficulty transitioning into their apartment, pretask requests could be used by a support provider to deliver an individualized set of pretask requests, such as "give me five," "shake hands," "say your name," "give me a fist bump," before saying "open the door now." Pretask requests involve identifying 3-5 simple responses that:

1. The person can already perform,
2. Require a very short time to complete,
3. Are from the same response class as the targeted, desirable behavior,
4. Have a high probability of being performed following presentation of a support provider request.

They are then followed by a "difficult" request that the individual has difficulty performing successfully, and is likely to resist via undesirable behavior. A request consists of an instruction to complete a task in which the person frequently engages in undesirable behavior.

There are three main situations in which to use pretask requests: **The first situation** is during "transitions" to avoid what is confusing or inappropriate. When an individual is changing from one task to another, pretask requests can be used to facilitate appropriate responding during the transition. This avoids giving the individual an opportunity to engage in undesirable behaviors. For example, when Neil is changing from putting the laundry away to getting cleaning supplies out, his support provider immediately says, "Neil, stand up," "give me five," "say your name," and "go to the closet in the laundry room." This avoids giving Neil the opportunity for undesirable behaviors (not going or saying, "I don't want to go to the laundry room") and immediately gives him desirable behaviors to engage in that result in Neil going to the closet in the laundry room.

The second situation is to strengthen the durable responding (or acquisition of skills) by the person. In this situation, pretask requests are interspersed in with tasks which the person has trouble performing or is still learning. This allows the individual to make a high density of correct responses and receive reinforcement while learning new tasks. For instance, if Angelo is learning new cooking skills, the support provider may intersperse some cooking tasks that he is familiar with (chopping vegetables, peeling fruit) when learning the new cooking skills.

In the third situation, pretask requests are used to interrupt a chain of behaviors that typically lead to undesirable responding. Delivering the pretask request early in such a chain increases the likelihood that the undesirable behavior will be avoided, and when the individual starts to engage in undesirable behaviors, the pretask requests are delivered so that the person is engaging in desirable behavior. This desired behavior is likely to continue rather than the undesirable behavior. For example, if Alejandro has an escalation sequence of behaviors (making an exasperated noise, looking angrily at the coworker, banging his hand on the wall, making a rude remark to the coworker) when he is presented with work tasks that involve working with others, his job coach could use pretask requests at the beginning of this chain of behaviors. When Alejandro is told to work with a coworker and he makes an exasperated noise, she could ask him to take a deep breath, put his hands in his pockets, give her a fist bump, put his hands on his hips, and take another deep breath. She could then praise him for complying, remind him that he did well yesterday doing a task with a coworker, and remind him of their prearranged secret signal if he needs help.

Guidelines for Using Pretask Requests

Pretask requests should only be used if there is a high enough level of reinforcement and antecedent practice for desirable behavior. Otherwise, pretask requests can inadvertently reinforce undesirable behavior. The support provider first needs to decide if one of these three situations is occurring. If so, then pretask requests may be effective. If not, then another strategy is called for.

Second, the support provider must assess if the individual is bored or frustrated during teaching sessions, is going from a more to a less reinforcing situation, is unclear about the transition, or if there is a chain to the inappropriate behaviors that the person is displaying.

Third, the support provider must determine what behaviors the individual reliably performs that may be used in the pretask requests (i.e., "take this," "put it on the table," "come here," etc.). For task variation, it is necessary to establish tasks that the person knows how to perform and enjoys doing.

Fourth, the person must be reinforced for following the requests.

And fifth, the support provider must establish the pretask requests as part of the individual's daily routines. It is important to emphasize that pretask requests are a preventative strategy and should not be used as a punishment procedure that follows undesirable behavior.

BEST PRACTICE RECOMMENDATIONS

1. Preventative procedures are focused on antecedent interventions that build skills that then prevent undesirable behaviors from occurring.
2. Changing the structure and environment of a situation can also be an effective preventative procedure.
3. A variety of preventative procedures can be combined as an effective intervention.

DISCUSSION QUESTIONS

1. How do you decide what type of intervention will be most successful with an individual?

2. Does it unnecessarily single out an individual to use an intervention, such as relaxation training or pretask request, when other individuals are not receiving that intervention in that environment (such as a work setting)?

3. Is it likely that these intervention procedures will to lead to generalized increases in desirable behavior or decreases in undesirable behavior?

EMPLOYMENT, COMMUNITY, AND HOME ACTIVITY SUGGESTIONS

1. Observe an individual with undesirable behaviors and list the types of undesirable behaviors you see. Match the type of preventative procedure that would be most effective as an intervention for each listed behavior.

2. Interview adults with disabilities about which preventative procedure(s) they would find most appropriate and beneficial to use.

REFERENCES

Archer, T., & Kostrzewa, R. (2012). Physical exercise alleviates ADHD symptoms: Regional deficits and development trajectory. *Neurotoxicity Research, 21,* 195–209.

Cowick, B., & Storey, K. (2000). An analysis of functional assessment in relation to students with serious emotional and behaviour disorders. *International Journal of Disability, Development and Education, 47,* 55–75.

Davis, M., Eshelman, E. R., & McKay, M. (2008). *The relaxation and stress reduction workbook* (6th ed.). Oakland, CA: New Harbinger Publications.

Goldstein, A. P., & Glick, B. (1994). Aggression Replacement Training: Curriculum and evaluation. *Simulation & Gaming, 25,* 926.

Goldstein, A. P., Glick B., & Gibbs, J. (1986). *Aggression replacement training: A comprehensive intervention for aggressive youth.* Champaign, IL: Research Press.

Hillman, C. H., Erickson, K., & Kramer, A. F. (2008). Be smart, exercise your heart: Exercise effects on brain and cognition. *Nature Reviews Neuroscience, 9,* 58–65.

Kazdin, A. E. (2013). *Behavior modification in applied settings* (7th ed.). Long Grove, IL: Waveland Press.

Manly, T., Hawkins, K., Evans, J., Woldt, K., & Robertson, I. H. (2002). Rehabilitation of executive function: Facilitation of effective goal management on complex tasks using periodic auditory alerts. *Neuropsychologia, 40,* 271–281.

Myles, B. S., Moran, M. R., Ormsbee, C. K., & Downing, J. A. (1992). Guidelines for establishing and maintaining token economies. *Intervention in School and Clinic, 27,* 164–169.

Singer, G. H. S., Singer, J. H. G., & Horner, R. H. (1987). Using pretask requests to increase the probability of compliance for students with severe disabilities. *Journal of the Association for Persons with Severe Handicaps, 12,* 287–291.

Wright, D. B. (2005). *Teaching and learning.* Sacramento, CA: Resources in Special Education.

EMPIRICAL RESEARCH SUPPORTING THAT THE INTERVENTIONS PRESENTED IN CHAPTER ARE EVIDENCE BASED PRACTICES

Bouvet, C., & Coulet, A. (2016). Relaxation therapy and anxiety, self-esteem, and emotional regulation among adults with intellectual disabilities: A randomized controlled trial. *Journal of Intellectual Disabilities, 20,* 228–240.

Brännström, L., Kaunitz, C., Andershed, A., South, S., & Smedslund, G. (2016). Aggression replacement training (ART) for reducing antisocial behavior in adolescents and adults: A systematic review. *Aggression and Violent Behavior, 27,* 30–41.

Claes, C., Van Hove, G., Vandevelde, S., van Loon, J., & Schalock, R. (2012). The influence of supports strategies, environmental factors, and client characteristics on quality of life-related personal outcomes. *Research in Developmental Disabilities, 33,* 96–103.

Cooper, K. J., & Browder, D. M. (1997). The use of a personal trainer to enhance participation of older adults with severe disabilities in community water exercise classes. *Journal of Behavioral Education, 7,* 421–434.

Guercio, J. M., Ferguson, K. E., & McMorrow, M. J. (2001). Increasing functional communication through relaxation training and neuromuscular feedback. *Brain Injury, 15,* 1073–1082.

Hedley, D., Cai, R., Uljarevic, M., Wilmot, M., Spoor, J. R., Richdale, A., & Dissanayake, C. (2018). Transition to work: Perspectives from the autism spectrum. *Autism: The International Journal of Research and Practice, 22,* 528–541.

Horner, R. H., Day, H. M., Sprague, J. R., O'Brien, M., & Heathfield, L. T. (1991). Interspersed requests: A nonaversive procedure for reducing aggression and self-injury during instruction. *Journal of Applied Behavior Analysis, 24,* 265–278.

LeBlanc, L. A., Hagopian, L. P., & Maglieri, K. A. (2000). Use of a token economy to eliminate excessive inappropriate social behavior in an adult with developmental disabilities. *Behavioral Interventions, 15,* 135–143.

Lee, D. L (2005). Increasing compliance: A quantitative synthesis of applied research on high-probability request sequences. *Exceptionality, 13,* 141–154.

Maki, A. L., Rudrud, E. H., Schulze, K. A., & Rapp, J. T. (2008). Increasing therapeutic exercise participation by individuals with acquired brain injury using self-recording and reinforcement. *Behavioral Interventions, 23,* 75–86.

McEntee, J. E., Parker, E. H., Brown, M. B., & Poulson, R. L. (1996). Case study: The effects of response interruption, dro and positive reinforcement on the reduction of hand-mouthing behavior. *Behavioral Interventions, 11,* 163–170.

Pérez-Cruzado, D., & Cuesta-Vargas, A. (2016). Changes on quality of life, self-efficacy and social support for activities and physical fitness in people with intellectual disabilities through multimodal intervention. *European Journal of Special Needs Education, 31,* 553–564.

Stocks, J. T., Thyer, B. A., & Kearsley, M. (1987). Using token economy in a community based program for disabled adults: An empirical evaluation leads to program modification. *Behavioral Residential Treatment, 2,* 173–185.

van Dongen, J. M., Coffeng, J. K., van Wier, M. F., Boot, C. R. L., Hendriksen, I. J. M., van Mechelen, W., Bongers, P. M., van der Beek, A. J., Bosmans, J. E., & van Tulder, M. W. (2017). The cost-effectiveness and return-on-investment of a combined social and physical environmental intervention in office employees. *Health Education Research, 32,* 384–398.

Verdonschot, M. M. L, de Witte, L. P., Reichrath, E., Buntinx, W. H. E., & Curfs, L. M. G. (2009). Impact of environmental factors on community participation of persons with an intellectual disability: A systematic review. *Journal of Intellectual Disability Research, 53,* 54–64.

GENERAL REFERENCES REGARDING TOPICS IN CHAPTER

Amendola, M., & Oliver, R. (2014). *Anger control training.* Champaign, IL: Research Press.

Hackenberg, T. D. (2018). Token reinforcement: Translational research and application. *Journal of Applied Behavior Analysis, 5,* 393–435.

Hayes-Skelton, S. A., Roemer, L., Orsillo, S. M., & Borkovec, T. D. (2013). A contemporary view of applied relaxation for generalized anxiety disorder. *Cognitive Behaviour Therapy, 42,* 292–302.

Hoover, J. J., & Ayllon, T. (2018). *How to use token economy and point systems.* Austin, TX: Pro-Ed.

Kazdin, A. E. (1977). *Token economy: A review and evaluation.* New York: Plenum Press.

Landrum, T. J., & Sweigart, C. A (2014). Simple, evidence-based interventions for classic problems of emotional and behavioral disorders. *Beyond Behavior, 23*(3), 3–9.

Lyon, C. S., & Lagarde, R. (1997). Tokens for success: Using the graduated reinforcement system. *Teaching Exceptional Children, 29,* 52–57.

Taylor, J. L., Novaco, R., & Brown, T. (2016). Reductions in aggression and violence following cognitive behavioural anger treatment for detained patients with intellectual disabilities. *Journal of Intellectual Disability Research, 60,* 126–133.

Table 6.1
Examples of Ecological Manipulations

Function is to Obtain Desirable Event:

Increase interest level of activity.
Change in activity.
Break activity into smaller segments.
Provide free time.
Provide outside activities that involve climbing, running, pushing, pulling, or lifting.

Function is to Obtain External Stimulation:

Seating with a peer.
Pairing with a peer.
Public acknowledgment of successes of the individual.
Information to access resources (e.g. counseling help, medical assistance).
Schedule regular conferences/checkins.
Pairing with advocate to maximize social involvement.
High reinforcement ratio/social praise.
Provide extra responsibilities in employment, community, and/or residential situation.

Function is to Obtain Attention:

Counseling services.
Social skills instruction.
Use of tutors/mentors.

Function is to Escape/Avoid:

Provide quiet space for calming down.
Provide isolated area for release of anger.
Use of Journal writing.
Prompting initiations and appropriate interactions.
Use of peer models and peer tutoring.
Use of clear/precise instructions.
Provide high probability requests prior to low probability request.
Clearly established rules and routines.
Clearly established consequences for both desirable and undesirable behavior.
Brief activities.
High interest activities.
Provide choice of activities.
Use a safety signal to indicate that activity is about to end contingent on appropriate behavior (e.g. we're almost finished).

Adapted from Cowick & Storey (2000).

Table 6.2
General Guidelines for the Implementation of Token Economies

1. Explain the behaviors that receive or lose points as well as the system, posted point values (cost or price), reinforcement menu, and redemption times and rules.
2. Instruction and role playing regarding desirable and/or undesirable behaviors, as well as for redeeming and/or losing points, should occur before initiating the token system.
3. Claiming reinforcers should involve a minimum of discussion and record keeping.
4. A regular routine for distribution and redemption should be developed to minimize interruption of instruction.
5. Pair praise with delivery of tokens.
6. Redemption and exchange periods may be schedule hourly, daily, and/or weekly.
7. Menu of reinforcers should specify the reinforcer options and costs, and be specified in advance.
8. There should be a variety of reinforcers with a variety of prices so that it is easy to purchase at least one reinforcer.
9. Tokens can be based upon a monetary system so that the individual can learn functional skills (counting, banking, interest accumulation, etc.) in conjunction with the token economy.

Adapted from Kazdin (2013); Myles, Moran, Ormsbee, and Downing (1992).

Table 6.3
Example of Anger Control Training Steps

Avoiding Trouble with Others

Steps:

1. Decide if you are in a situation that might get you into trouble.
2. Decide if you want to get out of the situation.
3. Tell the other people what you decided and why.
4. Suggest other things you might do.
5. Do what you think is best for you.

Adapted from Goldstein, Glick and Gibbs (1986).

Chapter 7

SELF-MANAGEMENT STRATEGIES

Key Point Questions

1. What is self-management?
2. Why are using self-management strategies advantageous for adults with disabilities?
3. What are the types of self-management strategies?
4. How are self-management skills taught?
5. How can self-management strategies be used to increase a person's positive behavior?

WINDOW TO THE WORLD CASE STUDY ONE

Theodore is identified as having a learning disability and Attention Deficit Hyperactivity Disorder (ADHD). He works in the central office of a bank where he oversees communications with the four local branches. Theodore is impacted in his organizational ability. One area, in particular, Theodore struggles with is organizing his work assignments which are beginning to cause both work performance and behavioral problems. When in meetings, Theodore follows directions to write his assignments down (which are done on a piece of paper from his loose-leaf binder). Once his assignments are written down, Theodore stuffs the work assignment paper in his briefcase along with any related handouts. Once at his desk and ready to work, Theodore has difficulty finding and organizing his assignments and materials. He dumps out the contents of his briefcase which usually consist of crumpled up papers, lunch wrappings, used up pens and various collected sticky notes. When the desired papers are found (often in a jumbled ball), they are usually torn, wrinkled and unreadable. This has caused such frustration and anxiety that Theodore will often be unable to do or complete his work assignments. On some occasions, he's so upset, he will leave work early taking a partial sick day.

Both Theodore and his supervisor are very worried about his lack of organization. A meeting was held with Theodore and his supervisor regarding the situation. Theodore's supervisor said that his work is excellent when it is completed but his lack of work completion, or late work completion, is a very serious issue and she has to place Theodore on probation. That night Theodore discussed the situation with his wife. It was decided that Theodore needed a better strategy for how he records his work assignments and how he stores paperwork and handouts in his briefcase (other than the haphazard strategy he's currently using). It was also discussed that, due to the fact that Theodore often moves from the main office to branch banks, he needs a way to learn to manage this task independently, yet be able to receive feedback from his supervisor that his new management system is working.

For this system, Theodore and his wife went shopping and bought five different colored spiral notebooks, one notebook for each location. Additionally, each notebook came with a two-sided pocket page. Theodore decided that he would write down his work assignments for each location in the designated color selected notebook (green for the main office, red for branch one, etc.). He would also put any handouts for each location in the notebook's pocket page. Theodore's wife designed a daily check-off list with the step-by-step instructions Theodore would follow and that Theodore would carry this check off list in his loose-leaf binder. This daily check-off list provided a section for each location. At prespecified times teach day, Theodore's smart phone would vibrate and provide a text prompt to assess whether he followed the steps on the checklist for organizing his materials and check off the boxes indicating completion for each completed step. If he missed a step, he would go back and complete it. Once this was done, he would send himself an email to confirm he had used the system correctly. This way he could share the emails with his wife at night so that she could reinforce his behavior. Theodore decided that in order to have a well-organized briefcase the following steps would be on the form:

☐ assignments written in notebook,

☐ handouts and/or materials placed in notebook pocket,

☐ notebook put in briefcase,

☐ pens and pencils put in side pocket of briefcase,

☐ other items (sticky notes, paperclips, etc.) put inside briefcase outside pocket,

☐ all wrappers and garbage thrown in trash.

Also included on the form is a line for the supervisor to sign and date confirming that Theodore correctly followed instruction and completed assignments along with any comments for corrective feedback, if needed.

WINDOW TO THE WORLD CASE STUDY TWO

Taylia is 22 and lives with her roommate, Nigar, in a nice apartment. Taylia works full time at a trendy boutique. Lately, Taylia and Nigar, who have been living together for a year, have not been getting along very well, even though they had been friends in high school. The two of them went out for pizza with their Independent Living coordinator, Allene, so that they could discuss their problems in a neutral location. After some discussion, the three of them came to the conclusion that the main problem is that Taylia has been having difficulty controlling her temper and has been yelling and cursing at Nigar. Allene helped them analyze the problem and it became clear that both Taylia and Nigar don't have a system for who will do what tasks at home. When Taylia thinks that Nigar didn't do something that she should have, such as putting the dishes away from the dishwasher, she "blows up" at Nigar.

Allene decides to implement a self-management strategy for the two roommates. She first works with Taylia and Nigar to come up with a weekly list of who will do what tasks on which days (Nigar will put away the dishes on Monday, Wednesday, Friday, and Sunday, and Taylia will on Tuesday, Thursday, and Saturday; Taylia will take out the garbage on Monday and Friday and Nigar will on Wednesday and Sunday). This clarifies who will do what tasks on what days. The schedule is put on the refrigerator door so that both roommates can see the schedule and then check off the tasks when they complete them. In addition, Allene put a list of anger management steps next to the schedule for what they can do when getting upset (close eyes, count to ten, tense and release muscles) in case one of the roommates did not do what they were supposed to do on the schedule. Allene then role-played the anger management steps with Taylia and Nigar right in front of the refrigerator (where they would most likely use them).

KEY POINT QUESTION #1: WHAT IS SELF-MANAGEMENT?

Self-management strategies promote learning in a less supervised setting (such as the lunchroom or grocery shopping) and facilitate as much independence as possible for the individual. Independence gives the person the opportunity to control how they behave. For the support provider, increasing the use of self-management strategies fades out the individual's reliance on the need for the support provider's constant prompting. Further advantages are outlined in Table 7.1.

Self-management broadly refers to specific procedures used by an individual to influence his or her own behavior (Browder & Shapiro, 1985). Terms such as self-regulation, self-monitoring, self-control, self-evaluation and self-reinforcement are often used interchangeably with the term self-management. Self-management may be viewed as giving the individual specific skills and strategies to control his or her actions. Control is transferred from the support provider to the individual through teaching the person skills and specific strategies to control or modify their own behavior. Ideally, the self-management process will involve the person (and/or support provider) in:

1. Recognizing there is a problem,
2. Seeing the problem as consisting of behavior(s) that need altering or changing,
3. Determining the natural contingencies currently controlling the behavior,
4. Arranging and/or changing those natural contingencies for supporting the desired behavior(s) to occur (Baer, 1984).

Through this self-management process, the chance of positively changing the behavior that has caused the problem will be increased. For example, in the Windows of the World Case Study One, Theo-

dore's inability to complete work assignments was caused by his behavior of just throwing his papers randomly in his briefcase. By changing the behavior of how he puts work assignments in his briefcase, he
was able to complete his assignments successfully. Using a self-management checklist, Theodore was able to respond to a cue (each step
on the checklist) and self-record his response by placing a check next
to completed steps.

KEY POINT QUESTION #2:
WHY ARE USING SELF-MANAGEMENT STRATEGIES
ADVANTAGEOUS FOR ADULTS WITH DISABILITIES?

The self-management process is useful when an individual has
become dependent on support providers for prompts, cues, instructions, or reinforcement for completion of tasks or other activities. Self-
management procedures can provide the person with a positive means
of transforming the need for external reminders and/or instructions
from the support provider to independently using a self-managed
prompt delivery process, thus taking control of their own behavior.

The first advantage for people using self-management strategies is
that it involves individuals in their own behavior change. Rather than
the support provider imposing structure for an individual to behave a
specific way, the person can use a self-management strategy that
guides them to change their own behavior. The result is that the individual is able to do tasks more independently, thus giving them more
control over their life. Being able to decide about how one behaves,
track one's own progress and have more "say so" gives the individual
more "empowerment" or "buy in," power and flexibility in their life.
For example, if a person has trouble remembering the directions for
a work task, a step-by-step task analysis checklist on their smart phone
can be used to list the order of the steps for the task. Once each step
is completed the worker can check off the completed step. This allows
the worker to be more independent while working and less dependent
on constantly asking the job coach for help. It is also very important
that this independence also decreases passivity or learned helplessness
that many adults with disabilities have.

The second advantage is that the successful use of the self-management strategy in one setting can often be easily used in another setting
(e.g., generalization across settings) such as using a checklist not only

for work tasks but also in community settings and in the person's home. For example, a checklist could be used for putting on clothing items at a work site (such as putting on gloves, mask, etc. for a job sterilizing instruments in the hospital). This type of checklist could also then be used in the home setting for getting ready for work.

Self-management strategies can be generalized with another behavior such as using a tally sheet to keep track of the times one greets co-workers appropriately while also using a tally sheet for recording talking to co-workers during a meeting instead of paying attention to the boss (this would be a behavior to be decreased). Most self-management strategies can be designed to be used any time of the day or in any situation. Keeping with the checklist strategy example, if a person has learned to use a checklist for monitoring work tasks, then they could also use it at home for doing chores, and so on.

These examples provide a picture of the versatility of a self-management strategy by showing that the use of a self-management strategy can be generalized across work sites, situations, behaviors, or other times of the day to monitor and assess one's own behavior. If a person learns to successfully use a self-management process in these ways, they are more likely to continue using it in the future. Self-management strategies provide great benefit to both the individual and support providers due to the reduced need for repeated instructions, reminders, support provider micromanagement, as well as an increase in independent behaviors.

A third advantage is that the person may keep track of progress and assess if the strategy is working. For example, using a step-by-step task analysis for completion of job tasks, a worker can determine if a step has been completed or missed. Doing so increases the likelihood that assignments will be completed and helps the worker to know if a step in the task needs more clarification.

Use of self-management strategies may allow for behaviors to come under control of naturally occurring cues or stimuli (e.g., the discriminative stimulus) and decrease the need for support providers to tell an individual when to move to an assignment's next step or change tasks. An example of a stimulus in self-management is the use of a digital timer on a smart phone to alert the individual when it's time to change tasks. The timer could be set two minutes before a work task is to be completed to signal the worker to finish up the step in progress and prepare for the next activity.

Initially, support providers may find that setting up a self-management process for an individual may be time consuming as an increase in "up front" teaching may be required. However, once a process is in place, the person's use of the strategy often frees up a support provider's time by not having to help that person with tasks, and enables the person to function more independently. Additionally, the individual can use the strategy in multiple situations and settings and use it as a self-assessment tool for monitoring her/his own progress, thus being able to decide on any needed future modification to the strategy. For example, a worker who is trying to interact more with co-workers could tally the occurrence of positive initiations towards co-workers. For every time the worker appropriately initiates an interaction with a co-worker, the worker puts a check on the tally card. At the end of the day, the worker tallies the checks for the day. At the end of the week, the worker graphs the tallies for each day. The worker then is able to see the progress or lack of progress and assess how to improve the behavior and to reinforce herself if she has met her goal. If the worker is providing herself with a reinforcer at the end of the week for good progress, she might also decide to reinforce immediately after a particular day where she has done an exceptionally good job of initiating towards co-workers.

KEY POINT QUESTION #3:
WHAT ARE THE TYPES OF SELF-MANAGEMENT STRATEGIES?

Self-management strategies need to be tailored to the needs of the individual and the appropriateness for the environment and the situation. The following are types of self-management procedures.

Antecedent Cue Regulation

Antecedents are information or stimuli provided before the behavior is to occur. Antecedent cue regulation involves the use of prompts that lead the person to the correct response. The antecedent prompt occurs before the behavior from the individual is supposed to occur. This prompt (cue) signals the person to perform the target behavior. Prompts may be in verbal, written, physical, audio, symbolic, or pictorial form. Examples of pictorial prompts for a supported employee might include pictures on their PDA depicting the items needed every day for a specific work task. The employee looks at the pictures when they start work and obtains the items shown. The pictures (antecedent) remind the worker to gather together the items. Initially, the job coach may verbally prompt the worker to look at the pictures but, as the behavior for using the pictures is repeatedly built into the routine, the job coach prompts will eventually fade out allowing the employee to become independent in completing this task.

CHECKLISTS: Using a checklist with written step-by-step instructions for completing a task, posting a chart listing work rules in a day planner with a space for marking that the rules were followed, or providing check lists for completing tasks at home such as cleaning the kitchen, taking out the trash, and picking up items in the living room are quick and easy self-management examples. Checklists may be on note cards, sticky notes, computer screen or digital device, or in notebooks. If desired, pictures or symbols can be used in place of words. A task analysis consists of written step-by-step instructions that lead the individual to a correct response (Storey & Miner, 2017). For example, a self-management system might list the items to be put away at the end of a work task using icons. These icons can be listed with check boxes next to them. The checklist can be used for leading a person to perform every step within a task (such as getting assignments and materials ready), to complete an entire task. For example, a janitor in an office would need to get cleaning supplies on the cart ready, put on gloves, and so on.

TIME-KEEPING DEVICES: Clocks and time-keeping devices (analog or digital) set to provide a tone as a reminder to perform an activity at a specified time, such as, taking medication or eating a snack. A clock face can be modified to replace a number on a clock face with a symbol for a specific task. This is advantageous when a task is done at the same time each day, as having lunch at 12:00 p.m. A picture of a lunch pack or sandwich and drink can be shown where the 12:00 hour is cueing the person that it is time to have lunch.

RECORDING DEVICES: Devices such as smart phones, laptops, or other electronic devices) can be prerecorded to deliver an audio cue. The person listens to the prompt, performs the task, and listens to the next prompt, and so on. Examples for using this type of recorded prompting are: following recipe steps, following directions for cleaning up an area of the home, or for following steps for shopping at the grocery store (getting a card, going to the first aisle, selecting an item, and so on. Many individuals find auditory cues more understandable than written instructions (or need both the written instructions and the auditory instructions paired together). This is especially helpful when learning a new task where correct sequence is important such as following a recipe or following job tasks when working in the cafeteria. Computer text to speech software can be used to read the prompts for each step, allowing the person to click on the next step. Many applications for delivery of visual and/or auditory prompting are now available to be downloaded into smart phones, mobile handheld devices or other electronic devices that can be used for prompting and self-management strategies (www.iprompts.com).

LISTS: Many individuals find it useful to have a list of steps to follow when they are angry or upset. For these situations, the person may keep a card in their pocket to pull out and read to help them reduce the agitation. Teaching an individual to use self-verbalization and self-monitoring in upsetting social situation can help them from losing self-control and responding impulsively (Lerner & Johns, 2009; Vargas, 2013). The individual can write questions on a card to help them "stop and think" before responding. They can create their own questions to follow. An example of this could be:

WHAT IF?
What Happened?
How did it make me feel?
Are there good reasons I need to tell someone who can help?
Try counting to 10 backwards to calm down.
If I am still upset and can't work, I will talk to the supervisor or support provider.

Pictures, icons, symbols, and graphic organizers also provide antecedent cues to a person. For example, a checklist using pictures or icons could also be used for work tasks or other tasks that have a sequence of steps.

GRAPHIC ORGANIZERS serve as a visual representation for following directions, keeping track of steps in a project, or as a reference to often used information in the workplace, such as rules, regulations, office procedures, or as a reminder to stay on task. Also, graphic organizers are useful self-management tools as they provide "cues" to stimulate newly learned information or to help organize information.

Graphics should be simple, use minimal text and eliminate unnecessary detail, keeping the message concise and clear (Lever-Duffy & McDonald, 2011), such as a planning matrix illustrating a time completion schedule for each process in a project. A calendar is a simple example of a graphic organizer. For more complex processes, flow charts and planning trees could be used. A planning tree can be used to show the goals and subgoals of a project with the sequence of tasks listed in each appropriate goal box (Forte & Schurr, 1996). See Figure 7.1 for example of a planning tree.

Self-Monitoring and Self-Recording as Part of the Self-Evaluation Process

Self-Monitoring And Self-Recording

Self-monitoring and self-recording involve an individual evaluating whether they have performed a behavior (self-monitoring) along with creating a written record of each time the behavior is performed (self-recording). In this process, the self-monitoring provides the opportunity for the individual to become aware of their performance (when they are performing the behavior as well as when they are not performing the behavior). If a person wants to increase their success rate for completing their home tasks (cleaning, cooking, laundry, etc.) by keeping a daily record to see which days they complete which tasks, then they may find it useful to see if there is a pattern for the non-completion, such as are there particular days when home tasks are not completed (see Figure 7.1). If Tuesdays turn out to be nonhome task completion days, the person can analyze the cause (perhaps every Tuesday is a long work day with feeling extreme fatigue in the evening). In this example, knowing when tasks are not being completed becomes valuable information in assessing how to address the problem. Knowing the possible cause, helps the person devise a solution which could be to arrange alternatives to doing home tasks on Tuesday (doing them other nights, eating out on Tuesday's, switching tasks with a roommate on different days).

Self-Evaluation

Self-recording of the data provides the tool for individuals to self-evaluate their performance to a standard (such as completing so many

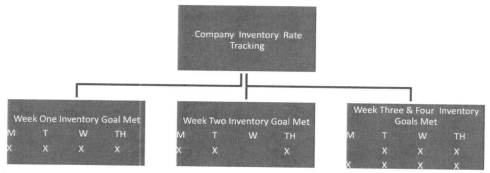

Figure 7.1 Planning Tree for completing a company's yearly inventory.

tasks at work per hour) or a self-selected goal (Storey & Montgomery, 2014). These two steps, self-monitoring and then self-recording, become part of a self-evaluation process providing an individual with the information on whether the behavior has occurred or if the targeted goal has been met and, in this way, gives the persons an active role for assessing their own progress. Additionally, this self-evaluation can often serve as a reinforcing activity, since it is completed independent of the support provider, and gives the individual feedback on the degree of success achieved on the targeted task. A useful and simple assessment tool for this is a checklist. A checklist helps the person identify key criteria for a task, such as reviewing their own work completion against listed criterion from the supervisor, and provide information for any needed revisions. This same checklist can serve as a conference tool with the supervisor or job coach in order to receive further feedback on progress (Culham & Wheeler, 2003). Targeted behaviors can be self-evaluated. An example of a simple self-evaluation strategy for a worker to improve getting along with others is to have a small card in their day planner for the worker to circle a happy face next to a picture or icon of people shaking hands when they have interacted positively with another person while at work. Initially, the criteria chosen might be that the person will interact positively with another at least three times during a day and when this is regularly accomplished, the criterion is increased for future work days. After the activity, the worker gives the card to the job coach for feedback and reinforcement.

Self-Recruited Feedback, Self-Determined Reinforcers and Choice of Reinforcers

Mank and Horner (1987) define self-recruited feedback as involving people in their own intervention and involves three components: (1) self-monitoring of the specific behavior, (2) self-evaluation of performance against a predefined criterion, and (3) recruitment of contingent feedback from the external environment. An example of self-recruited feedback is when a worker completes a specific task, self-evaluates her behavior, scores it, and then shares the information with the supervisor for feedback and reinforcement. One of the major advantages of self-recruited feedback is that it involves the supervisor in the evaluation and reinforcement process so that the supervisor is also given feedback on the person's positive performance and also provided an opportunity to reinforce the worker's desired behavior.

An example of self-recruited feedback is a worker at a library who is scanning returned books and placing them in the returned bin so that another worker can place them on the appropriate place in the stacks. When she completes a bin of returned books, Martha self-evaluates her behavior (she checks the bin to make sure that she scanned all of the books), pulls out a card from her pocket and puts a check mark next to the picture of a bin (scores her behavior), and then shows the card to her supervisor at the library who praises her and her task completion (feedback and reinforcement). An example for using this process is shown in Table 7.2.

Self-Punishment and Self-Management

If self-punishment is utilized in a self-management strategy it may involve a "response cost" procedure where the individual would lose points, tokens, or privileges that are already embedded in their program. The intent for using a response cost system is to target a behavior that needs to be decreased, such as spitting, destroying property, yelling at the job coach, and so on. An example of using a response cost in a self-management system would be when a worker gives herself 10 tokens at the beginning of the day and takes away a token each time she performs the target behavior to decrease. The worker and job coach can determine ahead of time how many tokens (8, 9, or 10 tokens) she must keep to receive the reinforcer at the end of the day. It should be remembered that people typically are more motivated to succeed when they are obtaining something they want rather than when they are losing something. However, using a response cost system in a self-management strategy can be effective for decreasing undesired behaviors when the process is used in conjunction with strategies that build new desired behaviors through the use of positive reinforcement. An example of this would be teaching the worker who yells at the job coach (behavior to be decreased) to count to 10 before responding when angry (alternative behavior) and then to use a calm voice to respond (desired behavior). When the worker performs the desirable alternative behavior, then they are positively reinforced with a compliment or a stronger reinforcer, such as points or a tangible reinforcer, if needed. If the worker does yell at the job coach then they would fine themselves a certain number of points.

KEY POINT QUESTION #4:
HOW ARE SELF-MANAGEMENT SKILLS BEST TAUGHT?

Snell and Brown (2006) outline the combination of components needed to set up a self-management tool such as deciding on the goal (what behavior needs changing), choosing a manner in which progress will be recorded (self-monitoring), evaluating if progress is being made (self-assessment) and deciding on a reward for progress made (self-reinforcement).

The following steps outlined by Koegel, Koegel, and Parks (1992) are helpful for setting up a self-management program:

1. Getting Ready
   a. Define behaviors
   b. Measure behaviors
   c. Choose a reinforcer
   d. Select an initial goal
2. Teaching Self-Management
   a. Get materials
   b. Teach identification of the behavior
   c. Record the behavior
   d. Reinforce self-management
3. Creating Independence
   a. Increase the amount of time the individual self-manages behavior

b. Fade reliance on prompts

c. Increase the number of response necessary for a reinforce

d. Fade the presence of the support provider.

Function of Behavior and Environment in Developing Self-Management Systems

The first step in designing the self-management system is for the individual to be able to describe and/or demonstrate the target behavior to change. Additionally, the individual and the support provider must understand the factors that influence the behavior in order to develop a self-management plan that will specifically address the target behavior. Depending upon the function (to get or to avoid) for the problem behavior, a self-management system may or may not be the correct tool to meet the person's need. Understanding the function of a behavior can also help determine situations when a self-management tool may not be the correct choice for intervening. If the functional assessment indicates the antecedents involve a person not understanding the task, has not learned the task, or the person is not attentive to or responsive to cues or consequences, then a different strategy should be chosen. An example of this would be where Muqali cannot successfully check off the systematic steps for completing a recipe because he doesn't understand the terms stated in the steps describing the cooking process. Once those terms are directly taught, then Muqali should be able to use the checklist. In those cases where an individual is not responsive to cues and consequences (reinforcers), the functional assessment process provides a means to delve deeper into assessing the person's specific behavioral needs for determining the best choice of interventions.

Teaching Self-Management

Individuals need to understand that a behavior is an action they perform They need to be aware of what it looks like or feels like in order to monitor whether the behavior has occurred or not. It is very important to understand that support providers will often need to directly teach the self-management strategy, demonstrating it and providing guided practice for the individual. Direct teaching of the self-management strategy is extremely important. This can be done through the support provider initially modeling for the person the strategy's components: recording, monitoring, and reinforcing. Role play would be another way to have the individual practice the strategy by moving through each component in a short period of time just to practice the skill. Only describing to the individual how to use the self-management strategy may not be enough for the person to then successfully use the system. Independent practice of the self-management strategy by the individual should include support provider supervision with delivery of reinforcement for using the strategy. Teaching should include reinforcement, prompts of encouragement and corrective feedback, when needed. Over time the frequency of reinforcers might be decreased to allow the natural occurring stimuli to control the desired behavior.

KEY POINT QUESTION #5: HOW CAN SELF-MANAGEMENT STRATEGIES BE USED EFFECTIVELY TO INCREASE A PERSON'S POSITIVE BEHAVIOR?

Involving the person directly in the self-management process is the most effective way to increase an individual's desirable behavior. For this reason, self-management strategies, such as keeping a written record of behaviors performed during a specific time and place, are often easy to use. Whether self-management strategies are designed for a single targeted behavior response (taking out the trash) or for a series of steps in a behavior (how to get ready for work), the design should be as simple and clear as possible for person's understanding and ease of use. Table 7.3 illustrates a self-management form for a single behavior and Table 7.4 illustrates self-management steps in a chain of behaviors.

Once a person has been directly taught a new skill or task, the individual can use a task analysis self-management form where each step in the new skill is listed and designed for the person to check off each step once performed. This is an ideal way for an individual to practice the new skill on their own without missing a critical step and causing an error in performing the skill. Additionally, a task analysis form may be used to help the person review a previously learned skill to maintain it or to relearn it.

A self-evaluation form can be used by a person to show how well they performed on a learned skill or how well they are mastering a target behavior needing improvement. A self-evaluation form is an effective way for a person to monitor their own progress and review the results with support provider for feedback. Table 7.5 provides an example.

Most importantly, self-management processes should be adapted to meet the individual needs, learning styles, and preferences of the person. For example, an individual may prefer a notebook to a checklist on the desk to keep track of tasks; other people may find a visible self-management procedure embarrassing or stigmatizing.

The following steps are provided for support providers to follow when setting up a self-management process:

1. Involve the individual in the process.
2. Collaborate with the person for each step in process and engage them in the design of the self-management form.
3. Adapt process to learning style and preference of the person.
4. Model the strategy.
5. Have the individual practice the strategy with support provider monitoring.
6. Provide praise and corrective feedback.
7. Have the individual use the strategy independently periodically checking for accuracy.
8. Once the person is competent in using strategy, allow independence. An occasional reminder to use it in appropriate situations may be needed.

BEST PRACTICE RECOMMENDATIONS

1. Self-Management Strategies should be an integral part of a support provider's instructional "tool kit" and be incorporated in a variety of settings and situations.
2. When developing a self-management strategy, consider using it in the beginning, middle and ending phases of instruction. Introducing self-management to a person in the beginning of learning a new skill may reduce errors in learning the task or process incorrectly.
3. Carefully assess the individual's learning needs, learning style, preferences and learning environment before developing a self-

management strategy to determine the appropriateness of the strategy. There may be considerable adaptation of a self-management strategy needed for an individual, or a different instructional approach needed altogether.

DISCUSSION QUESTIONS

1. How can technology support an individual's use of self-management in setting their own goals? In managing their own learning? In assessing their own progress?
2. How can using self-management strategies become a positive behavior support in addressing problem behavior?
3. In what ways can support providers provide self-management strategies to an individual without their use being stigmatizing for the individual?
4. Should a person always fade out the use of a self-management system once the original problem is resolved and/or the goal has been met?

EMPLOYMENT, COMMUNITY, AND HOME ACTIVITY SUGGESTIONS

1. Observe an adult with a disability or one without a disability who is having trouble with behavior and/or tasks. Make a list of 2 or 3 self-management strategies that might help the person. Write this need in the form of a goal for this individual.
2. Interview an individual who is having trouble with a behavior or a task. With the person, determine a self-management strategy that involves:
   a. defining the behavior for creating a self-management goal,
   b. choosing a system for monitoring the behavior,
   c. designing a form for recording data and assessing progress of the behavior,
   d. creating a list of self-reinforcers, and
   e. designing a timeline plan for the support provider and individual to review if the self-management plan is working or needs adjustment.

REFERENCES

Baer, D. M. (1984). Does research on self-control need more control? *Analysis and Intervention in Developmental Disabilities, 4,* 211–218.

Browder, D. M., & Shapiro, E. S. (1985). Applications of self-management to individuals with severe handicaps: A review. *Journal of the Association for Persons with Severe Handicaps, 10,* 200–208.

Cooper, J. O., Heron, T. E. & Heward, W. L. (2007). *Self-management. In applied behavior analysis* (pp. 575–612). Upper Saddle River, NJ: Pearson.

Culham, R., & Wheeler, A. (2003). *40 Reproducible forms for the writing traits classroom.* New York: Scholastic Teaching Resources.

Forte, I., & Schurr, S. (1996). *Graphic organizers and planning outlines for authentic instruction and assessment.* Nashville, TN: Incentive Publications, Inc.

Koegel, L. K., Koegel, R. L., & Parks, D. R. (1992). *How to teach self-management to people with severe disabilities: A training manual.* Santa Barbara, CA: University of California, Santa Barbara.

Lever-Duffy, J., & McDonald, J. B. (2011). *Teaching and learning with technology.* Boston: Pearson.

Lerner, J., & Johns, B. (2009). *Learning disabilities and related mild disabilities; Characteristics, teaching strategies and new directions.* Boston: Houghton Mifflin Harcourt.

Mank, D. M., & Horner, R. H. (1987). Selfrecruited feedback: A costeffective procedure for maintaining behavior. *Research in Developmental Disabilities, 8,* 91–112.

Snell, M. E., & Brown, F. (2006). *Instruction of students with severe disabilities.* Upper Saddle River, NJ: Pearson.

Storey, K., & Miner, C. (2017). *Systematic instruction of functional skills for students and adults with disabilities* (2nd ed.). Springfield, IL: Charles C Thomas Publisher, Ltd.

Storey, K., & Montgomery, J. (2014). Teaching skills to students. In K. Storey & D. Hunter, (Eds.), *The road ahead: Transition to adult life for persons with disabilities* (3rd ed.) (pp. 85–106). Washington, DC: IOS Press.

Vargas, J. S. (2013). *Behavior analysis for effective teaching* (2nd ed.). New York: Routledge.

EMPIRICAL RESEARCH SUPPORTING THAT THE INTERVENTIONS PRESENTED IN CHAPTER ARE EVIDENCE BASED PRACTICES.

Christian, L., & Poling, A. (1997). Using self-management procedures to improve the productivity of adults with developmental disabilities in a competitive employment setting. *Journal of Applied Behavior Analysis, 30,* 169–172.

Garff, J. T., & Storey, K. (1998). The use of self-management strategies for increasing the hygiene of persons with disabilities in supported employment settings. *Education and Training in Mental Retardation and Developmental Disabilities, 33,* 179–188.

Hughes, C., & Agran, M. (1994). Teaching persons with severe disabilities to use self-instruction in community settings: An analysis of applications. *Journal of the Association for Persons with Severe Handicaps, 18,* 261–274.

Mank, D. M., & Horner, R. H. (1987). Self-recruited feedback: A cost-effective procedure for maintaining behavior. *Research in Developmental Disabilities, 8,* 91–112.

Montgomery, J., Storey, K., Post, M., & Lemly, J. (2011). The use of auditory prompting systems for increasing independent performance of students with autism in employment training. *International Journal of Rehabilitation Research, 34,* 330–335.

Salend, S. J., Ellis, L., & Reynold, C. (1989). Using self-instruction to teach vocational skills to individuals who are severely retarded. *Education and Training in Mental Retardation, 24,* 248–254.

Storey, K. (2007). Review of research on self-management interventions in supported employment settings for workers with disabilities. *Career Development for Exceptional Individuals, 30,* 27–34.

GENERAL REFERENCES REGARDING
TOPICS IN CHAPTER

Hughes, C., & Scott, S. V. (1997). Teaching self-management in employment settings. *Journal of Vocational Rehabilitation, 8,* 43–53.

Michel, W. (2014). *The marshmallow test: Mastering self-control.* New York: Little, Brown and Company.

Rolider, A., & Axelrod, S. (2000). *How to teach self-control through trigger analysis.* Austin, TX: Pro-Ed.

Sarafino, E. P. (2011). *Self-management: Using behavioral and cognitive principles to manage your life.* Hoboken, NJ: Wiley.

Vohs, K. D., & Baumeister, R. F. (2016). *Handbook of self-regulation: Research, theory, and applications* (3rd ed.). New York: Guilford Press.

Watson, D. L., & Tharp, R. G. (2014). *Self-directed behavior: Self-modification for personal adjustment* (10th ed.). Belmont, CA: Wadsworth/Thomson Learning.

Yeung, A., Feldman, G., & Fava, M. (2010). *Self-management of depression: A manual for mental health and primary care professionals.* Cambridge, NY: Cambridge University Press.

Table 7.1
Advantages for Individuals and Support Providers using Self-Management

Advantage for the individual	*Advantage for support providers*	*Steps for implementing a self-monitoring strategy*	*Example*
Monitor and adjust own behavior	Provides remedies for noncompliant or disruptive behaviors	Choose one behavior to focus on (e.g., completing assignments)	Individual will complete assignments
Use of strategy increases appropriate behavior	Strategy Transfers management of the individual's behavior to the individual	Consider the type of antecedent prompting that was needed to get the individual to complete the task and the reinforcement being used.	Individual uses a self-monitoring chart showing 5 minute interval boxes that can be checked off indicating whether they are on task at end of each interval.
Improves work and social skills	Increases positive attitude of supervisor and coworkers toward the person	Design a self-monitoring strategy to replace the needed support provider prompting.	A smart phone along with the self-monitoring chart can be used. The smart phone is set to alert the person every 5 minutes to evaluate whether he/she is working on the task or not. At the end of each 5 minute interval, the person assesses whether he/she is on task or off task and checks the yes or no box.
Individual perceives him/herself as capable and successful	Increases time spent on other needed instructional tasks.	Collaborate with the individual on the use of the strategy. Clarify the behavior being self-monitored and the advantage to the person in using self-monitoring.	Person needs to stay focused on working in order to complete assignments. Monitoring her/himself will eliminate the constant support provider prompting which can be stigmatizing and disruptive to other workers.

continued

Table 7.1—*Continued*

Advantage for the individual	Advantage for support providers	Steps for implementing a self-monitoring strategy	Example
Person takes ownership of monitoring and evaluating her/his own behavior	Reduces need for constant supervision of the person	Teach the person how to self-evaluate her/his on task or off task behavior when the timer goes off. Give examples of what the "on task" behavior looks like, along with examples of what "off task" behavior looks like.	When the 5 minute timer goes off, person checks the "on" box if she/he is working on the task. Person checks the "no" box if not on task.
Removes support provider reminders that may be embarrassing in front of peers	Relieves support provider from constant prompting	Practice using the self-monitoring form in a simulation.	During the first use, monitor the process to make sure timer is working and person is correctly using the form. Be available to help the person with the process if required. Otherwise, allow individual to manage the process on their own.
Allows person to correct any errors, building confidence	Allows support provider to prevent future errors from occurring	Meet with person to review first use and make any necessary adjustments	Discuss how well the strategy worked with the person. Answer any questions and give corrective feedback and reinforcement.
Builds feelings of self-mastery	Frees support provider time from supervision	Instruct the person on how to count and record the on task time achieved.	Record the time amount of "on task" behavior achieved. A total of 30 minutes (6 intervals for 5 minutes each) for on task behavior is possible.
Builds confidence at each step and promotes feelings of success	Initial investment of planning and time can result in person learning to work on task.	Decide on a success level for reinforcement. Initially, any level of success in the use of the strategy should be reinforced. The level of reinforcement can be faded as person masters the strategy. In time, the feeling of independence and success in completing tasks may become the only necessary reinforcement.	Reinforcement can be a choice of a preferred activity or item from a pre-set rewards list. Initially (perhaps for first week), reinforce every day any use of the strategy. Second week, each day reinforce for 10 minutes "on task." Third week, each day reinforce for 20 minutes "on task." Fourth week, each day reinforce for 30 minutes "on task."

Table 7.2
Self-Monitoring, Self-Evaluation, Self-Determined
Reinforcement Example for a Work Site

Worker daydreams at work and is not focusing on tasks to complete.	Identification of the Problem
Worker needs to be focused on job tasks.	Determining behavior to be changed
Worker uses a timer (smart phone in pocket that vibrates) to go off every 2 minutes to alert him to be focused on job tasks.	Determining a solution
When the timer goes off, the worker observes whether she is focused on job tasks or not. If she is on task, she uses a tally sheet listing the time intervals and puts a plus mark next to that interval if she was focused on job tasks, or a zero mark if she was not focused on job tasks when the timer went off.	Self-Monitoring of target behavior
The worker decides that to start she will need 15 plus marks for each hour. When achieved she will increase by one the number of plus marks needed for the next work day.	Self-Determined Criteria
At the end of the hour, the worker tallies up the plus marks and if there are 15 or more checks she then provides herself with a reinforcer from a menu of preferred items.	Self-Evaluation of performance
When the worker has achieved her self-determined criteria and chooses to reinforce herself by having a breath mint (included on her self-reinforcement menu).	Self-Reinforcement

Table 7.3
Self-Monitoring form for a Single Behavior Example for a Work Site

Time Intervals Filing in Office: 10:00 – 10:35 Date:	Desired Behavior: Focused on job tasks. When the timer goes off decide if you are focused on the job task. Put a + for focused on the job task Put a 0 for not being focused on the job task
10:02	+
10:4	+
10:6	0
10:8	+
10:10	0
10:12	+
Total +	4
Self-Determined criteria	4
Met Goal?	[YES] NO
Choose self-determined reinforce?	[YES] NO
Keep Goal:	YES [NO]
Decrease Goal	YES [NO]
Increase Goal	[YES TO: 5] NO

Table 7.4
Self-Monitoring form for a Chain of Behaviors Example

Steps to be ready for Work	Completed Step: Circle yes or no.
Put on uniform	YES NO
Make lunch	YES NO
Get money for bus	YES NO
Check weather to see if coat needed	YES NO

Table 7.5
Self-Evaluation form with feedback for a Chain of Behaviors:
Example for a Work Site

Follow Steps to be Ready for Work	Completed Step: Circle Yes or No.	Supervisor Feedback
Personal belongings put away	YES NO	YES NO COMMENT:
Tool box on top of work station	YES NO	YES NO COMMENT:
Activity Folder with list of tasks to complete reviewed	YES NO	YES NO COMMENT:
First work task started	YES NO	YES NO COMMENT:
First work task completed	YES NO	YES NO COMMENT:

Chapter 8

SOCIAL SKILLS INSTRUCTION

Key Point Questions

1. Why are social skills important?
2. Is having social competence the same as having good social skills?
3. How are social skills best assessed?
4. What are instructional strategies for teaching social skills?

WINDOW TO THE WORLD CASE STUDY ONE

Dania works in the records office at a hospital. Her work is good and she is very popular with her coworkers. The only concern that her supervisor, Ms. Stiffler, has for Dania is that she does not take direction well from Ms. Stiffler. Just yesterday, Ms. Stiffler asked her to rework some forms for the department and Dania angrily replied she didn't want to do any work on it, that the form was fine as it was, and then walked away. This was not the first time an incident like this had happened where she was sassy and defiant at the supervisor's request. Adding to this concern about Dania's behavior, Ms. Stiffler had noticed that other workers in the office would snicker which seemed to egg Dania on. She wasn't sure of the cause for this behavior (perhaps Dania doesn't like her), but regardless of the cause, Ms. Stiffer decided that it was important to take immediate action and that the behavior should not be ignored. Therefore, Ms. Stiffler called the supported employment agency supporting Dania and reported what was happening. She informed Ms. Stiffler that if Dania didn't change her behavior, then she would be put on notice, and if there was still no improvement with her behavior she would be terminated from her position.

The supported employment director, Ms. Kasper, decided to handle the situation personally. She located a lesson from the Skillstreaming program on Responding to Difficult Requests. She knew she could appropriately include a role play for "responding to requests from the boss" into the lesson scenario for her agency's upcoming worker's Job Club that Dania had joined. The Skillstreaming lesson was included in the next job club meeting with all the group members enjoying the active role plays. During the Job Club meeting several people provided examples of difficult requests. Ms. Kasper then modeled the steps to use for responding. These steps were, (1) Listen to what the other person is requesting, (2) Restate back what you understand the person is asking, (3) If you disagree, ask the other person to explain anything you don't understand, (4) If you still disagree, politely provide the person with the information and reason you feel or think differently, and (5) Stop and think about the person's response and the best way to handle the situation. Ms. Kasper guided the members through the role plays and provided immediate corrections if steps were missed. Ms. Kasper made sure that Dania participated in several of the role-playing situations and that she displayed the appropriate responses and was reinforced (public praise) for her appropriate behavior. Ms. Kasper then phoned Ms. Stiffler to fill her in on what she had done, and that she would follow up with Ms. Stiffer weekly over the next several months making sure Dania was using the skills at work (generalization across settings). Fortunately, Dania was able to use the social skills appropriately at her work and the problem behavior no longer occurred.

WINDOW TO THE WORLD CASE STUDY TWO

Elise was working as an Independent Living provider for Ailene who was diagnosed as having Autism Spectrum Disorders. When they were out together running an errand to the bank to cash a check, Elise noticed that Ailene was engaging in several inappropriate behaviors at the bank. First, she talked way too loudly for the quiet environment. Second, she leaned in and put her head too close to the cashier. Thirdly, she asked the cashier inappropriate questions, such as, "How much do they pay you to handle all of this money?"

Elise decided to do some role playing with Ailene in Ailene's apartment to teach her appropriate interaction skills when at the bank. First, Elise modeled talking in a quiet voice, standing straight when at the counter, and asking appropriate questions to the cashier (such as, "how are you today?). They then took turns role playing the cashier or the customer. During the role plays Elise would say that she was going to make a mistake and asked Ailene to catch the mistake. She also asked Ailene to say what Elise was doing correctly (this is known as presenting positive and negative examples of the behavior). Elise made sure to praise Ailene for noticing mistakes, as well as when Ailene did well. Once Ailene was consistently displaying the appropriate behaviors, they went down to the bank to cash another check. Right before going in Elise reminded Ailene of the appropriate behaviors. Ailene went in and did very well. Elise praised Ailene for doing so well. She also made sure to go with Ailene to the bank a few more times to make sure Ailene was maintaining the appropriate skills.

KEY POINT QUESTION #1:
WHY ARE SOCIAL SKILLS IMPORTANT?

Just about every situation that an individual experiences with other people will require a social appropriate interaction. Acceptable social skills are necessary for success in all domains of living (at home, in community settings, on a date, and at work). The amount and variety of social skill needed is complex and learning successful social skills is a lifelong process. Through social interactions children learn social skills and these skills continue to develop and be refined as they grow. For example, a child quickly learns a set of behaviors (smiling, laughing, crying, babbling) she can use to gain approval and reinforcement from other people (usually mom and dad, at first, and then with siblings and familiar others). As a child grows older, her behaviors change to adapt to the expectations of significant people around her (such as parents' expectations for developmental age appropriate behaviors; a 5-year-old should act like a 5-year-old and not a 2-year-old). The child's social interactions are shaped by the responses of those around her. If her mom smiles back and gives her a tickle, she will continue to use that "smile" to obtain mom's positive reinforcement. These early simple interactional behaviors are continuously built upon until a complex system or repertoire of social behaviors is developed.

However, social skills don't stop developing at a certain age. How we interact with others is constantly being influenced by other people's reactions to us. If a reaction to a particular behavior (someone thanks us for helping them) is reinforced, we will be more likely to continue to use that behavior (help them or others). If a reaction is not favorable (we are yelled at by the boss for talking with coworkers rather than working), this punishment may cause us to be less likely to use that behavior again with that person. Notice the words "that person." Success with specific social behaviors varies across people, places, time and social situations. These varying factors add complexity for understanding and choosing the appropriate behavior to use in a specific circumstance.

Schumaker and Hazel (1984) define a social skill as "any cognitive function or overt behavior in which an individual engages while interacting with another person or persons. Cognitive functions include such capacities as empathizing with or understanding another person's feelings, discriminating and evaluating consequences for social behavior. Overt behaviors include the nonverbal (e.g., head nods, eye contact, facial expression) and verbal (e.g., what the person says) components of social performance." For example, Jasmine is criticized by her boss for not greeting a customer appropriately. Jasmine acknowledged that she greeted the customer incorrectly, that she realizes what she did wrong, and that it won't happen again in the future. This interaction involved decision-making capacity; processing and evaluating what is said and deciding how to respond. It also involved Jasmine's nonverbal behavior in standing near her boss as she spoke to her, having a serious expression on her face, using a serious tone of voice when responding, and making eye contact.

KEY POINT QUESTION #2:
IS HAVING GOOD SOCIAL COMPETENCE
THE SAME AS HAVING GOOD SOCIAL SKILLS?

Social Competence

Generally, a person is considered to have social competence if their interactions with others result in a positive effect, in other words how good the individual is at interacting with others (Foster & Ritchey, 1979). A socially competent person is judged by others (peers, supervisors, friends, coworkers, etc.) to be skilled at using specific social behaviors in specific social interactions. There is not one definition for "social competence" yet most definitions span from general attributes such as empathy and cooperativeness of the person to describing specific desired social behaviors such as taking turns, making polite remarks, or doing a kind act for someone (Sugai & Lewis, 1996).

Social Skills

As we can see from the definition above, social skills can be considered to be a component of social competence. Most of the professional literature agrees that social skills are learned, either directly (the supervisor instructing new workers on how they should answer the phone) or indirectly (responding appropriately to the check-out clerk at the grocery store after observing how previous customers in the line interacted with her). Though positive social skills are often learned without instruction, it may be necessary for an individual to learn specific social behaviors with instruction. This social skill instruction should be direct, systematically planned, and teach specific social behavior that results in the person's behavior being considered a positive interaction (with peers, supervisor, community members, etc.), and judged a positive social skill by peers, supervisor, community members, and so on (Gresham, 1986). Social skills include both verbal behaviors and nonverbal behaviors (e.g., physical mannerisms such as how to stand or to make eye contact). If an employee says, "Thanks a lot" (verbal behavior) to a coworker but has a sneer on their face (nonverbal behavior), the nonverbal behavior has changed the meaning of the exchange from a message of gratitude to a message of sarcasm. It's important, then, that instructors include nonverbal behaviors when teaching social skills.

Poorly developed social skills, lack of social skills, or an individual not using social skills they have learned, can present a barrier to success and social inclusion in work, community, or home settings. Research has shown that individuals with poor social relationships are more likely to develop behavior problems that can lead to employment failure, involvement with the criminal justice system, need for mental health services, and difficulties in relationships. Since the opinion and actions of others can have significant influence on the behavior of an individual, it is important for the support provider, especially when planning for the assessment and instruction of social skills, to keep in mind that individuals, besides the target person, will be an important component of the assessment and intervention. For this reason, using assessment strategies that rate the opinions of others on how important it is to learn a particular social skill, or to what degree the target person already has mastered the social skill, is necessary for determining what to teach. Also, focusing on teaching skills that help build friendships and creating opportunities to use these skills with others is a critical component in social skill teaching. For instance, teaching an individual how to carry on a conversation is an important skill with peers or others while conducting a social skill lesson which provides the individual with a model format for asking and answering questions in a conversation. After the instruction, the individual could use a check list to keep track of when they use their new conversation skills in other settings, such as in the cafeteria at work, on the bus, while shopping, and so on.

KEY POINT QUESTION #3:
HOW ARE SOCIAL SKILLS BEST ASSESSED?

There are many different ways to assess what social skills need to be taught (such as observing the person, asking the person, asking peers, supervisor ratings, etc.). Sometimes a variety of assessment tools will be used in order for the support provider to exactly pinpoint the skill deficit. When assessing social skills, it is important to take into consideration what is typical behavior for the person's age, gender, peer group, and any other cultural or societal behavioral norm. Decision for what instructional methods to use should always be directly related to the results of the assessment. Social skill assessment needs to be thorough and provide support providers with the following information:

1. A complete understanding of the social skill problem (skill deficit), including what social skill the person needs to learn (skill building) or if the skill is already known but not being used (performance deficit) what practice opportunities and reinforcement for using the skill can be provided.
2. How and where the skill should be taught.

3. The modality for how to teach it (using a lesson developed by the support provider, a social skills curriculum, incidental teaching).
4. How to evaluate if the new social skill has been learned (a system for measuring skill acquisition and use as outlined in Chapter 2).
5. A plan to monitor the ongoing performance (maintenance) of the social skill.
6. Is the social skill occurring in the criteria environment (the work site) or situation (greeting others) as well as in generalization of person's interactions with others? Knowing who, what, where, when and why an individual is performing a desired behavior can provide information for developing effective interventions (Sugai & Lewis, 1996) (see Table 8.1).

DIRECT OBSERVATION

It is important to know the person's strength in the social skill area, what social skills the individual already successfully performs, and to determine which social skills the person needs to develop. This can be done through direct observation methods (see descriptions in Chapter 2) or through a systematic functional assessment process involving direct observation (see description in Chapter 3) where information concerning the social skill is collected and measured. The purpose of the measurement is to identify positive social skills that are lacking (greeting coworkers appropriately), understand the specific social behavior presenting problems (using wrong words in greetings), identify replacement social skills (specific words to use in greetings), help with planning instruction for teaching the new social skill (such as role playing with the job coach), monitoring its use (frequency counts of appropriate greetings) and evaluating the effectiveness of the instruction (are appropriate greetings increasing?). Without this systematic approach to evaluate and address the target social skills, the intervention may not actually teach the individual the desired skill and result in an ineffective and inefficient solution (Horner, O'Neill, & Flannery, 1993), besides being a waste of valuable time.

Social skill assessment can be used for both an individual as well as a group of people to identify social skill deficits. There are many possible reasons an individual may be having difficulty in any particular social context. For example, it is possible that the person has not learned a specific skill (informal rules for greeting coworkers in the break room) or does not know in what situations to use it. For example, a worker greets the boss in the break room the same way that they would greet coworkers, not realizing that the informal rules for greeting the boss are different than for greeting coworkers. It could also be that the person knows a skill but is inconsistent in using it (the person knows how to asks coworkers if she can sit with them but instead sometimes quickly sits down at the table without asking), or due to insufficient practice of the skill and lack of strong reinforcement for using it, cannot use it effectively (the worker has self-rehearsed how to greet coworkers in the break room but in the actual situation only a small part of the rehearsed response is said, making the response ineffective). Also, there could be another behavior in the person's repertoire of behaviors that interferes with the person being able to successfully use the skill (the worker knows to walk away from the table in the break room if coworkers respond negatively to her asking to sit with them, but heightened anxiousness may prevent her from walking away which results in her just standing there feeling flustered).

Walker and Stieber (1998) recommend the following components as part of an assessment for an individual who has social skills deficits: (1) ratings of social skills from support providers or others, (2) ratings by peers to ascertain social status and possible rejection, (3) direct observation of social exchanges in different settings, and (4) review of records for regarding social skill deficits.

Interviews

An interview can be a written or oral assessment providing information that cannot be obtained through other measurement systems. Interviews can be conducted with the individual, support providers, coworkers, parents, or others and provide information through anecdotes and descriptions of specific situations as to why a person behaves in a certain way. These data can provide information on the context in which the behaviors are occurring, help define the behavior of concern, and choose appropriate social skill interventions. Interviews are considered an indirect measure as they are conducted after the behavior has occurred and most likely in a different setting (as opposed to an observation where one is directly assessing the behavior as it happens and where it is happening) and the influences that may increase the occurrence of the behavior.

Elksnin and Elksnin (2006) provide the following interview guidelines:

1. Establish the goal for the interview. Is the goal to obtain information, cooperation, or establish rapport?
2. Based on the goal, develop a list of potential questions to ask.
3. Identify ways the interviewee's perspective may differ from yours.
4. Identify sensitive topics to avoid during the interview.

Role Play

Role play is another way to identify if a person can perform a specific social skill. In role play assessment, the individual practices a specific social skill required in a given scenario. For example, a person would participate in a role play where they have to decide whether or not to express a concern about a work rule to their supervisor. The role play would allow the individual to demonstrate if they can appropriately and competently express their concern to their supervisors to comply with the work rule.

Scenarios can be practiced at home, in the community, or other settings such as the break room at work or at a job club (individual or small group instruction) and directed and controlled by the support provider. The support provider can create role play situations that require the use of the targeted social skill. Different settings (home, community, employment) where the person may need to use the skill should be included in the scenarios. McGinnis and Goldstein (1997) have created a commercial social skills program, Skillstreaming, which incorporates the role play strategy. Though Skillstreaming is designed for school-aged students it can easily be adapted for adults with disabilities. With any social skills assessment, preference should be given to assessing individual's ability to perform social skills in the criterion setting (the work site, in the community, or at home) where any competing contingencies might be occurring.

KEY POINT QUESTION #4: WHAT ARE INSTRUCTIONAL STRATEGIES FOR TEACHING SOCIAL SKILLS?

Preparing a plan to teach social skills should involve having instructional goals and objectives, a planned direct instructional sequence, an opportunity for the individual to demonstrate the behavior and a systematic assessment process to determine whether the skill has been learned or if the person needs more instruction (Sugai & Lewis, 1996). There should also be planned extension (generalization) activities for the individual to practice the new social skill in other settings (at home, at work, in the community), with other people, across times, and across behaviors with positive reinforcement provided. The use of the new social skill should be periodically monitored over weeks and months to see if the individual is still using the social skills successfully. Positive reinforcement should always be provided at these monitoring times to strengthen the skill use.

Published Social Skill Curricula

Examining the numerous published social skills curricula can serve as a starting point to teach commonly desired social behaviors. A list of available programs to consider is provided in Table 8.2. Although many of the skills in these programs are generic or focused on school-aged students, more intensive instruction for adults with disabilities who are having social skill deficits can be planned using the assessment tools provided in the programs. For selecting the most appropriate program, it is important to review the program content targeted and what methods are used to teach the social skills. Table 8.3 provides guidelines for criteria to keep in mind when selecting a commercial program.

Support Provider Designed Social Skill Instruction

Support Providers can design their own social skills instruction lessons once the social skills to be taught are identified. A direct instructional approach that incorporates role modeling, role playing and performance feedback can be planned (Peterson, Young, Salzburg, West, & Hill, 2006). A variety of strategies for teaching social skills should be used and every effort should be made to teach in natural environments using authentic contexts and targeting skills that the person values (Elksnin & Elksnin, 2006).

Generalization

Some individuals may learn to use a social skill in one setting, time, or with a person or group but will not use it in another similar situation. Helping a person to generalize a new learned social skill can be done using the following guidelines (Brown & Odom, 1994; Smith & Giles, 2003):

1. Use language similar to the language the person will encounter in the natural setting the social skill will be used.
2. Use a variety of role models so that the individual doesn't associate the social skill with only that one role model and thus will be more likely to generalize the skill across people.
3. Include all the behaviors in the behavior chain when teaching a social skill. For instance, when teaching "greeting" skills, besides teaching the typical response phrases for greeting, also teach the eye contact, voice inflection, and acceptable standing distance from person. More complex skills can be added to this chain (deciding what to say next, how to ask a question to engage the other person and how to end the conversation, etc.) as the individual masters the foundational skills.
4. Avoid teaching social skills only at a specific time. Use the teachable moments throughout the day by taking the time for incidental teaching by providing learning opportunities to use a social skill in the natural environment. People are more motivated to use the skill in real life situations. For example, if a worker is getting angry with coworkers and calling them names because they are not completing their assigned tasks, and also making it difficult for the worker to complete her tasks, this could be a good time for the job coach to address the situation and teach the skills for calming down, thinking aloud about what happened, and considering what other options she has for handling the problem, besides being angry with the coworkers and calling them names.
5. Just as any behavior needs to be generalized across people, times, behaviors, and settings, so too, learning and using social skills should be incorporated in these situations as much as possible.

Opportunities for social skill instruction can be embedded in these situations which will help to promote generalization of the social skill.

6. Once the person is determined to have mastered the targeted social skills, maintenance of the skill can be reinforced intermittently with fun activities, conversation with a friend, and such (Elksnin & Elksnin, 2006).

Incidental Teaching

Incidental teaching uses situations as they occur throughout the day and the natural interactions between the person and others to form the basis for practicing social skills (Elksnin & Elksnin, 2000). Providing explicit instruction at the moment when a social skill error is occurring is an effective way to teach an individual to read the social cues and respond appropriately. Support providers can point out non-verbal cues (gestures, facial expressions, voice tone, standing distance, etc.), characteristics of the environment, and any other factors present that indicate the need for an adjusted response. For instance, if a person is shopping in a grocery store and yells over to the check-out clerk who is assisting others, "Hey, where do I find sparkling cider?," this would be an instance for incidental teaching where the support provider could quickly and quietly prompt the person to observe that the clerk is helping someone else at the moment and that the person is in a situation where a more appropriate response would be to ask the clerk when they are not helping other customers or waiting their turn to be helped. The support provider could be in and out of that coaching moment in seconds and has not missed the opportunity for correcting a social error and guiding the person to the expected social behavior.

Modeling

A social modeling strategy found effective for teaching social skills (Cohen, 2011) is where the support providers, or peers, demonstrate how to perform the social skill, provide an opportunity for the person to practice it, and provide feedback and reinforcement. Cartledge, Gardner, and Ford (2009) found that individuals from culturally diverse backgrounds have had good success in social skill acquisition when peer-mediated instruction was used and they maintained these skills through the use of self-monitoring with recording their behavior on self-recording sheets (See Chapter 7 on self-management strategies). Peer modeling can be done with one-on-one individual instruction or in small groups. Only individuals who have mastered the skill should be chosen to be role models. Support providers should monitor peer sessions and assess if the individual is successfully learning the skills. Once the support provider has determined, through this assessment, that the individual has learned the skill, then role plays could be used to challenge the person's ability to adapt their new learned skill to unpredictable situations. In this way, a support provider can provide instruction on how to cope in difficult situations. Storey and Miner (2017) provide a format to for using this "coping" modeling:

1. Stop the role play after mistakes are made and correct the error.
2. Point out what the error was and why it was made.
3. Provide instruction on how to avoid the error.
4. Demonstrate the strategy used to avoid the mistake.

Multimedia and Video Modeling

Multimedia (virtual environments, simulations, videos, pictures, and other multimedia) can be very effective strategies for teaching social skills. Video peer modeling (VPM) and video self-modeling (VSM) are visual instruction ways to teach social skills. VSM involves the target person observing her or himself on video performing a skill to be learned, while VPM involves the target person observing a friend or other person on video performing the skill to learn. There is increasing research in this area indicating that individuals efficiently learn target social skills using video modeling (Gül & Vuran, 2010; Kennedy, Landor, & Todd, 2012; Sigafoos, O'Reilly, & de la Cruz, 2007). Video modeling eliminates support provider prompting, allowing the individual to completely focus on the model being presented. Convenience is another factor for using this tool. Support providers are able to manipulate the camera, zooming in and out, editing as necessary and the results can be viewed repeatedly by the individual. Another advantage is that it is easy to see the antecedent-behavior-consequence relationship in a video (as opposed to hearing a story about someone performing a behavior correctly). These situations can be manipulated so that the person can see both appropriate and inappropriate demonstrations of the social skill so that they can make the appropriate discrimination. For example, an individual could be videoed in a practice interview for a job. An interview error of the person frowning at times during the interview can be seen in the first recording. A second recording can show the person correcting the error and not frowning during the interview and smiling appropriately. The individual can then compare the correct behavior of smiling to the incorrect behavior of frowning in an interview. Facial expression, body language, voice tone, and emotions can all be seen and monitored using VSM (Prater, 2007).

Cognitive Modeling

Many problem-solving strategies are part of social skill curriculums wherein the particulars of a social interaction are discussed between the individual and the support provider. Core elements of these strategies involve the following components: a detailed account of what the person did, what happened, whether the outcome was positive or negative, and what the person will do in the same situation in the future. Support providers should assist the individual in identifying the specific behaviors that result in positive solutions, in addition to identifying the behaviors that caused an undesirable outcome. For example, if two roommates get into a verbal fight over who should take out the garbage, a support provider could help the two analyze the situation as to where the disagreement started. In this case, the support provider would guide the roommates through thinking about each step of the social exchange and locate the social error that caused the verbal fight and decide what a positive response would be. In this case, the roommates would identify the problem through asking, "Whose turn is it to take out the garbage, or who took out the garbage last time?" instead of "arguing." Analyzing, rather than arguing, should be used in the future to stay good roommates.

Social Stories

Social stories provide an individual with a narrative or script for appropriate behavior in a variety of situations and assists the person in understanding and rehearsing the steps needed to perform a target social skill. Support providers can design their own social stories or use published social stories. Many support providers create their own comic strip social stories or make video clips of someone acting out the skill. The following is an example of a support provider made social story for addressing how to behave when answering a question from a boss at work:

Answering the boss's question:

1. The boss asks me a question.
2. I know the answer.
3. I want to say the answer.
4. I look at the boss and make eye contact.
5. I say the answer.

This strategy allows for perspective taking and encourages the person to consider a range of responses to a specific situation. More information on social stories can be found at http://www.thegraycenter.org /social-stories.

Behavioral Rehearsal and Role Play

Behavioral rehearsal, embedded in social skill curriculums, such as the Skillstreaming curriculum, uses role play to provide opportunities for an individual to rehearse the needed social skill in social situation scenarios and receive corrective feedback and positive reinforcement. To avoid having the person practice an incorrect skill, prompting ahead of the rehearsal on what the appropriate behavior is (precorrection) minimizes the chance of the individual practicing social skill errors. Behavioral rehearsal/role play can be effective in small group instruction where individuals who are not role playing also have a responsibility in the role play process. These roles could include: a director role where the nonparticipant narrates what is going on or what the actors are doing, a note taker role that records a description of how the actor used the target skill, and a conflict observer role that records under what conditions the actor had to use the target skill. Concurrently, while role playing the scene, the actor can narrate what is happening and what they are thinking. This gives the support provider an opportunity to use precorrection and have the individual use the social skill successfully. These roles actively engage all the participants in the learning process and provide assessment information for the support provider in determining if the individuals understand the social skill and are able to use it in the appropriate context. At end of the role play, the support provider recaps what happened and describes the correct behaviors demonstrated. For example, for a role play where a person demonstrates how to handle being disturbed while working, the support provider would comment, "Vim looked directly at his coworker who was talking to him and said, "I can't talk to you now. I need to concentrate on what I am working on and not talk." It is important that the support provider avoid making comments about unrelated behaviors added into the role play (the person used wrong names, dropped something, laughed or fell out of character) and keeping participants focused on the target social skill they are learning (Sugai & Lewis, 1996).

BEST PRACTICE RECOMMENDATIONS

1. Teach social skills both formally and informally throughout the day, focusing on targeting immediate situations when a social skill error is made.
2. Teach social skills in the same systematic way you would teach any functional skill.
3. Use a variety of methods to teach social skills but give preference to strategies that use direct teaching and active learning strategies (role play, behavioral rehearsal, modeling) being sure to provide strong and ongoing reinforcement for correct social skill performance. For guidelines on choosing a published curriculum for teaching social skills see Table 8.3.

DISCUSSION QUESTIONS

1. How do you best decide which social skills to teach?
2. How do you decide if you should teach a social skill in a small group format or an individual one-on-one format?
3. Won't individuals gain social skills as they interact with others and learn appropriate skills? Is it really necessary to teach social skills?

WORK, COMMUNITY, AND HOME-BASED
ACTIVITY SUGGESTIONS

1. Observe people interacting in a specific environment such as a work site or community setting. Make a list of social skills that you see people using successfully, and social skills that are missing, and social skills that are not being used successfully. Use this list as a basis for selecting social skill lessons.

2. From the list above, choose two different strategies for teaching social skills. Compare the outcomes for each strategy to see which was more effective with individuals that you support.

REFERENCES CITED IN CHAPTER

Brown, W. H., & Odom, S. L. (1994). Strategies and tactics for promoting generalization and maintenance of young children's social behavior. *Research in Developmental Disabilities, 15,* 99–118.

Carter, J., & Sugai, G. (1988). Teaching social skills. *Teaching Exceptional Children, 20,* 68–71.

Carter, J., & Sugai, G. (1989). Social skills curriculum analysis. *Teaching Exceptional Children, 21,* 36–39.

Cartledge, G., Gardner, R., & Ford, D. Y. (2009). *Diverse learners with exceptionalities: Culturally responsive teaching in the inclusive classroom.* Upper Saddle River, NJ: Pearson.

Cohen, M. R. (2011). *Social literacy: A social skills seminar for young adults with ASDs, NLDs, and social anxiety.* Baltimore, MD: Paul Brookes.

Elksnin, L. K., & Elksnin, N. (2000). Teaching parents to teach their children to be prosocial. *Intervention in School and Clinic, 36,* 27–34.

Elksnin, L. K., & Elksnin, N. (2006). *Teaching social-emotional skills at school and home.* Denver, CO: Love Publishing Co.

Foster, S. L., & Ritchey, W. L. (1979). Issues in the assessment of social competence in children. *Journal of Applied Behavior Analysis, 12,* 625–638.

Gresham, F. M. (1986). Conceptual and definitional issues in the assessment of children's social skills: Implications for classification and training. *Journal of Clinical Child Psychology, 15,* 3–15.

Gül, S., & Vuran, S. (2010). An analysis of studies conducted video modeling in teaching social skills. *Educational Sciences: Theory and Practice, 10,* 249–274.

Horner, R. H., O'Neill, R. E., & Flannery, K. B. (1993). Building effective behavior support plans from functional assessment information. In M. E. Snell (Ed.), *Systematic instruction of persons with severe handicaps* (4th ed.) (pp. 184–214). Columbus, OH: Merrill.

Kennedy, H., Landor, M., & Todd, L. (2012). *Video interaction guidance: A relationship-based intervention to promote attunement, empathy and wellbeing.* Philadelphia, PA: Jessica Kingsley Publishers.

McGinnis, E., & Goldstein, A. P. (1997). *Skillstreaming the elementary school child: New strategies and perspectives for teaching prosocial skills* (2nd ed.). Research Press: Champaign, IL.

Peterson, L. D., Young, K. R., Salzberg, C. L., West, R. P., & Hill, M. (2006). Using self-management procedures to improve classroom social skills in multiple general education settings. *Education and Treatment of Children, 29,* 1–21.

Prater, M. A. (2007). *Teaching strategies for students with mild to moderate disabilities* (pp. 452–453). Upper Saddle River, NJ: Pearson.

Rogers, M. F., & Miles, B. S. (2001). Using social stories and comic strip conversations to interpret social situations for an adolescent with Asperger syndrome. *Intervention in School and Clinic, 36,* 310–313.

Schumaker, J. B., & Hazel, J. S. (1984). Social skills assessment and training for the learning disabled: Who's on first and what's on second? Part 1. *Journal of Learning Disabilities, 17,* 422–431.

Sigafoos, J., O'Reilly, M., & de la Cruz, B. (2007). *How to use video modeling and video prompting.* Austin, TX: Pro-Ed.

Smith, S. W., & Giles, D. L. (2003). Using key instructional elements to systematically promote social skill generalization for students with challenging behavior. *Intervention in School and Clinic, 39,* 30–37.

Storey, K., & Miner, C. (2017). *Systematic instruction of functional skills for students and adults with disabilities* (2nd ed.). Springfield, IL: Charles C Thomas.

Sugai, G., & Lewis, T. J. (1996). Preferred and promising practices for social skills instruction. *Focus On Exceptional Children, 29*(4), 11–27.

Walker, H. M., & McConnell, S. R. (1995). *The Walker-McConnell scale of social competence and school adjustment: Elementary version.* San Diego, CA: Singular.

Walker, H., & Stieber, S. (1998). Teacher ratings of social skills as longitudinal predictors of long term arrest status in a sample of at risk males. *Behavioral Disorders, 23,* 220–230.

EMPIRICAL RESEARCH SUPPORTING THAT THE INTERVENTIONS PRESENTED IN CHAPTER ARE EVIDENCE BASED PRACTICES

Baker-Ericzén, M. J., Fitch, M. A., Kinnear, M., Jenkins, M. M., Twamley, E. W., Smith, L., Montano, G., Feder, J., Crooke, P. J.; Winner, M. G., & Leon, J. (2018). Development of the supported employment, comprehensive cognitive enhancement, and social skills program for adults on the autism spectrum: Results of initial study. *Autism: The International Journal of Research and Practice, 22,* 6–19.

Botsford, K. D. (2013). Social skills for youths with visual impairments: A meta-analysis. *Journal of Visual Impairment and Blindness, 107,* 497–508.

Cavenaugh, B., & Giesen, J. M. (2012). A systematic review of transition interventions affecting the employability of youths with visual impairments. *Journal of Visual Impairment and Blindness, 106,* 400–413.

Chadsey, J. G., Linneman, D. Rusch, F. R., & Cimera, R. E. (1997). The impact of social integration interventions and job coaches in work settings. *Education and Training in Mental Retardation and Developmental Disabilities, 32,* 281–292.

Fisher, M., & Morin, L. (2017). Addressing social skills deficits in adults with Williams syndrome. *Research in Developmental Disabilities, 71,* 77–87.

Gül, S., & Vuran, S. (2010). An analysis of studies conducted video modeling in teaching social skills. *Educational Sciences: Theory and Practice, 10,* 249–274.

Murray, C., & Doren, B. (2013). The effects of working at gaining employment skills on the social and vocational skills of adolescents with disabilities: A school-based intervention. *Rehabilitation Counseling Bulletin, 56,* 96–107.

Park, H. S., Simon, M., Tappe, P., Wozniak, T., Johnson B., & Gaylord-Ross, R. (1991). Effects of a coworker advocacy program and social skills training on the social interaction of employees with mild disabilities. *Journal of Vocational Rehabilitation, 1,* 73–90.

Storey, K. (2002). Strategies for increasing interactions in supported employment settings: An updated review. *Journal of Vocational Rehabilitation, 17,* 231–237.

Storey, K., & Garff, J. T. (1997). The cumulative effect of natural support strategies and social skills instruction on the integration of a worker in supported employment. *Journal of Vocational Rehabilitation, 9,* 143–152.

Storey, K., Lengyel, L., & Pruszynski, B. (1997). Assessing the effectiveness and measuring the complexity of two conversational instructional procedures in supported employment contexts. *Journal of Vocational Rehabilitation, 8,* 21–33.

Storey, K., & Provost, O. (1996). The effect of communication skills instruction on the integration of workers with severe disabilities in supported employment settings. *Education and Training in Mental Retardation and Developmental Disabilities, 31,* 123–141.

Storey, K., Ezell, H., & Lengyel, L. (1995). Communication strategies for increasing the integration of persons in supported employment: A review. *American Journal of Speech-Language Pathology, 4,* 45–54.

Walsh, E., Holloway, J., & Lydon, H. (2018). An evaluation of a social skills intervention for adults with autism spectrum disorder and intellectual disabilities preparing for employment in Ireland: A pilot study. *Journal of Autism and Developmental Disorders, 48,* 1727–1741.

GENERAL REFERENCES REGARDING TOPICS IN CHAPTER

Barber, K. M. (2011). *The social and life skills menu: A skill building workbook for adolescents with Autism Spectrum Disorders.* Philadelphia, PA: Jessica Kingsley Publishers.

Cohen, M. R. (2011). *Social literacy: A social skills seminar for young adults with ASDs, NLDs, and social anxiety.* Baltimore, MD: Paul Brookes.

Gerhardt, P. F., & Crimmins, D. (2013). *Social skills and adaptive behavior in learners with autism spectrum disorders: Current status and future directions.* Baltimore, MD: Brookes.

Laugeson, E. A., & Frankel, F. (2010). *Social skills for teenagers with developmental and autism spectrum disorders: The PEERS treatment manual.* New York: Routledge.

Malouff, J. M., & Schutte, N. S. (2014). *Activities to enhance social, emotional, and problem-solving skills: Ninety activities that teach children, adolescents, and adults skills crucial to success in life* (3rd Ed.). Springfield, IL: Charles Thomas, Ltd.

Nangle, D. W. (2010). *Practitioner's guide to empirically based measures of social skills.* New York: Springer.

Newton, J. S., Olson, D., Horner, R. H., & Ard, W. R. (1996). Social skills and the stability of social relationships between individuals with intellectual disabilities and other community members. *Research in Developmental Disabilities, 17,* 15–26.

Prelock, P. A., & McCauley, R. J. (2012). *Treatment of autism spectrum disorders: Evidence-based intervention strategies for communication and social interactions.* Baltimore, MD: Paul Brookes.

Taubman, M., Leaf, R., & McEachin, J. (2011). *Crafting connections: Contemporary applied behavior analysis for enriching the social lives of persons with autism spectrum disorder.* New York, NY: DRL Books, Inc.

Timms, L. A. (2011). *60 social situations and discussion starters to help teens on the Autism Spectrum deal with friendships, feelings, conflict and more: Seeing the big picture.* Philadelphia, PA: Jessica Kingsley Publishers.

Volz, J. R., Snyder, T., & Sterba, M. (2009). *Teaching social skills to youth with mental health disorders: Incorporating social skills into treatment planning for 109 disorders.* Boys Town, NB: Boys Town Press.

Table 8.1
Environmental Social Skill Observation Form

WORK SETTING	SOCIAL SKILL	SOCIAL SKILL USED SUCCESSFUL	SOCIAL SKILL ATTEMPTED BUT UNSUCCESSFUL	SOCIAL SKILL NEEDED (Did Not Attempt)
During work	Working cooperatively on task			
	Joking with coworkers			
	Saying "Thank you"			
Entrance	Taking turns going through doorway			
Cafeteria	Making room at table			

Adapted from Elksin and Elksin (2006).

Table 8.2
Selection of Published Programs for Social Skills Instruction

The ACCEPTS Program (2012) (Walker et al), Middle School to High School ages
http://www.proedinc.com/customer/productView.aspx?ID=625&SearchWord=ACCEPTS%
20PROGRAM

CONNECTING WITH OTHERS curriculum, (Richardson et al, 2009) for K–12 grades.
https://www.researchpress.com/books/474/connecting-others

The EQUIP Program (2008) (Gibbs, Potter & Goldstein), adolescents, 12–17 yrs.,
http://www.researchpress.com/scripts/product.asp?item=4848#5134

The PREPARE program (Goldstein,1988) Middle School and High School Students
http://www.researchpress.com/product/item/5063/

PREPARE: A Pro-social curriculum for aggressive youth (Goldstein, 2010),
https://www.researchpress.com/books/818/prepare-curriculum

Skillstreaming Program (Goldstein & McGinnis, 1997) Pre K through12th grade,
http://www.skillstreaming.com/

Teaching Social Competence to Youth and Adults with Developmental Disabilities,
(D.A. Jackson, N.F. Jackson & Bennett, 1998) Adolescents and Adults, http://www.proed-
inc.com/customer/productView.aspx?ID=1428

Super Skills (Coucouvanis & Myles, 2005) curriculum targets skills often used for students
with autism spectrum disorders
https://autismawarenesscentre.com/shop/social-skills/super-skills-a-social-skills-group
-program-for-children-with-asperger-syndrome-high-functioning-autism-and-related
-challenges/

Table 8.3
Guidelines for Choosing a Published Curriculum

1. What instructional components are ncluded in the curriculum?
   (a) modeling,
   (b) video modeling,
   (c) role play,
   (d) direct instruction,
   (e) measurement,
   (f) rehearsal/practice,
   (g) prompting/coaching,
   (h) positive reinforcement/shaping, and/or
   (i) opportunities to practice.
2. Are the following programming considerations covered?
   (a) Are assessment procedures/instruments included?
   (b) Is the curriculum adaptable to individual needs?
   (c) Can the curriculum be used with small groups?
   (d) Can personnel implement the curriculum without specialized training beyond that described in the curriculum?
   (e) Is the cost reasonable and manageable?
   (f) Are strategies included that will promote maintenance and generalization of skills?

Adapted from Carter and Sugai (1988, 1989).

Chapter 9

COLLABORATION IN PROVIDING
POSITIVE BEHAVIOR SUPPORTS

Key Point Questions

1. Why is family involvement important in Positive Behavior Supports?
2. What Mental Health resources are available?
3. What are Wraparound services?

WINDOW TO THE WORLD CASE STUDY ONE

Melvin is 24 and lives independently in his own apartment, cooks for himself, and has a few good friends with whom he socializes with on a weekly basis. Melvin is diagnosed with schizophrenia and medication has helped reduced the disturbing thoughts/voices and anxiousness that were barriers to keeping his job and friends. His relationship with his family had also been broken due to threats he had made to his parents and close relatives. Fortunately, Melvin was able to work with a psychiatrist, Dr. Leath, who chose the correct medication and doses for addressing the anxiousness and the disturbing thoughts and voices. With his symptoms managed, Melvin was able to land a part-time job provided by a supported employment agency. The agency provided a job coach who checked in daily with his boss to see how Melvin was doing and would also observe Melvin's work performance twice a month, making sure he was handling the job well and getting along with others. His relationships with both family and friends improved and Melvin felt his life was better than it had been in a long time. Dr. Leath was so pleased with Melvin's progress, he discussed with Melvin the possibility of reducing his dosages to relieve the other minor symptoms Melvin was experiencing. Melvin agreed and a reduction plan was started. Since Dr. Leath was unable to monitor the effect of the dosage reduction by observing Melvin's behavior at his work or in his interactions with family, he asked Melvin to give his consent for Dr. Leath to collaborate on a weekly basis with Melvin's parents and job coach in order to find out if they were seeing any return of the disturbing behaviors Melvin had experienced before taking the medications. Melvin agreed as he absolutely did not want to experience again losing his job or the breakdown of his now healthy relationship with friends and family. Dr. Leath contacted the job coach and he agreed to send an email every Friday to report on Melvin's behavior. Dr. Leath also arranged with the parents to have a telephone call every 10 days (or as needed if the parents were concerned about a negative change in Melvin's behavior). It was decided that Melvin would check in with Dr. Leath at least every other day for the first week and then, if all was going well, the check in would be reduced to weekly. Melvin told Dr. Leath he felt secure in this plan and in knowing that other people who cared about him would be consulting with his doctor to make sure the old symptoms were not returning.

WINDOW TO THE WORLD CASE STUDY TWO

Franz lives in Sea View Apartments with a roommate. Sea View Apartments is a residential setting that provides services and supports to people who are not quite capable of living completely independently. It is a safe, stable environment offering services that range from 24-hour supervision to on-call assistance. Before moving to Sea View Apartments, Franz was living in his rural home with his retired parents who looked out for him. Franz had limited opportunities to meet other people or have a job since his home was not near a town. Franz's parents were also beginning to feel it was time for Franz to learn some independence as they would not always be there for him. Sea View Apartments seemed like a good place for Franz. Now, with the help of the Sea View Apartment's social worker and the job developer from a local supported employment agency, Franz has a job he goes to 3 days a week, a roommate (he chose through an interview process) and opportunities to go into town for shopping, movies, dinner, and just hanging out with new friends he met through the activities at Sea View. After a month at Sea View, Franz said, "Now I feel part of a community."

When Franz met his roommate, Marco, they discussed how they would share the apartment and who would do what to keep things neat and clean. Franz told Marco that he had Asperger syndrome which was the reason why he liked to have his own space with his things in the same place (and not touched by others), that he needed to keep a daily schedule, and especially a morning schedule for using the bathroom so he could get to work on time. Marco liked Franz right away (Franz had a cool sound system he brought with him) so Marco was fine with a set morning schedule, since he usually did not get up before 10:00 a.m. anyway. At first, Franz's part-time job at the bank and his excursions into town were stimulating and interesting for Franz, but after a few months, Franz noticed he wasn't feeling very well and thought it might be depression since every day he woke up feeling very unhappy. He realized he missed his parents and his life back home. Unfortunately, his home town was a 5-hour bus ride which did not make it easy to commute back and forth for a visit every weekend. At first, he tried to ignore his feelings but he missed the comfort and quiet of his rural home, the neighbors he knew, the local country store and talking to Thomas, the store manager. Franz started missing going to work one or two times a week. At first, Marco, did not think anything about it, but when Franz did not go to work for a whole week, stopped shaving, and started sleeping until noon, Marco became really concerned, knowing this behavior was not at all like Franz. Marco suggested Franz go to see the Sea View counselor. Franz wasn't sure about seeing the counselor since he didn't see how talking to someone would change his sad feelings. Marco suggested that he and Franz go together to see the counselor, Dr. Watt. Dr. Watt met with both Marco and Franz, and then with just Franz. Dr. Watt explained to Franz that what he was experiencing was fairly common for residents who first leave home and that he had an idea for a process they could use to help Franz. Dr. Watt had just been to a training on the Wraparound process and had been exploring how to incorporate this process which involved including the person's family, friends and community to assist in helping the person find solutions to their problems. Dr. Watt set up a meeting with Franz, Marco,

Franz's parents, Franz's best friend from high school (who attended a nearby university) and Rosario Moran, his boss at the bank. At the meeting, the team talked with Franz about his interests and strengths, his need to get back on his schedule, things he could do to feel less sad and, be able to talk out loud about his feelings and obtain medicine, if needed. From this first meeting, the parents decided they would make an appointment for Franz to see a doctor to assess for clinical depression, Franz and his best friend decided to get together for at least one activity a week, and Rosario said she would let Franz adjust his schedule to have a 4-day weekend to go see his parents whenever Franz felt he needed a visit. Also, Dr. Watt would meet with Franz once a week to monitor his progress, and his roommate, Marco, would remind Franz to monitor his self-recording (app on phone) for staying on schedule and going to work. Franz would also be responsible for making a list of reinforcers he could give himself by staying on his schedule each week. The team decided they would meet in two or three weeks to see how Franz was doing. Dr. Watt also offered for the team to email him or have an online video chat if meeting face-to-face was not possible. When Franc left the wraparound meeting he told the team, "I'm already feeling better."

KEY POINT QUESTION #1:
WHY IS FAMILY INVOLVEMENT IMPORTANT?

Parents[3] can be important allies and supports for providers. In many ways, parents play the critical role in the lives of their adult children with a disability, as they provide important information and insight about the individual. Additionally, under the Wraparound process (discussed in the next section), agency support providers who are case managers for transition age students who are young adults (18–22 yrs. of age) can participate in a postsecondary student's transition planning through the Individual Education Program (IEP)/Individual Transition Plan (ITP) process. In attending a student's IEP/ITP meetings in the last years of school, agency case managers and support providers may share in the responsibility of planning for needed

---

3. We will use the term "parents" in this chapter though we are including parents, siblings, grandparents, foster parents, and other adult care providers under this term.

positive behavior support services for a student having difficulties in sustaining vocational training, job placements, or participating in post-secondary education due to not having the appropriate behaviors for these adult settings. Working with the student, teachers and parents during this final transition phase from school to adult life will allow the support provider to initiate any needed follow along services to meet the student's behavioral needs. Table 9.1 provides an overview of benefits to support providers, teachers, parents, and students for successful agency, school and family collaboration.

It is important that support providers establish professional and positive contact with parents, but if they are working with young adults who are 18 and over, and not conserved, (a conserved person is one who has a legally appointed person, the conservator, who oversees their personal affairs due to their own incapability to do so), then the support providers need to ask the person's preference for people they want involved in their collaboration network of support and provide the adult person with the necessary consent forms to release information to the preferred people (although the support provider may feel certain people and/or parents may be helpful in the collaboration network and share their reasons with the adult person, if the adult person does not want their parents or certain people involved, then the support providers must comply with the legal mandates around confidentiality and privacy).

Table 9.2 provides a list of methods that support providers can use for communicating with parents. A variety of methods should be used with a focus on the communication preferences of the parents (providing parents with a list of options can be helpful). In these particular communications, support providers should be informing parents of what their adult child is doing well (a positive statement such as, "Miftah is doing a very good job of completing the list of tasks her boss gives her each day at work") more than what they are doing wrong ("sometimes Miftah's merchandise facing is a bit sloppy in terms of quality"). Support providers should always end the communication on a positive note ("If taking more time to organize the shelves, then Miftah will get assigned more work hours"). In communications and collaborations, support providers need to be aware of linguistic, cultural, ethnic, and socioeconomic differences between themselves and also among the different parents of their clients (Aguilar, 2010; Araujo, 2009; Sung & Clark, 2005).

The relationship between the support provider and parents should not be adversarial even though, unfortunately, it can sometimes become so. In these situations, it is important that the support provider have documentation (some form of written correspondence, such as emails, texts, or follow-up notes detailing a recent conversation) of the contact and content covered with the parents. Support providers need to analyze what they can do to improve the relationship with the parents rather than laying blame on the parents for the situation. Robinson and Fine (1994) suggest a six-step solution-oriented approach for collaboration. These steps can keep the focus on the tasks to accomplish and offer greater assurance of the participants' reaching resolution. These six steps are:

1. First, clearly state the purpose for collaborating together. This creates an atmosphere where the participants openly and non-defensively express an interest in discussing concerns and in working together to resolve those concerns.
2. Second, use accurate listening skills to explore the parent's view of the situation. The observations and inquiries should not be judgmental but are intended to further clarify the parent's views.
3. Third, both participants need to reach a common understanding of both the problem and the solution. The term "solution" refers to what the participants want to happen, both for the process and the outcome.
4. The fourth step is a review of options of appropriate interventions and outcomes.
5. The fifth step is the agreement on the specific intervention and outcome. The intervention should include specification of each person's role in carrying out the intervention, as well as a timetable. This helps to create a sense of accountability for all parties.
6. Finally, an evaluation of the success of the intervention and outcomes is important.

KEY POINT QUESTION #2:
WHAT MENTAL HEALTH RESOURCES ARE AVAILABLE?

In the United States, mental disorders are diagnosed based on the *Diagnostic and Statistical Manual of Mental Disorders,* fifth edition (*DSM-*

V). Depression, suicide, anxiety disorders, abuse, and substance abuse are all potential concerns for adults with disabilities. Even an individual who does not have serious mental health issues will face stressful or traumatic events that will affect their well-being (Cornell, 2006; Duchnowski & Kutash, 2008). A person's mental health condition is best viewed as being on a continuum or spectrum, as an individual is not necessarily either totally mentally healthy or unhealthy; thus, one's mental health condition can move around on the continuum depending upon life circumstances (Weare, 2000).

The website https://www.nimh.nih.gov/health/statistics/mental-illness.shtml of The National Institute of Mental Health states in 2016 that there was an estimated one in five U.S. adults (44.7 million) to have a mental disorder diagnosis in a given year. This represents 18.3 % of U.S. adults. Young adults between ages 18-25 had the highest prevalence for any mental illness at 22.1%. In a 2014 report, The Substance Abuse and Mental Health Services Administration's (SAMHSA) published a *National Survey on Drug Use and Health* (*NSDUH*) and found that 15.7 million adults in the United States reported having major depression in the past 12 months but one-third of those did not seek professional help.

Interventions for individuals with mental health needs may take place in outpatient treatment, day treatment, partial hospitalization, residential treatment, and inpatient care (Nelson, Sprague, Jolivette, Smith, & Tobin, 2008). These interventions may involve individual and/or group psychotherapies, case management, pharmacological, and psychosocial treatments or any combination of. It is important to note here that many adults with disabilities have been prescribed different pharmacological medicines which are often prescribed for undesirable behaviors. For example, Mohiuddin and Ghaziuddin (2012) suggest that at least 50% of persons with Autism Spectrum Disorders receive psychotropic medications during their life span. Mohiuddin and Ghaziuddin (2012) also found that out of 105 studies identified for their review on this topic, only 24 were randomized controlled trials. Thus, despite the common use of these medications in autism spectrum disorder, there are few well-controlled studies regarding the long-term efficacy and safety of the psychotropic medications.

However, as Flora (2007) has noted, there are many concerns with using drugs (prescribed or not) and that applied behavior analysis has a strong (if not stronger) empirical base for being an effective intervention for undesirable behaviors. We are not saying that pharmacological interventions are not effective, or unnecessary, but that their use needs to be viewed with caution. This is especially true with undesirable behaviors as there is sometimes a tendency to medicate the person so that the undesirable behaviors are suppressed rather than analyzing the function of the behavior and developing skills and positive behavior supports for the individual.

Mental health programs should be integrated into employment, community, and residential settings as much as possible with providing services where they are needed (this is a "push in" model). For example, in the employment setting the Human Resource Office could provide a "de-stress room" where an upset employee could calm down in a quiet private room. Additionally, an onsite mental health counselor, or social worker, could also be available for an employee to check in with if they are having a difficult time. An employee could provide permission to the counselor to collaborate with his/her family, doctor or therapist to provide more Wraparound support (see next section on "Wraparound"). This allows collaboration among support providers, counselors, psychologists, social workers, nurses, and police officers, rather than each providing their services in an isolated context. The logic is that the more complex the problem is, the more there is a need for a comprehensive cohesive system approach that involves a variety of supports from a team of professionals and others, such as family and friends (Adelman & Taylor, 1998). Adelman & Taylor (2015) suggest collaborating with a variety of resources and supports, such as:

• County and Municipal agencies (health, mental health, family social services, probation, sheriff, courts, fire, service planning, recreation and parks, library, housing).
• Mutual support and self-help groups.
• Postsecondary education institutions (community colleges, state universities, public and private colleges, vocational schools).
• Service agencies (Charitable agencies, volunteer agencies legal aid society).
• Service clubs and Civic groups (Lions, Rotary, Optimist, Soroptimists, etc.) veteran's groups, philanthropic foundations).
• Sports, health, fitness and outdoor groups (sports teams, athletic leagues, local gyms, Audubon Society).

- Community-based organizations (Neighborhood Watch, home-owner's association, economic development groups).
- Faith-based organizations (congregations, clergy associations).
- Ethnic associations and organizations.
- Special interest groups and clubs (science, art, literature, animal rescue and care, environment).

Exploring what local assets exist in the community can offer support providers expanded knowledge of potential services for meeting specific strengths, needs or interests of an individual client. Sometimes it is difficult to know where to start to look for help. The National Alliance of Mental Illness (NAMI) at https://www.nami.org provides resources and information on their national and regional websites. NAMI websites provide addresses, websites, and contact information for such agencies as County Health and Social Services Divisions, County Mental Health, Mental Health Crisis Units, Wellness and Recovery Centers, Community Organization Information, County Mental Health Committees and Boards, Regional Mental Health Service Offices, State Disability Community Action Networks, Parent Networks, National Mental Health Services Knowledge Exchange Network and other such local mental health agencies. Many NAMI local websites also list consumer-led peer support groups that provide help, such as Twelve Steps, Alcoholics Anonymous, Crisis Respite Services, Home-Based Family Therapy, Domestic Violence Groups, and Support Groups for depression, schizophrenia, mood disorders, bipolar and personality and psychotic disorders.

Community services may also be used to support intervention strategies. For example, Theresa, a support provider, is concerned about John, a client who is overeating at home after work because he says he is bored. The support provider knows the John likes to do tai chi and supports him in joining a tai chi class at the local gym before going home from work. The result is that John does not overeat at home on the days he goes to tai chi.

The focus is on prevention and promoting wellness for a specific individual. It can be that mental, emotional, and social health is the "missing piece" of positive behavior supports for many individuals (Weare, 2000). Mental health services should focus on:

Personal competencies: Social skills, problem solving skills.

Emotional well-being: Happiness or joy as well as understanding and being able to express one's emotions.

Thinking clearly: Having the ability to process information, make good decisions, set goals.

Ability to grow: To change positively, learn from experiences, and build skills.

Resilience: Having the ability to bounce back from stress and difficulties, moving on.

Emotional intelligence and Emotional literacy: The ability to identify, assess, and control the emotions of oneself, as well as the ability to express emotions productively.

Many adults with disabilities have a "dual diagnosis" where, for instance, they are diagnosed with having both an intellectual disability and a mental illness (it is of course possible that an individual may have more than two types of disabilities). For individuals with a dual diagnosis it becomes important to determine if there are positive behavior supports that are specific to a disability (such as teaching communication skills to a person who has both an intellectual disability and a mental illness) or if factors, such as determining the function of the behavior, are generic across all situations and individuals. For example, Gus is diagnosed with a panic disorder and also has an intellectual disability. Speaking quickly in response to someone is often difficult for Gus, but if given time to respond, he can usually speak the words he wants to say. However, when Gus's boss gives him a short deadline (e.g., "I need this in 15 minutes") he often experiences a panic attack which makes it even more difficult for him to use the strategy the counselor gave him for calming down (which is to tell the boss he is feeling anxious and to ask to take a quick break in the staff room). Normally, he could do this in most situations when he is feeling anxious but "deadlines" send him into a panic and he cannot get even one word out, let alone the two sentences for using the strategy. Gus's support provider knew Gus used a smart phone and taught him how to record the two sentences and also placed an icon on the screen so he could tap it for fast access when he needed to use the "panic" strategy. Now when the boss gives him a short deadline that Gus becomes anxious about, he can press his "panic button."

KEY POINT QUESTION #3:
WHAT ARE WRAPAROUND SERVICES?

Wraparound services are a team-based planning process (not a specific intervention or service) to providing community-based care for individuals with complex mental health and related issues. The team includes the individual, family members, service providers, and members of the family's social support network. Team members work together to create, implement, and monitor a plan to meet the needs of the person. The focus is on proactively organizing supports and services across agencies to develop comprehensive interventions.

Wraparound services are based upon:

1. Engaging the individual, caregivers, and families in a strengths-based process.
2. Identifying priority needs.
3. Assembling an integrated team that provides the basis for collaboration.
4. Managing the work of the team so that cross-system, solution-based problem solving occurs.
5. Building the individual and family's self-efficacy and social support.
6. Setting goals and monitoring success over time (Bruns, Sather, Pullmann, & Stambaugh, 2011).

The purpose of the wraparound process is to bring together the individual and their family with needed supports such as medical coordinators, family and adult peer-to-peer support partners, mental health workers, social workers, and so on, to develop comprehensive interventions (rather than piecemeal approaches from each individual or agency) to meet the needs of the person, their family, and others. Wraparound is not based on any single theory of intervention; wraparound is best understood as a planning process and a philosophy of care (Eber, Hyde, & Suter, 2011).

Wraparound is operationalized as a process with activities that occur across four distinct phases in which a team is formed that develops, monitors, and continuously revises a plan that is focused on achieving success as defined by the individual, their family, and relevant others (Eber, Hyde, Rose, Breen, McDonald, & Lewandowski, 2009; Walker 2008):

PHASE I: ENGAGEMENT AND TEAM DEVELOPMENT: This phase provides the foundation for success by building positive relationships and support networks among the person, the family, and the team members. During this phase, a wraparound facilitator meets with the individual and family to engage them in the process, address concerns and explain how this process is different from traditional interventions, and help them to decide who they want on their wraparound team. Baseline measurements are established during Phase I for continued updating and evaluation of the success of the intervention.

PHASE II: INITIAL PLAN DEVELOPMENT: In this phase, the facilitator helps the individual, family and team reach consensus and buy in on the desired outcomes. Both the needs and strengths are used to identify specific interventions as well as to clarify roles for all team members.

PHASE III: PLAN IMPLEMENTATION: This phase starts the intervention process to effectively meet the needs of the individual by combining supports such as child care, mentoring, social networking with specific interventions such as counseling, or and addressing medical issues. Wraparound teams can also arrange supports for the parents or other family members who support the individual, such as assisting family members in accessing stable housing, recreation opportunities, and social supports. Supports can also come from or be provided to support providers as well as for meeting the unique needs of the individual.

PHASE IV: PLAN COMPLETION AND TRANSITION: In this final phase, the person and their family are transitioned from the ongoing wraparound team to progress monitoring through less intensive structures, such as support agency contacts. Movement to Phase IV is determined by the ability of the individual and their family to continue successful functioning with supports and skills that have been developed, and to continue interventions as necessary, such as a self-management system at home, counseling services, or access to appropriate medical services.

BEST PRACTICE RECOMMENDATION

1. Interventions need to be comprehensive in order to be effective and may involve the person's network of support, such as parents and individuals designated in the Wraparound Process.
2. Mental health services need to be pushed into employment, community and residential settings to reach and serve a greater number of people with mental illness and other types of disability.
3. Support providers need to focus on prevention and finding activities that promote wellness through focusing on the person's strengths, interests and preferences.

DISCUSSION QUESTIONS

1. How often and under what circumstances should parents and support providers communicate?
2. How do you handle a situation where the person does not want their parents and/or other family members involved even though you feel they could really help providing intervention support?
3. How do you build a successful relationship with adversarial parents?

EMPLOYMENT, COMMUNITY, AND RESIDENTIAL ACTIVITY SUGGESTIONS

1. Interview other professionals about an individual with complex support needs and analyze supports in terms of medical, mental, social, academic and other support needs. Analyze what a comprehensive intervention package might need to entail.
2. Follow this interview up with the individual and their family with analyzing the supports in terms of medical, mental, social, academic and other support needs. How are the viewpoints of the individuals and their family similar and/or different? Analyze what a comprehensive intervention package might need to entail.

REFERENCES

Adelman, H. S., & Taylor, L. (1998). Reforming mental health in schools and expanding school reform. *Educational Psychologist, 33,* 135–152.

Adelman, H. S., & Taylor, L. (2015). *Mental Health in Schools: Engaging learners, preventing problems, and improving schools.* New York: Skyhorse Publishing.

Aguilar, E. (2010). Teaching secrets: When the kids don't share your culture. *Education Digest, 76,* 52–54.

Araujo, B. E. (2009). Best practices in working with linguistically diverse families. *Intervention in School and Clinic, 45,* 116–123.

Bruns, E., Sather, A., Pullmann, M., & Stambaugh, L. (2011). National trends in implementing wraparound: Results from the state wraparound survey. *Journal of Child and Family Studies, 20,* 726–735.

Cornell, D. G. (2006). *School violence: Fears versus facts.* Mahwah, NJ: Lawrence Erlbaum.

Duchnowski, A. J., & Kutash, K. (2008). Integrating PBS, mental health services, and family-driven care. In W. Sailor, G. Dunlap, G. Sugai, & R. Horner (Eds.), *Handbook of positive behavior support* (pp. 203–231). New York: Springer.

Eber, L., Hyde, K., Rose, J., Breen, K., McDonald, D., & Lewandowski, H. (2009). Completing the continuum of schoolwide positive behavior support: Wraparound as a tertiary-level intervention. In W. Sailor, G. Dunlop, & G. Sugai (Eds.), *Handbook of positive behavior support* (pp. 671–703). New York: Springer.

Eber, L., Hyde, K., & Suter, J. (2011). Integrating wraparound into a schoolwide system of positive behavior supports. *Journal of Child and Family Studies, 20,* 782–790.

Flora, S.A. (2007). *Taking American off drugs: Why behavior therapy is more effective for treating ADHD, OCD, Depression, and other psychological problems.* Albany, NY: State University of New York Press.

Mohiuddin, S., & Ghaziuddin, M. (2012). Psychopharmacology of autism spectrum disorders: A selective review. *Autism, 17,* 645–654.

Nelson, C. M., Sprague, J. R., Jolivette, K., Smith, C. R., & Tobin, T. J. (2008). Positive behavior support in alternative education, community-based mental health, and juvenile justice settings. In W. Sailor, G. Dunlop, & G. Sugai (Eds.), *Handbook of positive behavior support* (pp. 465–496). New York: Springer.

Robinson, E. L., & Fine, M. J. (1994). Developing collaborative home-school relationships. *Preventing School Failure, 39,* 9–15.

Sung. J. B., & Clark, G. M. (2005). Incorporate diversity awareness in the classroom: What teachers can do. *Intervention in School & Clinic, 41,* 49–51.

Walker, J. S. (2008). How, and why, does wraparound work: A theory of change. Portland, OR: National Wraparound Initiative, Portland State University.

Weare, K. (2000). *Promoting mental, emotional, and social health: A whole school approach.* New York: Routledge.

EMPIRICAL RESEARCH SUPPORTING THAT THE INTERVENTIONS PRESENTED IN CHAPTER ARE EVIDENCE BASED PRACTICES

Austin, K. L., Hunter, M., Gallagher, E., & Campbell, L. E. (2018). Depression and anxiety symptoms during the transition to early adulthood for people with intellectual disabilities. *Journal of Intellectual Disability Research, 62,* 407–421.

Bernstein, A., Chorpita, B. F.; Rosenblatt, A., Becker, K. D., Daleiden, E. L., & Ebesutani, C. K. (2015). Fit of evidence-based treatment components to youths served by wraparound process: A relevance mapping analysis. *Journal of Clinical Child and Adolescent Psychology, 44,* 44–57.

Cooney, P., Jackman, C., Tunney, C., Coyle, D., & O'Reilly, G. (2018). Computer-assisted cognitive behavioural therapy: The experiences of adults who have an intellectual disability and anxiety or depression. *Journal of Applied Research in Intellectual Disabilities, 31,* 1032–1045.

Fuller-Thomson, E., Carroll, S. Z., & Yang, W. (2018). Suicide attempts among individuals with specific learning disorders: An underrecognized issue. *Journal of Learning Disabilities, 51,* 283–292.

LaPorte, T. M., Haber, M. G., & Malloy, J. M. (2016). Wraparound team composition, youth self-determination, and youth satisfaction in transition services. *Journal of Behavioral Health Services and Research, 43,* 611–629.

Lechtenberger, D., Brak, L. B., Sokolosky, S., & Cccrary, D. (2012). Using wraparound to support students with developmental disabilities in higher education. *College Student Journal, 46,* 856–866.

Lorenc, T., Rodgers, M., Marshall, D., Melton, H., Rees, R., Wright, K., & Sowden, A. (2018). Support for adults with autism spectrum disorder without intellectual impairment: Systematic review. *Autism: The International Journal of Research and Practice, 22,* 654–668.

Man, J., Kangas, M., Trollor, J., & Sweller, N. (2018). Clinical practices and barriers to best practice implementation of psychologists working with adults with intellectual disability and comorbid mental ill health. *Journal of Policy and Practice in Intellectual Disabilities, 15,* 256–266.

Mendenhall, A. N., Kapp, S. A., Rand, A., Robbins, M. L., & Stipp, K. (2013). Theory meets practice: The localization of wraparound services for youth with serious emotional disturbance. *Community Mental Health Journal, 49,* 793–804.

Nevill, R. E., & Benson, B. A. (2018). Risk factors for challenging behaviour and psychopathology in adults with Down syndrome. *Journal of Intellectual Disability Research, 62,* 941–951.

Painter, K. (2012). Outcomes for youth with severe emotional disturbance: A repeated measures longitudinal study of a wraparound approach of service delivery in systems of care. *Child and Youth Care Forum, 41,* 407–425.

Perera, B., & Courtenay, K. (2018). Mental health services for people with intellectual disability in the United Kingdom. *Advances in Mental Health and Intellectual Disabilities, 12,* 91–98.

Roberts, L., & Kwan, S. (2018). Putting the C into CBT: Cognitive challenging with adults with mild to moderate intellectual disabilities and anxiety disorders. *Clinical Psychology and Psychotherapy, 25,* 662–671.

Salloum, A., Johnco, C., Lewin, A. B., McBride, N. M., & Storch, E. A. (2016). Barriers to access and participation in community mental health treatment for anxious children. *Journal of Affective Disorders, 196,* 54–61.

Shimoyama, M., Iwasa, K., & Sonoyama, S. (2018). The prevalence of mental health problems in adults with intellectual disabilities in Japan, associated factors and mental health service use. *Journal of Intellectual Disability Research, 62,* 931–940.

GENERAL REFERENCES REGARDING TOPICS IN CHAPTER

Bottke, A. (2018). *How to connect with your troubled adult children.* Eugene, OR: Harvest House Publishers.

Hazen, E. P., Goldstein, M. A., & Goldstein, M. C. (2011). *Mental health disorders in adolescents: A guide for parents, teachers, and professionals.* New Brunswick, NJ: Rutgers University Press.

Kazdin, A. E. (2018). *Innovations in psychosocial interventions and their delivery: Leveraging mprove the world's mental health.* New York, NY: Oxford University Press.

Leach, J. (2015). *Improving mental health through social support: Building positive and empowering relationships.* Philadelphia: Jessica Kingsley Publishers.

Shatkin, J. P. (2015). *Child & adolescent mental health: A practical, all-in-one guide.* New York: W. W. Norton & Company,

Simkins, S. (2009). *When kids get arrested: What every adult should know.* New Brunswick, NJ: Rutgers University Press.

Volz, J. R., Synder, T., & Sterba, M. (2009). *Teaching social skills to youth with mental health disorders: Incorporating social skills into treatment planning for 109 disorders.* Boys Town, NB: Boys Town Press.

Weist, M. D., Lever, N. A., Bradshaw, C. P., & Owens, J. S. (2014). *Handbook of school mental health: Research, training, practice, and policy* (2nd ed.). New York: Springer.

Ziomek-Daigle, J., & Cavin, J. (2015). Shaping youth and families through positive behavior support. *Family Journal, 23,* 368–373.

Table 9.1
Benefits of Support Provider/Parent Collaboration

Benefits to Support Providers of a Productive Parent-Support Provider Relationship

1. Greater understanding of the individual's strengths and needs.
2. Access to more meaningful reinforcers (tangible and activity).
3. Increased opportunities for reinforcement (trans-environmental programming).
4. More cooperation from parents.
5. Easier to face hard decisions together rather than alone.
6. Avoiding potential problems such as implementing an intervention that has been unsuccessfully tried before.

Benefits to Parents of a Productive Parent-Support Provider Relationship

1. Takes away sense of helplessness in dealing with the adult service system.
2. Have an advocate (support provider) within the system.
3. Inside view of what is going on in the person's employment, community, and home environments.
4. Greater access to resources and services.
5. Better understanding of what the person can do in employment, community, and home environments.

Table 9.2
Effective Strategies for Communicating with Parents

1. Phone calls.
2. Emails.
3. Texts.
4. Mailed notes home.
5. Journal back and forth between support provider and parents.
6. Support Providerblog, social network site, or agency website posting how individual or family can best contact for assistance.
7. In person meetings or online (for example, skype).
8. Introductory letter.
9. Introductory video.
10. Home visits.
11. Regular progress reports.
12. Agency newsletters.

Chapter 10

BEHAVIOR SUPPORT PLANS

Key Point Questions

1. What are Behavior Support Plans and why are they important?
2. What Components should be in a Behavior Support Plan?
3. How should the Competing Behavior Model be used to decide upon potential interventions?
4. What is an example of a Comprehensive Behavior Support Plan?

WINDOW TO THE WORLD CASE STUDY ONE

Martin is a nineteen-year-old man who has a dual diagnosis of an intellectual disability and a mental health disability. Martin also has difficulty processing verbal language. In the past, hyperactivity has been a problem interfering with his learning, but currently this behavior has improved. Martin has started attending a program for intellectual disabilities at a local liberal arts college. However, he was referred for a Functional Behavior Assessment because of a number of concerns regarding his conduct at the college. Specifically, staff at the college who directly support the students with intellectual disabilities have reported that he has become increasingly aggressive (e.g., hitting, kicking, scratching, etc.) towards staff and sometimes peers who happen to be close to him. This aggression often happens when Martin refuses to move from one activity to another and is prompted by staff who are attempting to physically guide him. Administrators at the college have become increasingly concerned and are starting to question if the program for the students with intellectual disabilities is a good fit and if it should be closed down at the end of the semester.

Because of the potential dangerousness of these behaviors, the staff from the program have asked for a Functional Assessment to assist them in positively impacting his behavior at the college.

The purpose of the functional assessment was to analyze specifically the aggressive behaviors that interfere with Martin's functioning at college, to determine the function of these behaviors, and to provide recommendations for teaching him alternative skills aimed at decreasing the occurrence of these undesirable aggressive behaviors.

The behavior assessment conducted consisted of the following components:

1. Record Review.
2. Interviews with the direct care staff at the college, the behaviorist previously assigned to Martin's case when he was in high school, and Martin's mother and father.
3. Direct observation forms and reports from previous assessments.
4. Description of behavior from direct observation.
5. Daily data collection tools employed by the previous behaviorist.

WINDOW TO THE WORLD CASE STUDY TWO

Lucien is a twenty-four year old man who has been diagnosed with Autism Spectrum Disorders. He lives in an apartment with his roommate, Kushim, who also has ASD. They both receive supported living services to help the two of them with activities of daily living (cooking, cleaning, bathing, shopping, etc.) and also to support Lucien who has challenging behavior. Lucien was referred for a Functional Behavior Assessment because of a number of concerns regarding his conduct in his home. His supported living staff as well as his parents are very concerned about Lucien, but are unsure what to do and they hope that the Functional Behavioral Assessment will give them a plan of what they should do to help support Lucien. Specifically, supported living staff reported that he has become increasingly aggressive towards staff and sometimes his roommate, Kushim. In addition, Lucien will sometimes engage in self-injurious behaviors of biting his hand and hitting his head. Staff members have tried a number of strategies to help the situation, such as reminding him to be good, blocking his aggression and self-injurious behavior, reprimanding him, and denying him access to activities but none have worked well, if at all.

KEY POINT QUESTION #1: WHAT ARE BEHAVIOR SUPPORT PLANS AND WHY ARE THEY IMPORTANT?

Behavior Support Plans are the professional documents that demonstrate a coherent and rational plan of support. They are part of the legal, administrative, and professional standards for quality in positive behavior supports. Behavior Support Plans are formats for clearly defining exactly what will be done to reduce undesirable behaviors and to increase positive behaviors. A written Behavior Support Plan (BSP) provides a guide for all individuals responsible for its implementation.

An effective written plan provides a clear strategy for monitoring progress. The BSP also provides a format for modifying support procedures in response to ongoing changes in the behavior of the student and the contexts within which that behavior occurs.

It is critical that there is a logical connection between assessment information collected (e.g., understanding the function of the undesirable behavior), and the development of the behavior support plan. Function-based behavior support interventions and plans are more likely to be effective and efficient than interventions that are not tied to the function of the undesirable behavior (Ingram, Lewis-Palmer, & Sugai, 2005; Newcomer & Lewis, 2004).

Horner, O'Neill, and Flannery (1993) note that a BSP should result in these outcomes for the individual: (a) a reduction of the undesirable behavior, (b) an increase in health and safety for the individual, (c) an increase in positive activity patterns for the individual, and (d) an increase in the choices and preferences for the individual. Horner, et al. (1993) provide three assumptions for developing BSP's:

1. The BSP will be hypothesis driven (how events in a person's life can be modified to positively influence their behavior).
2. BSP's will have multiple components.
3. BSP's will be uniquely shaped by the context of the setting.

KEY POINT QUESTION #2: WHAT COMPONENTS SHOULD BE IN A BEHAVIOR SUPPORT PLAN?

O'Neill, Albin, Storey, Horner, and Sprague (2015) outline four themes that are important in the design of behavioral support plans:

1. The BSP should identify how support personnel will change their own behavior and not just focus on how the undesirable behavior of the adult with a disability will change.
2. The BSP should be directly based on the function of the behavior.
3. The BSP should be technically sound—that is, consistent with the principles of applied behavior analysis and based upon best practices in the field (also known as evidence-based practices).
4. The BSP should be a good fit with the values, resources, and skills of the people responsible for implementation of the BSP.

Behavior Support Plans Describe the Behavior of Plan Implementers

Behavior Support Plans are designed to alter patterns of undesirable behavior by the adult with a disability. This process, however, involves changing the behavior of coworkers, family members, staff, or others in the various settings in which the person needs supports. BSP's describe what support providers and others will do. It is the change in the behavior of the support providers that will result in the positive behavior change of the adult. A good BSP defines in detail the changes expected in the behavior of relevant support providers, family members, or staff. The focus on the behavior support plan should be on reducing undesirable behavior and increasing positive desirable replacement behaviors.

Building from Functional Behavioral Assessment Results

Two strategies have proven useful to improve the link between functional behavioral assessment and the design of a behavior support plan (O'Neill et al., 2015). The first strategy is simply to ensure the summary statements from the functional assessment that identify the proposed function(s) of problem behavior are listed in the behavior support plan (O'Neill et al., 2015). An example of a summary statement is "When Louie is asked to complete a difficult work task, he will throw items to the floor in order to escape from the difficult work task." These summary statements provide the foundation for the plan, and all procedures defined in the behavior support plan should be logically consistent with the summary statements. If, for example, the summary statement indicated that the function of the undesirable behavior is to obtain staff attention, the intervention should involve extinction of staff attention following undesirable behavior and a positive reinforcement schedule of staff attention when the undesirable behavior is not occurring (DRO or DRI).

A second strategy has been to build a "competing behaviors model" of the functional behavioral assessment summary statement and define how the model must be changed to ensure that appropriate behaviors will "compete" successfully with undesirable behaviors (O'Neill et al., 2015). The competing behavior model is discussed in detail in response to Key Point Question #3 in this chapter.

Behavior Support Plans Need to Fit the Setting Where They Will Be Implemented

Behavioral support procedures should be technically sound as well as a good fit with the values, resources, and skills of the people who will implement the procedures. The goal is to design a BSP that will be both effective and possible to implement.

If the BSP is to lead to change in the behavior of staff and other support providers, the procedures need to (a) fit the natural routines of the setting; (b) be consistent with the "values" of the people in the setting (they need to indicate a willingness to perform the procedures); (c) be efficient in terms of time, money, and resources; (d) be matched to the skills of the people who will carry out the procedures; and (e) produce positive results (a reduction in the undesirable behavior and increases in positive behavior (O'Neill et al., 2015).

KEY POINT QUESTION #3: HOW SHOULD THE COMPETING BEHAVIOR MODEL BE USED TO DECIDE UPON POTENTIAL INTERVENTIONS?

As previously discussed, it is critical that there be a link between the BSP and the functional behavioral assessment results (e.g., the function of the undesirable behavior for the student). It is common for clinicians to conduct a functional behavioral assessment and move directly into the write-up of the behavior support plan. However, O'Neill et al (2015) recommend the use of a competing behavior model to define the features of an effective environment and to ensure that the intervention is based upon the function of the behavior. These features are then used to select the specific strategies that will make up the BSP.

The use of competing behavior pathways is key to BSP because "it increases the link between intervention procedures and functional assessment results; it increases the fit between the values, skills, resources, and routines of the people who carry out the plan and the procedures that will be employed; it increases the logical coherence among the different procedures that could be used in a multielement plan of support; and it increases the fidelity with which the plan is ultimately implemented" (O'Neill et al., 2015, p. 79).

Constructing a competing behavior model involves three steps. First is building a diagram of the functional behavioral assessment summary statement for each undesirable behavior. Second, define desired positive behaviors and appropriate replacement behaviors for the undesirable behaviors and the consequences associated with them. The third step is to identify potential intervention procedures across four intervention categories (i.e., setting event; antecedent; behavior/ teaching; consequence) that will promote positive behaviors and make undesirable behaviors irrelevant, inefficient, and ineffective (O'Neill et al., 2015). An example of these steps is provided in Figure 10.1.

How to Identify Potential Interventions

One of the most difficult issues in Positive Behavior Supports is in deciding what intervention or interventions to use to support the individual. When the function(s) of the undesirable behavior is understood, it becomes possible to identify multiple intervention strategies that are logically linked to that function(s) and are Evidence Based Practices. There are a wide variety of interventions that may be appropriate and likely to be effective for the individual. The competing behavior model form provides a framework for identifying potential intervention strategies. An important element of identifying interventions is to be able to analyze possibilities in a logical manner that covers all facets of the situation that need to be considered. Figure 10.2 provides a flowchart of variables to consider in identifying potential interventions. The strategies included in Figure 10.2 illustrate potential examples and are not intended to be exhaustive lists.

KEY POINT QUESTION #4: WHAT IS AN EXAMPLE OF A COMPREHENSIVE BEHAVIOR SUPPORT PLAN?

In this section, we provide an example of a comprehensive behavior support plan using Martin from Case Study One at the start of this chapter. Each section in the following behavior support plan provides a model to follow.

Behavior Support Plan

RECORD REVIEW. Martin is diagnosed as having both an intellectual disability and a mental health disability. He also experiences difficulty with "extreme" hyperactivity but, as reported in the psychologist's evaluation from the school district that previously served him, the degree of hyperactivity has diminished over the two years. Martin is currently receiving services through the Disabled Students Programs and Services department (in which the program for students with intellectual disabilities is a part) at the college he attends.

INTERVIEWS AND INFORMAL OBSERVATIONS. The following people provided valuable information regarding the history and description of behavior.

Support Specialist, DSPS Program for Students with Intellectual Disabilities, Ms. Fannin. Ms. Fannin was interviewed using the Functional Assessment Interview Form (FAIF) from O'Neill et al. (2015). From that interview, the undesirable behavior of concern was identified to be aggression as manifested by biting, kicking, scratching, hitting, and spitting at staff and peers. Results from the FAIF indicated that Martin probably engaged in these behaviors both to escape from staff attempts to support him during transitions and sometimes to get a preferred item or activity.

Mr. Hanson, Previous Behaviorist from the School District. Mr. Hanson stated in reports that many of Martin's high risk times are during transitions, especially if demands are placed on him to transition quickly from one activity to another or if staff physically prompt him during transitions. Mr. Hanson also expressed concern regarding the difficulty that Martin had in asking appropriately for preferred items or activities.

Ms. Berman, Previous School Psychologist from the School District. Ms. Berman had assessed Martin and she noted in her report that Martin does "these things" to get out of something (such as a prompt to transition or when he is bored). In Ms. Berman's estimation, Martin needs to be challenged more and that his undesirable behaviors may serve as a way of him saying, "I need something stimulating to do."

Parents. Martin's parents were also interviewed using the FAIF. His parents expressed the concern that Martin may be engaging these behaviors as a way to express frustration or an inability to express his wants or needs. His parents also expressed an escape function specifically when "Martin thinks he's in trouble." Finally, his parents expressed the need to give Martin additional time to transition. For example, telling Martin a transition will happen in five minutes instead of when the transition is to happen.

DSPS records. The DSPS staff have maintained academic and behavioral records for Martin regarding his performance while at college. Martin is currently working on goals related to academic performance, expressive and receptive language, and undesirable behavior related to transition. In addition to work samples for academic progress, the DSPS staff have also taken frequency data records on actual aggressive actions that led to physical contact. No record was kept of aggressive attempts.

Identify the Undesirable Behavior

Operational Definitions of Behavior

Definition of Aggression:

- *Aggression to Others:* Any episode of physical assault towards staff or peers that results in or has the potential to result in harm to that person.
- *Positive Examples (occurrences of the behavior):* biting, kicking, hitting, or scratching another person or attempts to bite, kick, hit, or scratch another person.
- *Negative Examples (nonoccurrences of the behavior):* hitting own head, slamming own head into wall, smashing objects, or verbal threats towards others.

Select a measurement system to obtain representative data given the dimensions of the behavior and the logistics of observing and recording:

- Frequency data record during each class situation (e. g, transition time, academic class, social situation outside of class, physical prompt by staff) would be an appropriate and easy way in which to collect data on Martin's aggression.

Select a schedule of observation and recording periods:

- Continuous recording of frequency data throughout the school day would be a reasonable method for staff to collect data.

FOLLOW UP INTERVIEWS: Staff and parents were previously interviewed using the FAIF from O'Neill et al. (2015). It would be possible, but not critical, to conduct follow-up interviews after the intervention has been implemented to see if interviewees believe that progress is being made and if the function of the behavior remains the same.

ANALYSIS OF DATA: Since frequency is the data collection system being used, a line graph across school days would be a logical way to visually represent the data (as long as the length of the school day for Martin is constant throughout the week) and could easily be visually interpreted to determine if the intervention is being successful in reducing the frequency of Martin's aggressive behaviors. It would also be possible to have separate graphs for each class period or other times (such as lunch) to determine if there were different patterns of aggression across the different classes/times.

FUNCTION OF BEHAVIOR:

- *Setting Events:* Martin engages in aggression to terminate physical prompts during transition times or to obtain desirable objects or activities.
- *Maintaining contingencies:* Based on the data collected and information obtained through interviews and record review, it appears that the undesirable behavior functions to terminate a physical prompt during transition times or to obtain a desired object or activity.

SUMMARY STATEMENTS:

Topography and Episode

- During transitions from activity to activity and when he wants a desired object or activity, Martin is likely to engage in aggressive behaviors towards others. He also can be aggressive when he wants a desired object or activity and does not know how to ask appropriately for the item or activity.

Environmental Intervention: How do we prevent the target behaviors from occurring?

1. Martin's aggression occurs most often during transition times and Martin may then be likely to escape the prompts to transition by aggressing towards staff or lashing out at a peer.
2. By avoiding physical prompts, physical aggression should decrease. However, Martin needs to be able to transition successfully so other types of prompts such as peer modeling, video modeling, self-management systems (antecedent cue regulation, self-monitoring, and self-recording), and positive reinforcement.

Antecedents and Precursors

Aggression is likely to occur during:

1. Group activities especially during "transition from activity to activity;"
2. Transitions from preferred activities to less preferred activities;
3. In response to an "unpredictable change in routine;"

Contextual Fit of the Intervention

Step 1

Martin's plan is presented to the DSPS team and ratified. Behavioral Goals and objectives are presented and ratified. Roles and responsibilities are assigned, and the plan is put in place.

Step 2

The primary "Players" are walked through each step of the plan and instructed on data collection tools and suggested teaching strategies (one week from Plan's ratification).

Step 3

Martin's plan is implemented with initial weekly consultation from Dr. Skinner, a private consultant hired by the college. Consultation includes data review, implementation integrity, and suggested minor modification to existing plan (as needed). It is decided that implementation should continue for three months with a team meeting held thereafter to discuss progress on Behavioral Goals and Objectives.

Step 4

Once Martin has mastered the alternative skills or behaviors, the plan should be modified to reflect more flexibility in implementation. For example, Martin could be allowed to transition by himself for some of the transitions throughout his day. Data should be collected for an additional month then faded to probes done weekly.

Proactive Strategies

Key Routines

1. Prior to all transitions, Martin should be specifically notified that a transition will take place. For example, say, "Martin, in three minutes it will be time to go to your Writing Strategies class." Prompt Martin to respond acknowledgment that he has heard the prompt. If Martin does not respond, say, "Martin, look at me {gain eye contact}, in three minutes it will be time for Writing Strategies." Again, prompt Martin to respond acknowledgment. After Martin responds, let him continue and repeat at one minute prior to the actual transition time.

2. Martin will specifically taught strategies to use in transitions and for asking for preferred items or activities. These instructional strategies should include least to greatest prompting strategies, modeling, role playing, feedback, error analysis and correction

procedures, generalization strategies, and video modeling (Storey & Miner, 2-17).

Setting Events

1. Martin enjoys and is successful at Math and during Computer instruction times. These teaching activities are key opportunities to facilitate replacement skills and behaviors.
2. Martin also responds well to consistency, predictability, and structure in his environment and thus it will be important to make sure that these components are in place.

POSITIVE REINFORCEMENT. When Martin is not engaging in aggressive behaviors he will receive praise every five minutes (Differential Reinforcement of Other Behavior) from his class assistant. After every class period if he has not had any incidents of aggression his class assistant texts his parents to let them know and at home that evening if Martin has not had any aggression during the day his parents reinforce that behavior with preferred food items and extra time on his iPad playing a favorite game of his choice.

NEGATIVE REINFORCEMENT. Martin is often negatively reinforced for his aggression when the demand or transition is removed following his aggression. Therefore, every demand or transition must take place even if Martin engages in aggression. There may be a delay between the demand and Martin's complying to the demand but the demand cannot be removed.

COMPETING BEHAVIOR. Description of how alternative behavior/skill will serve the same function as the target behavior and Increase appropriate behavior.

- Topography of behavior/skill: Martin has, at a very low frequency and with prompting, expressed his need to escape or to prolong an ongoing activity (such as computer). Martin will say, at times, the word "no." It is not known if Martin means, "No, I do not want to," or "No, I do not understand what I need to do." Further, Martin will, at times, express that he is unclear of the expectation or that he is angry. These expressions are usually given after staff have prompted him when they see he is upset. If Martin expresses this feeling, respond by giving him a choice to switch activities or to take a break.

- Description of how alternative behavior/skill will serve the same function as the target behavior:

   1. Martin can engage in successful transitions during transition times.
   2. If Martin is given the skills to appropriately request an object or activity then he will not have to engage in undesirable behaviors during those times.
   3. Martin should be afforded with feedback on his behavior with specificity. When Martin engages in the appropriate transition response, give feedback and praise, and allow the transition to happen.

- Steps to teach alternative behavior/skills:

   1. Martin will be afforded one to one attention for all transitions during his day. It is recommended the same staff assume this responsibility to ensure consistency and predictability of intervention.
   2. Martin should be prompted to use his words to express wants and needs. One method of accomplishing this is to provide Martin with choices and giving Martin the opportunity to make a choice. The initial goal is to get Martin to practice the replacement behaviors to obtain an item or an activity. Prompting Martin and modeling the correct response should be used if it becomes apparent that Martin is unable to state his wants or needs.

Consequence Strategies

How to Respond to Target Behavior

- What to do if antecedents/precursors occur:

   1. Use physical proximity but not physical prompts for all transitions. Martin sometimes will bolt off. As long as he's safe (and others are safe), walk over to him and verbally redirect. Following instructional style described above, follow through. Provide specific praise once Martin starts to comply.

2. Have peers give feedback about aggression such as, "Martin, please do not _____ me . . . use your words."
3. Give Martin feedback on his behavior. For example, "Martin, it's not ok to hit, use your words."

- What to do if target behavior occurs:

  1. Take a step away from Martin, state in calm voice, "NO," and prompt him to use his words.
  2. Use approved strategies for escaping holds such as pinches and grabs. Use approved strategies for deflecting hits and kicks. Use brief escorts or containment when level of dangerousness is eminent and threatens Martin's safety or the safety of others.
  3. Use supervised Time Out (TO) for situations that pose a continued risk for Martin or others. Have supervision view at all times but do not verbally engage Martin while in TO.

- How and when can Martin return to reinforcement schedule:

  As soon Martin begins to comply to staff directions consider the incident over, move forward and catch Martin being good. Remember, all behavior is communicating something and the communicative intent may change. Do not assume that Martin's challenging times are personal towards you or are going to last the entire day. Each moment is a chance for success and to practice the alternative behaviors.

- What to do when alternative/skills occur:

  1. Consistently give Martin contingent and specific feedback on his behavior and provide incentives developed by the DSPS for school and by his parents for the home. Give feedback to the other environment on Martin's successes at school/home.
  2. Provide preferred activities for demonstrating the alternative skills (give Martin what he's requesting).
  3. Always use praise and combine with primary reinforcers for tasks that are very difficult for Martin to do. The goal is for you and your instruction to be the discriminative stimulus, not the food.

PUNISHMENT PROCEDURES. It was decided that punishment procedures were not needed at this point in time.

SAFETY OR CRISIS PLAN. During any instance of Martin's aggression or attempted aggression staff should follow the policy and training on safety for themselves, other students, and Martin. Safety training will take place at the beginning of Fall and Spring semesters, or as needed, for all staff who teach or support Martin.

MONITORING AND EVALUATION. Martin's DSPS will case manage the data collection of both problem behavior and replacement behaviors. If a detrimental trend occurs, the support team will be advised and revisions made to the behavior support plan.

COLLABORATION WITH OTHERS. Martin's DSPS staff and parents should be specific in the daily communication book on phases that "work" for Martin. Cross-environmental consistency will aide Martin in learning that using his words works for him as much as aggression. Also, cross-environmental consistency will reduce behavioral contrast.

MAINTENANCE. If Martin continues to demonstrate maintenance of alternative skills, the plan should be revised during the next normal annual review to reflect interventions that are as "normalized" as possible.

REFERENCES CITED IN CHAPTER

Bambara, L. M., & Kern, L. (2005). *Individualized supports for students with problem behaviors: Designing positive behavior plans.* New York: Guilford Press.

Bambara, L. M., & Knoster, T. (2009). *Designing positive behavior support plans* (2nd ed.). Washington, DC: American Association on Mental Retardation.

Horner, R. H., O'Neill, R. E., & Flannery, K. B. (1993). Building effective behavior support plans from functional assessment information. In M. E. Snell (Ed.), *Instruction of students with severe disabilities* (4th ed., p. 184–214). Columbus, OH: Merrill.

Horner, R. H., Sugai, G., Todd, A. W., & Lewis-Palmer, T. (1999-2000). Elements of behavior support plans: A technical brief. *Exceptionality, 8*(3), 205–215.

O'Neill, R. E., Albin, R. W., Storey, K., Horner, R. H., & Sprague, J. R. (2015). *Functional assessment and program development for problem behavior: A practical handbook* (3rd ed.). Stamford, CT: Cengage Publishing Company.

Storey, K., & Miner, C. (2017). *Systematic instruction of functional skills for students and adults with disabilities* (2nd ed.). Springfield, IL: Charles C Thomas Publisher, Ltd.

EMPIRICAL RESEARCH SUPPORTING THAT THE INTERVENTIONS PRESENTED IN CHAPTER ARE EVIDENCE BASED PRACTICES

Benazzi, L., Horner, R. H., & Good, R. H. (2006). Effects of behavior upport team composition on the technical adequacy and contextual fit of behavior support plans. *Journal of Special Education, 40,* 160–170.

Borgmeier, C., Loman, S. L., Hara, M., & Rodriguez, B. J. (2015). Training school personnel to identify interventions based on functional behavioral assessment. *Journal of Emotional and Behavioral Disorders, 23,* 78–89.

Burke, M., Hagan-Burke, S., & Sugai, G. (2003). The efficacy of function-based interventions for students with learning disabilities who exhibit escape-maintained problem behaviors: Preliminary results from a single-case experiment. *Learning Disability Quarterly, 26,* 15–26.

Codding, R. S., Feinberg, A. B., Dunn, E. K., & Pace, G. M. (2005). Effects of immediate performance feedback on implementation of behavior support. *Journal of Applied Behavior Analysis, 38,* 205–219.,

Cook, C. R., Crews, S. D., Wright, D. B. Mayer, G. R., Gale, B., Kraemer, B., & Gresham, F. M. (2007). Establishing and evaluating the substantive adequacy of positive behavioral support plans. *Journal of Behavioral Education, 16,* 191–206.

Hagermoser-Sanetti, L. M., Collier-Meek, M. A.; Long, A. C. J., Byron, J., & Kratochwill, T. R. (2015). Increasing teacher treatment integrity of behavior support plans through consultation and implementation planning. *Journal of School Psychology, 53,* 209–229.

Ingram, K., Lewis-Palmer, T., & Sugai, G. (2005). Function-based intervention planning: Comparing the effectiveness of FBA indicated and contra-indicated interventions plans. *Journal of Positive Behavior Interventions, 7,* 224–236.

Matson, J. L., & Wilkins, J. (2009). Factors associated with the questions about behavior function for functional assessment of low and high rate challenging behaviors in adults with intellectual disability. *Behavior Modification, 33,* 207–219.

McClean, B., & Grey, I. (2012). A component analysis of positive behavior support plans. *Journal of Intellectual and Developmental Disability, 37,* 221–231.

McVilly, K., Webber, L., Sharp, G., & Paris, M. (2013). The content validity of the Behaviour Support Plan Quality Evaluation tool (BSP-QEII) and its potential application in accommodation and day-support services for adults with intellectual disability. *Journal of Intellectual Disability Research, 57,* 703–715.

Strickland-Cohen, M. K., & Horner, R. H. (2015). Typical school personnel developing and implementing basic behavior support plans. *Journal of Positive Behavior Interventions, 17,* 83–94.

GENERAL REFERENCES REGARDING TOPICS IN CHAPTER

Albin, R. W., Lucyshyn, J. M., Horner, R. H., & Flannery, K. B. (1996). Contextual fit for behavioral support plans: A model for a goodness of fit. In L. K. Koegel,

R. L. Koegel, & G. Dunlap (Eds.), *Positive behavioral support: Including people with difficult behavior in the community* (pp. 81–98). Baltimore, MD: Paul H. Brookes Publishing Company.

Asher, M. J., Gordon, S. B., & Selbst, M. C. (2010). *The behavior problems resource kit: Forms and procedures for identification, measurement, and intervention.* Champaign, IL: Research Press.

Bambara, L. M., & Knoster, T. P. (2009). *Designing positive behavior support plans.* Washington, DC: American Association on Intellectual and Developmental Disabilities.

Cipani, E. (2018). *Functional behavioral assessment, diagnosis, and treatment: A complete system for education and mental health settings.* New York, NY: Springer Publishing Company.

Feeman, R., Baker, D., Horner, R. H., Smith, C., Britten, J., & McCart, A. (2002). Using functional assessment and systems-level assessment to build effective behavioral support plans. In R. H. Hanson, N. A. Wieseler, & C. Lakin (Eds.), *Crisis: Prevention & response in the community* (pp. 199–224). Washington, DC: American Association on Mental Retardation.

Manente, C. J., Maraventano, J. C., LaRue, R. H.;, Delmolino, L., & Sloan, D. (2010). Effective behavioral intervention for adults on the autism spectrum: Best practices in functional assessment and treatment development. *Behavior Analyst Today, 11,* 36–48.

O'Neill, R. E., Hawken, L. S., & Bundock, K. (2015). Conducting functional behavioral assessments. In R. L. DePry, F. Brown, and J. Anderson (Eds.), *Individual positive behavior supports: A standards-based guide to practices in school and community-based settings* (pp. 259–278). Baltimore, MD: Paul H. Brookes.

Ryan, C., & Baker, B. (2014). *The PBIS team handbook: Setting expectations and building positive behavior.* Minneapolis, MN: Free Spirit Publishing.

Sugai, G., Horner, R. H., Sprague, J. R. (1999). Functional-assessment-based behavior support planning: Research to practice to research. *Behavioral Disorders, 24,* 253–257.

Sugai, G., Lewis-Palmer, T., & Hagan, S. (1998). Using functional assessments to develop behavior support plans. *Preventing School Failure, 43,* 6–13.

Figure 10.1

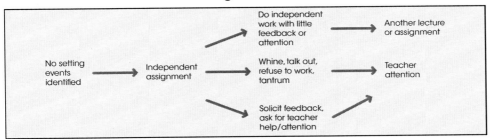

O'Neill, R. E., Albin, R. W., Storey, K., Horner, R. H., & Sprague, J. R. (2015). *Functional assessment and program development for problem behavior: A practical handbook* (3rd ed.). Stamford, CT: Cengage Publishing Company.

Figure 10.2

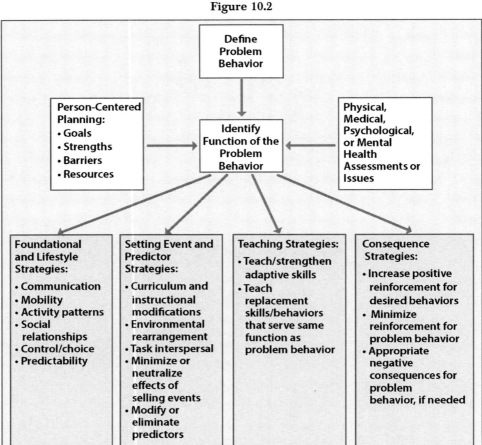

O'Neill, R. E., Albin, R. W., Storey, K., Horner, R. H., & Sprague, J. R. (2015). *Functional assessment and program development for problem behavior: A practical handbook* (3rd ed.). Stamford, CT: Cengage Publishing Company.

Appendix
J18

RESOURCES FOR POSITIVE BEHAVIOR SUPPORTS

It is important to join professional organizations, read professional journals, and visit web sites. Here is a list of suggestions. Joining an organization will help you in your professional development and assist you in staying current in the field.

Journals

American Journal on Intellectual and Developmental Disabilities
Autism Advocate
Autism Research Review International
Behavior Analysis in Practice
Behavior Modification
Behavior Therapy
Behavioral Disorders
Education and Training in Autism and Developmental Disabilities
Focus on Autism and Other Developmental Disabilities
Intellectual and Developmental Disabilities
International Journal of Disability, Development and Education
International Journal of Positive Behavioural Support
Intervention in School and Clinic
Journal of Applied Behavior Analysis
Journal of Autism and Developmental Disorders
Journal of Behavioral Education
Journal of Emotional and Behavioral Disorders
Journal of Positive Behavior Interventions
Research and Practice for Persons with Severe Disabilities
Research in Autism Spectrum Disorders

Resources

The Association for Behavior Analysis
550 West Centre Avenue, Suite 1
Portage, MI 49024
269/492-9310
www.abainternational.org
mail@abainternational.org

The Association of Positive Behavior Support
P.O Box 328
Bloomsburg, PA 17815
570/441-5418
www.apbs.org
tknoster@bloomu.edu

B. F. Skinner Foundation
18 Brattle Street Ste. 451
Cambridge, MA 02138
www.bfskinner.org
info@bfskinner.org

Cambridge Center for Behavioral Studies
550 Newtown Rd, Suite 950
Littleton, MA 01460
978-369-2227
store@behavior.org
www.behavior.org

Council for Exceptional Children
2900 Crystal Drive, Suite 100
Arlington, VA 22202-3557
888-232-7733
www.cec.sped.org

National Alliance for the Mentally Ill
3803 N. Fairfax Dr., Ste. 100
Arlington, VA 22203
800/950-6264
www.nami.org

National Center for Learning Disabilities
32 Laight Street, Second Floor
New York, NY 10013
888/575-7373
www.ncld.org

TASH
1101 15th Street NW, Suite 1212
Washington, D.C. 20005
www.tash.org

American Association on Intellectual and Developmental Disabilities
501 3rd Street, NW Suite 200
Washington, D.C. 20001
800/424-3688
www.aaidd.org

Autism Society of America
 4340 East-West Hwy, Suite 350
 Bethesda, MD 20814
80/ 328-8476
http://www.autism-society.org/

Relevant Web sites

Behavior Homepage
www.state.ky.us/agencies/behave/homepage.html

Intervention Central
www.interventioncentral.org

Positive Behavioral Supports and Interventions
www.pbis.org

The Challenging Behaviour Foundation
http://www.challengingbehaviour.org.uk

AUTHOR INDEX

SUBJECT INDEX

227

ABOUT THE AUTHORS

Keith Storey, Ph.D., BCBA-D, is currently a Clinical Director at Juvo Autism and Behavioral Health Services in Oakland, California. He is also a Professor Emeritus at Touro University in Vallejo, California. Dr. Storey has over forty years' experience working with individuals with disabilities, including six years as a classroom teacher. His professional and research interests include transition from school to adult life, functional analysis and positive behavioral supports, supported employment, inclusion, and curriculum development. Dr. Storey is the recipient of the 1988 Alice H. Hayden Award from The Association for Persons with Severe Handicaps; the 1996 Hau-Cheng Wang Fellowship from Chapman University, which is presented for exceptional merit in scholarship; and the 2001 Robert Gaylord-Ross Memorial Scholar Award from the California Association for Persons with Severe Disabilities. He is a member of the Illinois State University College of Education Alumni Hall of Fame. He has published over 100 journal articles on a wide variety of topics. Dr. Storey has published the books *Case Studies in Transition and Employment for Students and Adults with Disabilities, Positive Behavior Supports in Classrooms and Schools: Effective and Practical Strategies for Teachers and Other Service Providers, Case Studies in Applied Behavior Analysis for Students and Adults with Disabilities, Systematic Instruction of Functional Skills for Students and Adults with Disabilities, The Road Ahead: Transition to Adult Life for Persons with Disabilities, Walking Isn't Everything: An Account of the Life of Jean Denecke,* and *Functional Assessment and Program Development for Problem Behavior: A Practical Handbook.* He currently serves on the editorial boards of *Career Development and Transition for Exceptional Individuals, Journal of Vocational Rehabilitation, Education and Training in Autism and Developmental Disabilities, Journal of Positive of Behavior Interventions,* and *Research and Practice for Persons with Severe Disabilities.* He previously served on the editorial boards of *Education and Treatment of Children, Vocational Evaluation and Career Assessment Professional Journal,* and Exceptionality. Dr. Storey's amazon author page is at amazon.com/author/keithstorey and his Goodreads author page is at https://www.goodreads.com/author/show/105547.Keith_Storey. You can reach him at keith.storey@tu.edu.

Michal Post is currently teaching education and special education credentialing courses for a San Francisco Bay Area university. She has over 35 years working in field of education including the role of General Education Teacher, Special Education Teacher, Inclusion Specialist, Transition and Employment Specialist, Instructor for Community College Disabled Students Program Services classes, and Student Teacher Supervisor for two universities. She has over 20 years of direct experience in providing transition and employment services to adults with disabilities, and in providing trainings for teachers and support staff for including children with special needs in general education settings. For over 13 years she has shared her experience through annual presentations at both national and international professional conferences on topics such as self-management strategies, supported employment strategies, and behavioral supports for students with autism. She has published articles in *Teaching Exceptional Children, Journal of Vocational Rehabilitation, International Journal of Rehabilitation Research, Education and Training in Autism and Developmental Disabilities, Research in Practice for Persons with Severe Disabilities,* and *Journal of Autism and Developmental Disabilities.* Michal has been the project coordinator for three personnel preparation grants from the Office of Special Education and Rehabilitation Services with two for preparing teachers and service professionals to serve students in transition planning for adult life and the other providing comprehensive training for teachers serving students on the autism spectrum. She has also co-authored with Keith Storey *Positive Behavior Supports in Classrooms and Schools; Effective and Practical Strategies for Teachers and Other Service Providers.*

Concrete reflective = why?
Abstract reflective = what?
Abstract active = how?
Concrete, active = what if?